# Semiotics and Communication:
## Signs, Codes, Cultures

# COMMUNICATION TEXTBOOK SERIES

Jennings Bryant—*Editor*

---

Intercultural Communication
W. Barnett Pearce—*Advisor*

---

CARBAUGH • Cultural Communication
and Intercultural Contact

LEEDS-HURWITZ • Semiotics and
Communication: Signs, Codes, Cultures

# Semiotics and Communication: Signs, Codes, Cultures

**Wendy Leeds-Hurwitz**
*University of Wisconsin-Parkside*

**LEA** LAWRENCE ERLBAUM ASSOCIATES, PUBLISHERS
1993   Hillsdale, New Jersey                    Hove and London

Cover photo: Cuna jaguar, in the collection of the Milwaukee Public
Museum, catalog number 65951/28220. Photo by Don Lintner,
University of Wisconsin-Parkside.

Lawrence Erlbaum Associates, Inc., Publishers
365 Broadway
Hillsdale, New Jersey 07642

**Library of Congress Cataloging-in-Publication Data**

Leeds-Hurwitz, Wendy.
    Semiotics and Communication : Signs, Codes, Cultures / Wendy Leeds-
Hurwitz.
        p.    cm.
    Includes bibliographical references and index.
    ISBN 0-8058-1139-7 (c) — ISBN 0-8058-1140-0 (p)
    1. Semiotics.   2. Communication.   I. Title.
P99.L44   1993
302.2—dc20                                                      92-923
                                                                   CIP

Books published by Lawrence Erlbaum Associates are printed on acid-free
paper, and their bindings are chosen for strength and durability.

Printed in the United States of America
10   9   8   7   6   5   4

# Contents

## FIGURES AND TABLE

# Acknowledgments

This book has taken several years to write with many people playing a role in the process. Barnett Pearce played instigator by asking what my next book was about before I was fully ready to answer that question. By the time we finished talking several hours later, I knew what I wanted to write. His constructive comments on several drafts are greatly appreciated.

The first three chapters were written while I was a Fellow at the Center for Twentieth Century Studies at the University of Wisconsin-Milwaukee, and I thank the regular staff there (Kathleen Woodward, Director, and Carol Tennessen, Program and Publications Coordinator) as well as the other Fellows from 1990–1991 (Marcus Bullock, Gwynne Kennedy, Panivong Norindr, Marina Perez de Mendiola, Helena Pycior, Roby Rajan, and Rolando Romero) for creating an environment conducive to thinking and writing.

When I returned to the University of Wisconsin-Parkside, my regular academic home, my students were presented with an incomplete draft of this volume as their text in an advanced seminar on semiotics. They were remarkably patient with the process, actively contributing to it, both in the originality of their insights and the questions they required me to answer. Through the many excellent projects and final exams they prepared, they demonstrated that undergraduates *can* learn difficult theory, if only they are shown what to do with it.

Many of my examples are the result of class discussions of how to ground theoretical concepts in specific data. We applied semiotic theory specifically to weddings, chosen because they are complex events, carefully planned and organized, yet readily accessible to analysis, and so weddings serve as a continuing theme throughout this volume. Though it would now be difficult to identify each case with the originating student, I want at least to name them all and thank them as a group. In the fall of 1991 they were: Joanne Beardslee, Marie Boris, Karen Carlson, Jason Caspers, Ronda Coats, Margaret Coca, Sue Glanz, Eric Hall, Debra Halvorson, Nicole Janaky, Sharon Kowalke, Mark Lauer, Joel Meadow, Sarah Minasian, Michelle Myles, Judith Neumiller, Melissa Patterson, Kimberly Pinti, Karen Pitsoulakis, Georgette Sampson, Dan Schmidt, Lenora Schmidt, Karen Semonson, Robert Smith, Chris Summers, Carmen Tenuta, Christina Witt, and Darin Zimpel.

And in the spring of 1992: Beth Adelsen, Suneeta Akkinapalli, Judy Bostetter, Gretchen Cole, Daphne Cook, Debbie Denjo, Rachel Donahue, Christopher Dunbar, Rob Fox, Jordanna Gastrow, Heather Good, Diane Hendrickson, Dennis Kaczanowski, Lisa Krebs, Sue Kusz, Amber Lundskow, Bill Ohm, Sharon Pastorino, Renee Pughsley, Tim Radke, Jennifer Rakowski, Becky Richards, Richard Sosa, Kirsten Tenges, and Laura Wakefield.

My first introduction to many of the ideas presented in this volume came from graduate courses at the University of Pennsylvania in the 1970s. Dan Ben-Amos was the most explicit about the value of semiotic theory and the most adamant about the need to read early, original sources. Dell Hymes continues to question what semiotic theory has to offer that cannot be discovered elsewhere; this volume provides a longer answer than I have yet given him, perhaps it will prove persuasive. Don Yoder, Henry Glassie, Barbara Kirshenblatt-Gimblett, Ken Goldstein, and Ray Birdwhistell all introduced me to the significance of food, clothing, and objects as communication, though each was interested in similar material for quite different reasons.

Yves Winkin, Steve Murray, and Mort Leeds read an early draft of this manuscript, the first two for content, the third for fluency; many of their suggestions were incorporated. Stuart Sigman, John Stewart, and Klaus Krippendorff asked serious questions about the endeavor as a whole, making me think carefully about what I was saying.

In reading my final draft, Barnett Pearce suggested that photographs would be particularly valuable for some of the examples. Though his comment created a great deal of last-minute work, it was a valid suggestion, and I am grateful for it. I have enjoyed my many conversations with the various copyright holders and thank them all for permissions to include illustrative material. Formal acknowledgments for permission to reprint photographs accompany the photos in the text. I would like to particularly thank two individuals for help above and beyond the call of duty: Nancy Lurie, at the Milwaukee Public Museum, for the entire morning she spent guiding me through their anthropology collection and Don Lintner, from the media services department of my university, who not only took several of the photographs printed here (including the cover) but reproduced many of the others from photographs sent to me.

In addition, Kate Owen took time out of a family gathering to photograph an authentic pasty. Kim Avery created Fig. 3.3 on short notice. And my department secretary, Pam Barsuli, helped substantially in the typing of final changes to the manuscript. My editor, Hollis Heimbouch, was supportive throughout the entire process, but especially during the quest for appropriate illustrations.

Being an academic is not a 9-to-5 job and actively requires the support of family members. As with everything else I have written, this volume would never have been finished without the considerable tolerance of odd working hours and numerous requests to "just wait until I finish this page" on the part of my husband, Marc, and son, Aaron.

# Prelude: Why Semiotics?

Several years ago, I asked students in a class to record everything they ate for a week, everything they wore for a week, and to draw a diagram of every object present in their living rooms during that week. Removing names, I presented summaries of their data, randomly sorted. My students and I were all a bit surprised at the ease with which they were able to match foods to clothing and living room furnishings. What seemed obvious and simple to them as social actors was astonishing in its complexity to them as social analysts. They knew through their participation in the system that someone whose living room included silver service, a mirror, and family photos should be matched to multicourse dinners and to clothing that came in sets (e.g., sweaters purchased to go with pants); they knew that someone with one old couch, two mismatched chairs, and posters taped up on the living room walls was most likely the person eating pizza for breakfast.

They found it easiest to make gender distinctions in any category. Women were most likely to have framed prints and photographs of family members in their living rooms, to eat vitamins with their dinner, to wear accessories (belts, jewelry, scarves) with their clothing; men were most likely to have an aquarium or sports equipment in the living room, to eat desserts, to wear sweatpants and T-shirts. After gender, they distinguished between what Ray Birdwhistell termed *pads* (temporary living spaces) and *nests* (more permanent living spaces).[1] Someone with a pad was more likely to skip lunch, have minimal variety of clothing, and few or no extras in the living room (''extras'' being defined as anything beyond basic furniture and lamps). With some further effort they could also distinguish between student-designed nests and parent-designed nests (some of the students were the ages of other students' parents, so they were clearly describing role distinctions rather than age distinctions). A parent nest was more likely to include silver service and antiques in the living room; a student nest was more likely to include bookshelves. Of the three social codes, they found objects the most immediately revealing and clothing the most difficult to interpret without knowing more details than had been recorded initially.

We wanted to talk about the ties among these three social codes and to describe the ways in which choices in one could seemingly be predicted from choices in another, yet we had trouble explaining what we knew and how we knew it. In particular, my students were surprised at the extent and certainty of their own practical knowledge and at the fact that they could not readily verbalize the rules they followed in making decisions. Ultimately, the feeling of frustration stemming from that discussion is what led me to write this book. I felt then, and still feel today, that the connections among social codes are important, something people should be able to talk about. It seems inappropriate to let the lack of available terminology shut down that conversation before it even begins.

This volume is designed to close the gap between what we are able to do as social actors and what we are able to describe as social analysts. What we do as participants in the system seems obvious and easy and does not generally require much thought or deliberation. But sometimes explaining that same behavior as social analysts is difficult if not impossible, not the least because the right words are not always available. It seems to me that some of the words needed are to be found within *semiotics*, and so this book introduces that language.

My ultimate goal is for readers to use the theoretical material presented in this book for their own ends, applying it to whatever examples are of greatest importance to them. I refer here both to colleagues and to students, in fact to anyone who may discover that semiotic theory provides a useful tool for insight into daily life. Abstract theorizing alone can be decidedly cold and unrewarding; but I have always found my students willing to plow through difficult material if there was a sufficiently enticing goal at the end. There are few more enticing goals than understanding one's own behavior and that of others. In order to ensure the accessibility of this book to a variety of audiences, I have buried technical and historical details as well as extensive suggestions for further reading in endnotes, where they are available for those who are interested but easily skipped over by those who are not.

The "we" used in these pages refers to me, the author, together with you, the reader. We are both social actors, you and I, in that we are active participants of the cultures in which we live. We are also both social analysts, if only by virtue of the discussion of social interaction that I am writing and you are reading. These two roles cannot be separated—there is no social analyst who is not also a social actor, despite the frequent academic fiction to the contrary, in communication as in other fields.[2]

*Wendy Leeds-Hurwitz*

## NOTES

1. I have never seen this idea of Birdwhistell's in print, but learned it from his lectures in a class entitled "Communication Codes and Modes" at the University of Pennsylvania in 1977.
2. When this manuscript was copyedited, the title "Prelude" was changed to "Preface." I objected strenuously to the change and, much to my delight, the original title was subsequently returned. I argued that there is a difference of connotation between the two terms and that, particularly in a volume about connotation and other aspects of meaning, the distinction is a relevant one. After completing Part I, the reader is invited to consider the subtle difference between a prelude, with connotations of music and the direction of attention to an uncommon choice of word, and a preface, with connotations of a dry academic text, and business as usual. In searching for precedent, I discovered that Brady (1991) wrote a preface to the entire volume he edited, but a prelude to each chapter. It seems completely appropriate that his volume concerns poetics, specifically the connections between art and science. My use of the term was not drawn from Brady, because I had not read it when I wrote my first draft; presumably someone else's prelude influenced me.

# Introduction:
# Communication and Semiotics

The field of communication includes, among other things, the study of meaning, the study of how people convey ideas for themselves and to one another, whether through words, food, clothing, objects, or in other ways. Yet there are precious few words available to describe how exactly people convey meaning to themselves and others. Communication is not the only field to consider the study of meaning a central topic, and so when we want more vocabulary words than are available for discussing meaning, we can look to other fields for help, borrowing their words, adapting them to our own needs.

This volume proposes one such borrowing from another field. It suggests that semiotics has paid a great deal of attention to describing how people convey meanings and thus has developed a vocabulary we can borrow for our own uses. The point, of course, is not to use these new vocabulary words as trophies, for their own sake, to impress others with the obscure words we know but they don't. We borrow vocabulary only when it suits our needs better than the words currently available, and we stop borrowing when we have figured out how to say what is important.

This volume presents a set of terms as well as a set of ideas about how to use these terms and demonstrates what the terms permit us to do that we couldn't do so easily before. The goal is not to present vocabulary words for their own sake, for that would serve only to hide meaning, but rather to supply words for use in analyzing our own behavior and that of others. Because all words have their own history and because it seems to me inappropriate to borrow these words without understanding any of their history, some brief background is given for the field of semiotics from which the words are borrowed and for the traditional uses of each of the words discussed.

We all make assumptions when we present our views. To the extent I am able to make them explicit, this volume makes the following assumptions:

1.  that the social world is a rich and complex place with frequent subtleties of implication;
2.  that people are ultimately responsible for creating the meanings they use;
3.  that meaning is often conveyed through minor details of everyday behavior, nonverbal as well as verbal;
4.  that meanings change as often as the people who use them require; and
5.  that the ultimate goal must be to explain real behavior in real contexts.

Students of communication must use whatever tools best serve in the task of unlocking meaning from interaction. If one place to find such tools is semiotics, then it will prove profitable to spend a little time learning what semiotics has to offer. This volume serves as a starting point for those who would pursue semiotic theory as an aid to the goal of understanding communicative behavior.

This volume contributes to an understanding of semiotics in two major areas: (a) It synthesizes those parts of semiotic theory most valuable to the study of communication, placing particular emphasis on signs and codes; and (b) It extends the existing theory through discussion of possible relationships, particularly among codes. My first goal is to propose semiotic theory as a tool in the study of meaning useful to those in communication, especially those with an interest in social interaction; to do so requires paring semiotic theory down to the bare essentials. For me there are a few basics from semiotics that have been useful in understanding communicative behavior; I assume these should be equally useful to others. I try to present these theoretical concepts in such a way that they can be immediately applied to actual instances of human social behavior, for to me theory is not in and of itself tantalizing. To this end, what is presented is a new synthesis of semiotic theory, different from any available elsewhere.

Specifically, of the possible topics within semiotic theory, my emphasis is on *signs* (the smallest elements of meaning in interaction) and on *codes* (sets of related signs and rules for their use). Several types of signs are described; one of these, *symbols*, is pointed to as the most relevant for communication research. Equally, several types of codes are described; one of these, *social codes*, is suggested as the most relevant for communication.

My second goal is to extend semiotic theory in a new direction. Semiotic analysis has generally stopped at the boundaries of a single sign or code, but I argue here for a new emphasis on the *relationships* between signs (in codes) and between codes (in cultures). This implies the continuation of study beyond the code to some larger entity. We need to create new terms to describe what occurs when these codes are viewed in conjunction with one another, as in fact occurs in everyday life. I propose some of that new terminology in chapter 7.

Briefly, it is my argument that in addition to an understanding of the theoretical assumptions of semiotics, involving primarily the key concepts of *sign*, *code*, and *culture*, there is a special fit between semiotics and nonverbal communication. As currently studied, nonverbal communication is parsed into a series of channels (or types of behavior) generally confined to movement of various body parts (such as facial expressions, eye gaze behavior, the amount of space between participants in an interaction, the use of touch) having little impact on one another. No participant could make the mistake of thinking that the use of touch is unrelated to how we move our bodies or the distance between people; they are separated only temporarily by analysts in order to make research easier. But we as analysts have gone perhaps too far in our efforts to make research easy, forgetting to ever recombine the separate elements again. To me, the purpose of studying nonverbal communication is to aid the understanding of social interaction as a whole. Lotman pointed out the problem of emphasizing the separate parts of a topic of study rather than the whole with a vivid metaphor: "if we put together lots of veal cutlets, we do not obtain a calf. But if we cut up a calf, we obtain lots of veal cutlets" (as translated from the Russian in Eco, 1990, pp. xii–xiii).[1] He emphasized the importance of establishing at the start whether we are interested in the cutlets or the calf.

Semiotics can potentially aid the effort to understand what occurs during social interaction. This is demonstrated specifically using several codes of behavior that are appropriately termed *nonverbal*, though only occasionally have they been studied under that label. Traditionally most studies of nonverbal behavior within communication have stopped at the edges of the physical body, as if such additions as clothing have no bearing on the interaction.[2] But we do not interact as physical beings; we interact as social beings. One has only to consider the effect of removing participants' clothes in a casual interaction to be reminded of their significant role.

The three social codes that serve as focus in this volume are food, clothing, and objects. These three are chosen in part because of the extensive literature already available for each—they have been widely accepted as significant forms of behavior to study—and in part because they are so basic to interaction, so central to people's lives. We take them so much for granted that we tend to ignore them, yet each is essential. These three are proposed as useful focal points for study, but that does not mean they can serve exclusively. Some comments are made about language in particular, that most significant social code, because it would be inappropriate to ignore language just as it would be inappropriate to ignore food or clothing or objects. Only the physical constraint of preparing a volume with a finite number of pages prevents me from including more comments on additional social codes.

What remains is a twofold task: (a) to introduce semiotics to a communication audience, showing why it is particularly significant given the currently proposed focus on symbols as the unifying concept of the discipline; and (b) to illustrate the theoretical material with numerous examples chosen from studies of food, clothing, and objects showing particularly why they should be studied in conjunction rather than separately as has generally been the case to date.

Researchers have known for a long time that there is a close connection between vocabulary and ideas.[3] Although it is generally true that any idea can be expressed in any language, eventually and in roundabout terms, having particular words for ideas certainly makes them easier to discuss. A new invention is described despite the lack of words for it: "Horseless carriage" was a phrase used by those first confronted with cars, most descriptive not of what it was but of what it wasn't. Once a new invention becomes a common sight, a new word gains currency to facilitate discussion of the new thing or idea ("automobile"); if that word is long and the need for its use great, it will gradually be shortened ("car"). Similarly, it facilitates the discussion of how meaning is created through interaction to have an appropriate set of vocabulary words available.

A good number of the examples included in these pages analyze food, clothing, and objects in their wider cultural context, and this context is not always an American one. Even when the focus is the United States, some of the discussion is about subcultural groups. It is important to me that this volume integrate intercultural assumptions whenever possible, one of these being that there are many solutions to common problems around the world, not all of them identical. *Food, clothing, and objects serve as classic sites for the study of cultural divergence around common themes.* Everyone eats, but every group develops different assumptions about what is eaten and in what way or what foods are highly prized. There have been recent suggestions that intercultural concerns be integrated into interpersonal communication, but this is still an infrequent approach; there is as yet much room for experimenting with various combinations of the two.[4]

My goal is not to present one more description of semiotic terminology or history of semiotic theory; numerous books have provided both.[5] To the contrary, I avoid discussions of theory for its own sake. I am more interested in enabling readers to directly apply semiotic concepts to their own experiences of everyday life than encouraging readers to join arcane discussions of terminology. That is one of the reasons why food, clothing, and objects serve so well as examples: It should be easy to move from potentially dense theoretical material to applying key concepts to the dinner you ate last night or the clothes you wear today.[6] Eco's (1973b) article, "Social Life as a Sign System," serves in some ways as the justification for this approach. He argued that the best way to understand communication is as a system of social codes. We do this all the time as participants; we might also try it as analysts.

One way of describing this endeavor is to explain that it uses theory in the study of *praxis*. (Praxis can be roughly defined as "situated knowledge"—using what you know theoretically in order to do something.) Theory is only a tool in a more concrete endeavor: understanding why and how people do what they do. Barthes spoke of the need "to decipher the world in order to remake it (for how remake it without deciphering it?)'' (1982a, p. 352). His tool of choice in the effort to decipher the world was semiotics; I also find it valuable for that purpose. Before we can change the world, we must understand how it works; semiotics is valuable to the extent that it increases our understanding.

Fiske pointed out, ''Communication is too often taken for granted when it should be taken to pieces'' (1983, p. x). Semiotics is one appropriate tool to use in the endeavor to take apart, to unlock, interactional meanings. The goal is that each person should be capable of critically, analytically understanding his or her own behavior and that of others. After learning to unpack meanings, if anyone chooses to change anything as a result of what has been learned, that is fine, but telling others what to do and how to do it is not my plan. My goal is understanding, and understanding must precede change. Taking the world figuratively to pieces is one part of understanding. Ultimately, effective change must come from those who create meanings themselves, it cannot be imposed from the outside.

As with any tool, the potential uses of semiotics must be explained, its capabilities made clear, and demonstrations of how to use that tool must be supplied. Thus this volume is divided into three major parts. ''Part I: Semiotic Theory and Communication Theory'' provides a brief introduction to the field of semiotics, beginning with an overview of history in chapter 1 and stressing two key semiotic concepts: signs (emphasizing symbols) in chapter 2 and codes (emphasizing social codes) in chapter 3. In this way, Part I presents the basics but no more. ''Part II: From Semiotic Theory to Communication Behavior'' demonstrates what to do with the theory in a few choice contexts by providing an initial analysis of three social codes: food, clothing, and objects. Briefly, they are all forms of nonverbal communication and so logically function as part of the field of communication. Elsewhere (in semiotics, in anthropology, in folklore, in history) they have already been studied to good effect. It may be useful to incorporate them more thoroughly into the field of communication. As with semiotics as a whole, the point is not to claim another's territory, but rather to examine communicative behavior traditionally omitted but logically appropriate to the field of communication. Semiotics is the theoretical construct; food, clothing, and objects are particular aspects of behavior appropriately studied using that theory. These expand the traditional boundaries of communication, just as study of discourse expands the traditional boundaries of rhetoric, nonverbal communication expands interpersonal communication, or cultural studies expands our understanding of mass media.

''Part III: From Communication Behavior to Semiotic Theory'' suggests the final step of moving beyond single codes considered independently to whole cultures, considered as sets of codes, and presents a beginning vocabulary for discussing social codes as they interrelate. Each culture is composed of a set of mutually influencing social codes, thus it becomes important to have available theoretical terms for the analysis of these interrelations. Culler said, ''If we are to understand our social and cultural world, we must think not of independent

objects but of symbolic structures, systems of relations which, by enabling objects and actions to have meaning, create a human universe" (1981, p. 25). If
this volume is successful, it will demonstrate the potential value of making that
shift, of moving from single signs through codes to entire cultures, Culler's "human universes."

But first a cautionary note. This volume is about both semiotic theory and
communication theory. The majority of the time, semiotic theory has center stage;
where exactly does communication theory fit into the picture? We cannot borrow
the tools of semiotics until we are sure we have a toolbox to put them into; that
is, we must be sure which basic framework in communication we are using.[7]

Although rarely phrased explicitly in these terms, the study of communication, particularly but not exclusively the study of interaction, is primarily about
how *structure* connects to *process*. I take structure to mean the social forms available to people as they participate in events; I take process to mean the ways in
which they use those forms while interacting, simultaneously creating a new structure for the future. People constantly move between what is given in social life
through a new construction modifying the old to a completely new structure. For
example, men who meet professionally have traditionally shaken hands. Women
professionals did not have a place in the handshaking ritual for a long time—the
fact that they were women overrode the fact that they were professionals. Over
time, the fact that they were professionals became paramount and so increasingly
they are included in the handshake ritual. Younger professionals today generally
assume that women will shake hands just as men will, for they have the model
provided the first time they saw a women shake hands. This is an example of
how structures change to meet revised social assumptions.

There can be no process without structure, no structure without process. All
one can observe is process: people doing things with other people. But people
rely heavily on preexisting structures: ideas they have about what is appropriate,
norms they have internalized, assumptions they make about what is possible. We
may separate structure and process occasionally in an attempt to understand them;
however, this should be understood as foregrounding one over the other temporarily, to see it better, never considering one to the exclusion of the other.

Lofland stated the basic problem concisely: "How, simultaneously, are we to
speak of that which seems fluid and that which seems solid? How to appreciate
within the same sentence/paragraph that which is emergent and that which per-
sists generation after generation?" (1988, p. 308). As used here, structure
represents that which appears solid, and process represents that which appears
fluid. Though as analysts we have less practice than we might at combining the
two, we have substantial practice as social actors. Each time a person speaks to
another person, he or she makes use of words heard before and interaction patterns that are recognizable (the structural aspect), combining those words and
those patterns of interaction in new ways to fit the current needs (the processual
aspect).

Traditionally most social sciences have given the greater weight to structure: Researchers generally emphasized pattern over individual occurrence.[8] But there is no pattern without individual event. Equally, we as social actors cannot be expected to successfully create the social world anew each time we interact with someone; we must have the option of using "behavioral repertoires."[9] That is, we know what we have previously experienced, we have been told about additional experiences by others, and we draw on that accumulated knowledge of prior experience when we interact. We take bits and pieces from our past experiences and recombine them in new ways, inserting new elements. We do not have to create all the bits and pieces ourselves each time we attempt to chat with a friend or perform a task; if we did, we would be overwhelmed and could never move past that first interaction. Culture and communication both are in a continual state of flux, *emerging through* interaction; they are not monolithic wholes, unchanging over time.

Structure is both antecedent to and subsequent to process. That is, it comes before, and it comes after, but we can never actually see it in the present. It is "jam tomorrow and jam yesterday—but never jam today," as put by Lewis Carroll (1871) in *Through the Looking Glass*. What exists today is process: The recombining of elements from the past into a new present in turn becomes the past that influences tomorrow's present. People use the structure of the past to create the process of the present interaction, in so doing creating a modified structure that is available for use in creating the next interaction, and so on.

Process generally refers to the active, changing aspect of social interaction; structure refers to that which is static, unchanging. But upon close inspection, one discovers that nothing is static in social life; everything is change. The terms must be revised: we must learn to study both at the same time as well as the interactions between them. It is this problem that Rawlins resolved by referring to the combination of structure and process as "an incessant achievement" (1992, p. 7).[10] His phrase appropriately credits the creative nature of even mundane, everyday interactions. They do not simply occur, they must be actively, mutually, created by their participants. As S.F. Moore put it, "the fixed in social reality really means the continuously renewed" (1975, p. 235).

Ultimately, we must study both process and structure together, to do justice to either. Turner, known primarily for his work on the ritual process, provided first a phrase to combine them adequately ("the processual structure of social action," 1974, p. 13) and then a caveat: "It has sometimes been forgotten by those caught up in the first enthusiasm for processualism that process is intimately bound up with structure and that an adequate analysis of social life necessitates a rigorous consideration of the relation between them" (1985, p. 156). It is likely that any one analysis will emphasize one over the other, however, because no one has yet devised an appropriate method of describing both simultaneously.

The remainder of this volume foregrounds structure over process. That is, it describes an essentially structural model as one way to understand process, specifically the process of interaction. Semiotics is generally considered to be more clearly valuable in understanding a frozen moment in time, in understanding the underlying pattern, rather than particular actions. Yet the frozen moment is not separate from, but a resource to, the person acting.[11] If semiotics is valuable in the study of at least one part of what occurs, it is worthy of attention.

John Stewart argued that communication researchers should move away from "semiotic, representational accounts and toward a focus on the situated, emergent, constitutive, paradigmatically oral-aural and person-defining features of languaging" (1991, p. 372). My response would be that there is value in both: We cannot completely escape structure, therefore we study it, but such study should be one part of the study of process, not permitted to overwhelm it. I assume the use of structural resources in constructing the process of interaction, thus study both, for it is a unique combination of both that we as participants simultaneously use and create. By itself, semiotic theory does not prohibit studying the situated, the emergent, or the constitutive, though it has not often been so used; handled with care, it can encourage, not preclude, such attention.

During the course of interaction, one recombines materials currently available in new ways; rhetorical scholars call this *inventio* when it occurs in speech.[12] *Inventio* is no less useful as a concept applied to nonlinguistic behavior: Everything one does is either a recombining of old elements or a deliberate attempt to move away from the old and create something new. In either case there is a focus on the old, on the preceding, on tradition. Whether continuing or rejecting the past, the behavior known and taken for granted is the focus. There is no choice; one cannot convey meaning if one moves entirely away from that which has occurred before: How would anyone understand? There is no creation *ex nihilo* (out of nothing) in social interaction. Likewise, one cannot repeat exactly what has occurred in the past, for the mere act of repeating changes the behavior, making it a second rather than another first occurrence.

This image reveals everything in the social world to be constantly in flux: People recreate what they know in the process of each interaction that occurs, each interaction being influenced by all past interactions and, in turn, influencing all future interactions. For example, first there are human relationships; then buildings are designed taking these into account; then, in their turn, the buildings influence the types of relationships available to our children (Carlisle, 1982, p. 20).

The connection between past and future may be more fragile than is generally assumed. As Levi-Strauss pointed out, "the balance between structure and event, necessity and contingency, the internal and external is a precarious one" (1966b, p. 30). It requires deliberate action to maintain social organization; one must repeat enough of the past to give coherence to the present. Thus, social interaction can be understood as a process of negotiating a succession of discrete social acts. Each social act is novel in detail but predictable in general outline, in overall organization.

Communication thus outlined appears as constant motion, an apparent impossibility. It is made possible because not all elements are in motion at the same time: Everything moves, yes, but not all at once. Today people modify some parts of the greeting ritual while maintaining others (we still shake hands in professional encounters as previously, but now with women as well as with men); tomorrow it will be new parts of the behavior that change (we cannot yet know what, perhaps we will change the age requirements, including children).

Despite the difficulty of pinpointing what to emphasize when foregrounding process over structure, it is appropriate to make some initial suggestions. All social codes serve as the nexus of a series of important dichotomies useful to the study of communication: individual/social, tradition/creativity, stasis/change, product/process, consensus/conflict, public/private, part/whole, and occasionally sacred/secular.[13] These dualities appropriately serve as a starting point in the effort to move beyond studies emphasizing structure to an integration of communication process with structure. Each is briefly summarized here, being brought up again as appropriate throughout the volume.

I begin with the most significant: the connection between the *individual* and the *social*.[14] Ultimately, there is no social group (culture, subculture, community, family) without the individuals who make it up; similarly, in most contexts no one individual alone can function without the larger group. Despite the existence of established social codes and typical expectations for their use, the individual maintains an enormous degree of choice; it is just that those choices are made from within societal constraints.

The control exerted by social expectations can be treated as a resource rather than a restriction. Knowing what is expected, we can flaunt expectations in minute or substantive ways. When girls in a Catholic grade school are required to wear uniforms, they generally find ways to express their individuality despite rather rigidly enforced guidelines: They wear sweaters on top of the uniforms to hide them or develop a secondary code of hair ribbons (or shoelaces or jewelry or hats).

To the extent that the individual chooses to act in expected ways, we speak of *tradition*; to the extent that there is departure from the expectations, we speak of individual *creativity*. Synonyms for tradition are custom, convention, expected norms, the usual, the regular, the ordinary. Tradition stands for all of the past ideas communicated from one person to another that stand as precedent for any future ideas. Tradition defines the present in terms of continuity with the past, drawing a similar bridge to the future.

Tradition is partially constituted through actual performance, yet it is impossible to ever duplicate any prior performance exactly; therefore, each performance actually combines tradition with creativity. Because no one conveys meaning unless there is some overlap with previous examples, one cannot escape tradition. When wedding invitations ''request the honour of your presence,'' they use one of the traditional markers of formality, the British spelling of *honor*, not commonly maintained in other contexts in the United States. Even invitations that are contemporary in other ways (using color or simplified wording) often spell out the full names of the bride and groom and the day and date of the wedding. As with every other object, word, and deed created or performed, each invitation can be described as ultimately a unique exercise in combining tradition with creativity.

*It is an intensely creative act to manipulate a particular form in such a way that the result is sufficiently consistent with cultural expectations to be interpretable while simultaneously sufficiently innovative to be interesting.* People take pleasure in such creative social acts, whether their own or those of others. Even when they think they are not being creative, using the word in its artistic sense, they often are creative in the social sense. When a class of mine was given the choice of writing their own final exam questions and answering them, one student began her essay by commenting that she was not terribly creative and so would simply write me a letter explaining everything she had learned during the semester. Despite her explicit denial, this was nonetheless a creative and original response, one no other student invented.

Closely tied to tradition is the concept of *stasis*: When traditions are maintained, they are static, and the situation is one of stasis. Closely tied to creativity is *change*: Being creative, by definition, implies doing something different. Presumably what my student meant by saying she wasn't creative was that she didn't feel her product was terribly artistic or beautiful in any way. Yet it was socially and intellectually creative (the main kind of creativity teachers encourage anyway). Social life requires a balance of stasis and change: Too much stasis is boring; too much change results in confusion.

Anthropologist David Schneider said: "Social action requires commonality of understandings; it implies common codes of communication; it entails generalized relationship among its parts mediated by human understanding" (1976, p. 198). In outlining the subject matter for the study of other cultures, he has no less outlined the subject matter for our own; in outlining the field for anthropologists, he provides light to other scholars as well. Communication researchers who wish to understand the structure underlying social action need equally to focus on the "common codes of communication" permitting "commonality of understandings." To me, this is most readily studied through the social use of material objects as vehicles to convey ideas and meanings.

Change, no less than tradition, is one of the hallmarks of social life. Lotman and Uspensky said: "The necessity for continual self-renewal, to become different and yet remain the same, constitutes one of the chief working mechanisms of culture" (1978, p. 226). This is often forgotten, and we think of change as odd, continuity as normal. Rather it is both, together, that constitute the normal way of things.

Different communities choose to emphasize creativity versus tradition at different times and in different ways. It is possible to use a home primarily as a display of traditional good taste or to use it primarily as a site for displaying individual creativity. G. Pratt (1982) documented two communities in Vancouver where one that may best be defined as those having old money did the former;

the second, defined as those having new money, did the latter. Both are valid approaches to homes, but it is significant that they chose to divide the world in this way. Somehow as social actors we come to learn what is viewed as appropriate in our own communities, and act accordingly.

Each social fact is a *product*; to arrive at each product one goes through some sort of *process*. In communication, product is used particularly often in reference to mass media items (an ad is one product, a television show another), but the term can refer equally to social interaction. A conversation is no less a product than an ad, though less visibly concrete, and far more obviously a joint production of all the participants. What one does in creating a social product is referred to as the process. Sometimes the process and the product are quite separable (the social process of creating an ad is quite different from the physical ad that results); other times they are harder to disentangle (the process of having a conversation is an event, hardly distinguishable from the conversation considered as product). Here the distinction may be one of point of view: whether we as analysts emphasize the process of negotiating necessary to interaction, or if we look to the outcome as separable from the event itself.

Within any interaction there is room for both *consensus* and *conflict*. Consensus occurs when traditions, goals, or expectations of the participants overlap considerably. Conflict is more frequent when these traditions, goals, or assumptions diverge, it being harder to agree when people do not even share sufficient grounds for mutual understanding.[15] This is not to imply that understanding is sufficient for agreement, only necessary. One reason so much interaction follows traditional guidelines is the level of comfort and lack of effort it permits; conflict often takes more time and effort and thought than consensus. If there is a fight every time dinner is served within a family over whether dinner time arrives according to the clock, regardless of who is currently at home, or according to when family members walk in the door, regardless of what hour the clock reports, more time will be spent fighting than eating. A study by Ellis demonstrated how one major cause of domestic violence in Britain can be attributed to exactly this clash in definitions of dinner time: The wife prepares dinner at the usual time, but the husband does not arrive; when he arrives several hours later, the food is cold, and he beats her for not having a hot meal immediately to hand (Ellis, 1983).

Though true of all social codes, in particular food, clothes, and objects are the places where the *private* and the *public* worlds meet. People have great control over their own use of items in these categories; at the same time, they have perhaps less control than they might assume. Also, though modern Western culture gives great emphasis to privacy, the public world is granted more emphasis elsewhere in the world. "Privacy cannot be the dominant value in any society. Man has to live in society, and social concerns have to take precedence" (B. Moore, 1984, p. 274).[16] Clearly both have significant roles to play.

People learn their ideas about appropriate or "good" behavior from others and model their own private behavior after what they see demonstrated publicly.[17] At times there is specific censorship by others (as when employees are told directly not to wear sandals to work, for example, or when taxi drivers in Kenosha find their dress code legislated by the city government), though most often self-censorship alone requires us to conform. In theory I could eat anything I want for breakfast, especially when no one else is witness; in fact, like the majority, I tend to eat what are considered "breakfast" foods: cereal, eggs, toast, and so forth. A choice of ice cream or steak or pizza carries with it an implication of deliberate nonconformity, even if I am the only witness to the act. Small social facts such as these convey meaning, so they are granted time and study.

It has been suggested that public space is currently increasing at the expense of privacy. Levrant de Bretteville referred to this as the *parlorization* of our homes, using the parlor as metaphor:

> Parlorization thus implies the establishment of a space for displaying possessions or wares to visitors, a place to sit in formal attire engaging in genteel conversation. The parlor's expressive equipment—its furnishings and appointments—communicates what we would have others think of us, while real personal and individual content is devalued and displaced, shoved behind the scenes along with the variety of activity that flourishes in loosely ordered space. (Levrant de Bretteville, 1979, p. 35)

This concept may be valuable metaphorically to describe a larger process as well, not limited only to the use of space within homes.

The same behavior changes substantially when moved from a private to a public location. J. Finkelstein pointed out that dining in a restaurant may appear to be quite similar to dining at home, but it entails a quite different degree of sociality. In the restaurant, "we are relieved of the responsibility to shape sociality," thus eating out destroys precisely that which it appears to encourage, "our participation in the social arena" (1989, p. 5). By eating in a restaurant, the primary social actors permit secondary others to make decisions regarding food and context, in this way significantly limiting their range of expected behavior, refusing to take charge and design the event themselves. Entertaining in the home leaves them no such choice: They must make all the decisions, retaining control, increasing their participation in the social arena.

The most obvious dichotomy, yet the least studied, is that between the *part* and the *whole*.[18] As used here, the part refers to any small, generally too small, piece or bit of behavior; too small, that is, for adequate analysis. And the whole refers to the larger context within which it can be said to make sense: all of the information necessary to take into account if that bit is to be interpreted appropriately. The concern here is less with structure, hierarchy, or size, than with the human need to join small, individually meaningless bits (behaviors, words, things) into coherent, meaningful wholes. Synonyms for wholes, depending on who is doing the writing, are set, system, matrix, and pattern. Gregory Bateson and Margaret Mead were in some ways a most unlikely couple, but they shared and passed on to their students and colleagues an overriding concern with the nature of pattern in the world.[19]

Depending on the event studied, there may also be a relevant distinction between the *sacred* and the *secular*. In the modern-day United States, the sacred refers primarily to whatever formal religious traditions are followed within a particular community whereas the secular refers to virtually everything else. A study of ritual oratory, though initially based on language use within a church setting, for example, could be expanded to compare that linguistic code with language use of the same participants outside the church. Some of the time they make use of some of the same techniques but to different ends. Martin Luther King, Jr. used just this technique: By moving linguistic structures typical of the sacred uses of language into the secular sphere, he maintained a connection with the religious force generally attributed to the sacred setting, otherwise absent from the secular world, giving his words particular resonance and authority.

As a further example of the connections between the sacred and the secular, Dyen, in a study of *pysanky* (Ukrainian Easter eggs given elaborate designs through the use of a wax resist technique), described two types of rituals incorporating the eggs. One is private and sacred, the other public and secular. In both, the *pysanky*, as objects, are combined with foods and clothing chosen for their ability to be equally indicative of ethnic identity. The private, sacred ritual takes place in church and emphasizes the priest blessing the eggs (see Fig. I.1).

> Families place their finished eggs [*pysanky*] in a basket along with the holiday foods to be eaten on Easter Sunday, cover the basket with an embroidered cloth, and take it to church to be blessed by the priest in a special ceremony, either on Holy Saturday evening or on Easter morning. Each family then gives the priest a decorated egg as a token of respect. (Dyen, 1988, p. 100)

Although not explicitly mentioned here, family members normally dress up, most likely in traditionally embroidered blouses or shirts.

This private, religious ritual is matched to a public, secular ritual for selling the *pysanky* (see Fig. I.2). They are grouped with other objects considered indicative of Ukrainian ethnic identity (such as Easter candles) and sold together with traditional Ukrainian foods (such as *pirohi*) by people wearing traditional Ukrainian clothing (again the embroidered shirt or blouse). Understanding the connection between these two rituals in the minds of community members, despite the obvious distinction that one is sacred whereas the other is secular, is essential to understanding their meaning.

Each of these dualisms—individual/social, tradition/creativity, stasis/change, product/process, consensus/conflict, public/private, part/whole, and sacred/secular—is brought up again throughout this volume. Some are given great attention, others only minimal notice. All are potentially valuable topics in the study of communication, thus, they are included here, however briefly. Certainly they

FIG. I.1.   Ukrainian *pysanky*. In the collection of the Milwaukee Public Museum, catalog number 431780/24816 a-e. Photo by Don Lintner, University of Wisconsin-Parkside.

FIG. I.2.   Ukrainian basket with *pysanky*. Photo courtesy of The Balch Institute for Ethnic Studies.

are not new topics for this field or any other, but they are rarely presented together, as the coherent package they form.[20] They are part of how current researchers understand communication, assumptions we take for granted before we even begin to discuss semiotics.

## NOTES

1. Eco (1990) then proposed a less graphic image for the squeamish, describing how putting together branches and leaves will never equal a forest, but in walking through a forest one discovers the nature of leaves and branches (1990, p. xiii). Either metaphor provides a clear image of the delicacy with which we must begin our study of the whole, and of the danger of carelessly dividing it into smaller parts for the purpose of study.

2. Obviously there are exceptions to this. Knapp and Hall (1992), for example, included a chapter on clothing; Roach and Musa (1983) discussed clothing as part of nonverbal communication. Note, however, that the majority of the references cited in both are by researchers outside the discipline of communication.

3. Study of this connection generally goes by the name "the Sapir-Whorf hypothesis" after Edward Sapir and Benjamin Lee Whorf, known for their serious consideration of the matter. The classic reference is Whorf (1956).

4. See Gudykunst and Ting-Toomey with Chua (1988) for the most obvious proposal, that traditional research concerns in interpersonal communication be applied to intercultural settings; see Carbaugh (1990), Leeds-Hurwitz (1990a, 1992a), and Pearce (1989) for more subtle integrations of interpersonal and intercultural concerns.

5. As Jameson pointed out, "We need, not one, but many, introductions to this 'semiotics' " (1987, p. vi). Semiotics is complex; no single introduction has to date been sufficient for all audiences.

6. This is how I hope to step outside of the problems with semiotic theorizing that Krippendorff (1990) outlined: Encouraging people to use semiotics as a tool for understanding their own lives, it may be possible to avoid inappropriate objectivism.

7. For further discussion of some of the issues introduced later, see Pearce (1989), Leeds-Hurwitz (1989), Leeds-Hurwitz and Sigman with Sullivan (in press).

8. Turner (1985, pp. 151–173) documented the shift within anthropology from structural assumptions to a new emphasis on process; S. F. Moore (1975, 1978) provided extensive discussion of the connections between a structural view and a process view as applied to actual behavior.

9. See Leeds-Hurwitz and Sigman with Sullivan (in press) for elaboration.

10. Rawlins spoke solely of relationships; it is my expansion of his idea to apply it more generally to other aspects of social interaction.

11. Threadgold (1986) discussed at length the way in which three semioticians (Voloshinov, Halliday, and Eco) resolved the relationship between structure and process through situating both in dialogic interaction, particularly emphasizing language with text as the basic unit of study. The original statements used in his analysis are Voloshinov (1929/1973, p. 117), Halliday (1978, p. 135), and Eco (1976).

12. My thanks to Barnett Pearce (personal communication) for this point.

13. This is my preferred set of dichotomies; other lists have been presented by others with different agendas in mind. The philosopher W. T. Jones (1961, pp. 20–42) proposed what he called the seven *axes of bias*: order/disorder, static/dynamic, continuity/discreteness, inner/outer, sharp-focus/soft-focus, this-world/other-world, spontaneity/process. Jones applied these to art, science, metaphysics, and political theory. Closer to home, in recent discussions of communication theory, Gronbeck (1988) presented a set of "knots" to be untied: information/knowledge, individual/society, continuity/ change, form/content, self/role. And Rawlins (1992) divided his dialectics

of friendship into those he deemed contextual (public/private, ideal/real) and those he deemed interactional (independence/dependence, affection/ instrumentality, judgment/acceptance, expressiveness/protectiveness). What is common to all these lists is the understanding that dualities can be helpful in thinking through the complexity of real life.

14. The most influential book on the topic, for both sociology and communication, is probably G. H. Mead (1974).

15. See Freeman, Littlejohn, and Pearce (1992) for further discussion of conflict, particularly moral conflicts, defined as "those in which the participants not only differ about what they want, believe, or need, but also lack shared criteria by which to adjudicate their differences" (p. 312).

16. See Spierenburg (1991) for a description of the rise of the private sphere in Western Europe in the 1800s; see Cromley (1990) for description of the issues involved in achieving balance between public and private space within New York City apartments in the late 1800s.

17. Perhaps a better word choice would be *moral*. See Birdwhistell (1970a) for a description of what constitutes moral behavior in interaction. Note the connections between his use of the term and that of Freeman et al. (1992).

18. Lerner (1963) provided an early attempt to address the issue within a variety of disciplines.

19. This is reflected clearly in the writings of M. C. Bateson, their daughter (1984, 1989); see also Bateson and Mead (1942); G. Bateson (1979).

20. I once presented a conference paper on a closely related set of concepts, arguing then that they served as common themes for the fields of communication and folklore. Just now that point seems less critical to me than their value as a way of framing abiding concerns within communication.

# Semiotic Theory and Communication Theory

Part I of this book is intended to provide a strong theoretical foundation for the study of semiotics within communication. Chapter 1 provides an historical overview and necessary background to the study of *semiotics*. This chapter is hardly a complete summary of the field of semiotics (whole books have been written on the topic) but is designed to provide basic information particularly of value to communication scholars. After a brief history of the establishment of the field by its major figures, discussion of various definitions and the potential contributions of semiotics, the common use of linguistics as a model for other semiotic codes, is described. The connections between culture, communication, and semiotics serve as the focus of the chapter; interrelated definitions of each demonstrate their overlap, providing common ground for later elaboration. Think of this chapter as the portal, or doorway, to the remainder of the book; it presents the obvious beginning point.

Chapter 2 introduces *signs* as the basic building blocks of semiotic theory, as informally agreed upon by nearly all authors writing on the topic. If this one concept is understood, all else will follow; if it is fuzzy, little else will make sense. The origins of the concept are described, followed by a select list of basic terms useful in its study. These have been chosen from the vast number of terms invented to date, for researchers in semiotics have proposed more new vocabulary than anyone can reasonably be expected to remember. Of the three major types of signs, the one most important to researchers in communication, *symbols*, serve as the focus of the majority of the chapter. Continuing with the metaphor of chapter 1 as the doorway, chapter 2 presents the first object of study; that object is noticed, picked up, examined, and described.

Chapter 3 places signs into their proper context, *codes*. Signs rarely appear alone; they appear in groups. These groups, together with the rules for their use, are known as codes. After defining the term, the characteristics of all codes are described in detail and three major types of codes are outlined; the majority of the chapter discusses *social codes*, the type most relevant to communication. Because the term code has appeared frequently in the communication literature, a brief review of how it has been used previously is provided. Past uses of the term are similar but not identical to that described here. Here the angle of vision changes: The object of study presented in chapter 2 no longer appears alone in an empty room; the remainder of the room, its proper context, is now visible and other objects appear and can be examined as well.[1]

Together these chapters are intended to provide sufficient theoretical grounding for the doing (the practice) of semiotics; the basics are laid out as clearly as possible, the details ignored. Extensive footnotes recommending further reading are provided for anyone wishing to follow up any of the ideas presented. It is not my intent to provide a complete overview of semiotics as it currently stands; others have attempted that, more or less successfully. Because semiotic theory has its own agendas, not identical with those of communication, some parts of semiotics are more useful to communication than others. I attempt to focus on what seem to me the most essential and valuable parts. Others would certainly have chosen differently; they may yet write their own books. It is important to stress, however, that Part I of this book is not intended to stand alone. It is but prelude to the second part: applying the theory to concrete examples of behavior.

Any theory can be thought of as a tool kit, and semiotics is no exception; applying theory to data involves turning passive knowledge about each tool and how it functions into active knowledge of how various tools are actually used. Despite the fact that theory alone is always a bit dry to read (just as trying to memorize the names and functions of unfamiliar tools is difficult), it comes alive when joined to examples taken from everyday life (as one learns the names and functions of tools more completely through using them to build something new). As with the first bird feeder a young carpenter makes, the edges of our semiotic analysis may not be perfectly squared, but a homemade object can have value to its creator despite its flaws. We learn best in the process of doing; so we must each eventually use semiotic theory ourselves to analyze behavior if we are to find value in it. At the same time, just as a good carpenter studies her tools before using them the first time, learning their names and hearing their functions from someone more experienced, so I begin this foray into semiotics with an overview of theory.

**NOTE**

1. Following this metaphor, chapters 4 through 6 examine three different rooms in a single house. Chapter 7 steps back yet further, discussing the connections between these (and potential other) rooms, and the house as a whole.

# Chapter 1

# Introducing Semiotics

Communication is a young field, yet it covers a broad area. Recently, to resolve much dispute about exactly what constitutes the definition of the field, Cronkhite (1986) proposed ''the study of human symbolic activity'' as one emphasis shared by all subfields. His definition has been noticed and is gaining acceptance, but one obvious implication remains undeveloped: the connections between communication and *semiotics*, the theoretical area most directly identified with the study of symbolic behavior. With others, it makes sense to me that Cronkhite's proposal points to a reasonable focus for the field of communication; I have no problem in identifying my research as contributing to the study of human symbolic activity. Yet as others have previously studied this topic, we may find it profitable to discover what the semiotic literature contributes to our understanding of communication.[1]

This chapter briefly introduces semiotics: its origins, the definition of the field, and the connections between semiotics and the related field of linguistics, concluding with closely related definitions of culture, communication, and semiotics to demonstrate their areas of overlap. Semiotics is uncommonly broad; this volume makes no pretense of supplying a complete history even of the major ideas. Rather it presents a concise introduction to selected aspects, those that seem to me potentially most valuable for the field of communication. This summary in no way substitutes for a more thorough reading of original sources, but as an introductory synthesis, it may provoke interest in particular authors or ideas.[2]

## ESTABLISHING THE FIELD OF SEMIOTICS

Independently, but at approximately the same point in time, Ferdinand de Saussure, a linguist in Switzerland, and Charles Sanders Peirce, a philosopher in the United States, described the need for a field to study the meanings conveyed through signs and symbols (see Figs. 1.1 and 1.2).[3] Both felt something important was missing in the currently existing fields of study and wanted to remedy the situation. For both authors the standard references are to books published by others on their behalf after their deaths; as a result their influence was greater on future generations than on their contemporaries.

Saussure's statements introducing *semiology* come from a compilation of notes taken by several of his students based on lectures given between 1907 and 1911, published after his death as *Course in General Linguistics*. The quote most often cited as responsible for establishing the field follows:

> A science that studies the life of signs within society is conceivable; it would be a part of social psychology and consequently of general psychology; I shall call it semiology (from Greek *semeion* "sign"). Semiology would show what constitutes signs, what laws govern them. Since the science does not yet exist, no one can say what it would be; but it has a right to existence, a place staked out in advance. Linguistics is only a part of the general science of semiology; the laws discovered by semiology will be applicable to linguistics, and the latter will circumscribe a well-defined area within the mass of anthropological facts. (Saussure, 1916/1969, p. 16)

Note that he, being a linguist, proposed semiology as a science placing the study of language into a broad context; similar concerns by others later led to the development of pragmatics and sociolinguistics.

Peirce, unlike Saussure, wrote his own papers (enormous numbers of them, in fact), though the majority remained unpublished during his lifetime. The larger quantity of available quotes from Peirce about *semiotics* (which he actually used in the singular, *semiotic*), encourages disputes among his followers as to exactly what he intended (as with all authors, he changed his mind on a variety of details over the years). From his writings, one commonly cited justification for establishing the new field, to be matched to that of Saussure presented previously, follows:

> Logic, in its general sense, is, as I believe I have shown, only another name for *semiotic*, the quasi-necessary, or formal doctrine of signs. By describing the doctrine as "quasi-necessary", or formal, I mean that we observe the characters of such signs as we know, and from such an observation, by a process which I will not object to naming Abstraction, we are led to statements, eminently fallible, and therefore in one sense by no means necessary, as to what *must* be the characters of all signs used by a "scientific" intelligence, that is to say by an intelligence capable of learning by experience. (Peirce, 1931/1958, Vol. 2, para. 227)

FIG. 1.1. Ferdinand de Saussure. Photo courtesy of the Library of Congress.

FIG. 1.2. Charles Sanders Peirce. Photo courtesy of the Peirce Edition Project, Indiana University, Indianapolis.

5

Here the study of signs is narrowed rather than broadened; it is related to logic rather than the broader society.

As is clear from these quotes, a fundamental distinction between the two efforts exists: Peirce studied *logic*; Saussure studied *behavior*. Despite this distinction, it should be obvious that logic is one part of what governs behavior. As a result, these two separately established fields of study have substantial areas of overlap. It has become common in the United States to use the term semiotics to refer to the entire field (to all of the work of Saussure and Peirce as well as the followers of both), in deference to the fact that Peirce devoted the greatest amount of time and effort toward developing the groundwork of the discipline and in an attempt to consolidate rather than draw fine distinctions between areas of related research.[4]

Within the field of communication Peirce has been the more influential to date, and the Peircian tradition is proposed as potentially the most valuable in a recent argument by Switzer, Fry, and Miller (1990).[5] Yet I would recommend Saussure as the less obscure and more readily applicable to actual behavior.[6] Saussure's scant comments have been expanded by his many followers, so there is no dearth of material available for inspiration. In particular, there is an entire strand of related research by scholars known collectively as the Russian Formalists and the Czech Structuralists (surprisingly often ignored within both current semiotics and communication as studied in the United States), heavily influenced by Saussure, demonstrating an early interest in applying semiotics to various aspects of culture.[7] Their work is particularly valuable when applying semiotics to material aspects of communicative behavior, as proposed in Part II of this volume, and is described in some detail in the introduction to that section. Thus, the approach followed in this book technically is *semiology*, though the term *semiotics* is used, because it has found favor as the more general term.


## DEFINING SEMIOTICS

The accepted definition of semiotics today generally is phrased as either "the study of signs" or "the study of signs and sign systems." (Briefly, a sign is something present that stands for something absent, as a cross represents Christianity; a sign system, also termed a code, is a collection of signs and rules for their use.) Defining semiotics in this way is brief but vague. What does it mean to say one studies signs? What exactly are signs? Why are they worthy of attention in the first place? What difference do they make in the world? These are issues addressed by many authors. In comments specifically intended for an audience of nonspecialists, Wray provided a useful beginning:

> Semiotics is the study of signs. On that and little else, all "semioticians" seem to
> agree. Specifically it is the study of semiosis, or communication—that is, the way

any sign, whether it is a traffic signal, a thermometer reading of 98.6° F, poetic imagery, musical notation, a prose passage, or a wink of the eye, functions in the mind of an interpreter to convey a specific meaning in a given situation. Broadly defined, semiotics includes the study of how Sherlock Holmes makes meaning out of Hansom tracks, how deoxyribonucleic acid conveys hereditary traits, how an historian sees significance in an old church registry, or how Baudelaire's view of the world can be approached through a pattern of words arranged on paper. (Wray, 1981, p. 4)

Wray introduced two new terms, *semiosis* and *semiotician*. Briefly, semiosis is understood to be the active form of the word semiotics, more formally defined as "the process of making and using signs" (Sless, 1986, p. 2). The term semiotician moves outside the realm of semiotic behavior to its study: It is the name for someone who studies semiotics. Anyone who performs semiotic analysis figuratively dons a T-shirt reading "Semiotician at work." (Because everyone engages in semiotic behavior, there is no need of a special word for someone *doing* semiosis). Three ideas are particularly noteworthy in Wray's quote: (a) the facile equation of semiosis with communication, not uncommon for semioticians, though usually passing unremarked within the field of communication; (b) the basic description of what the study of signs actually involves (here described as studying how something functions in the mind of an interpreter to convey a specific meaning in a specific situation); and (c) the breadth of activity included in the study of semiotic behavior.

What is important here is not merely that semiotics includes a lot of things that other people would never have grouped together, which is interesting but not terribly enlightening, but that it explains how they are similar. In each case, whether it be a traffic signal or poetic imagery, something (the sign) conveys meaning—meaning that would not otherwise be obvious, or that we could not otherwise present in such a condensed form. Some signs have practical functions: A traffic signal is a fast way for people to follow a set of rules in common, without spending a great deal of time and effort discussing these rules each time they find themselves in the same predicament (at a crossroads with other cars going other directions, needing a fast and easy way to arrange who should go when, so the cars do not crash). Others have less practical function but no less significance. Poetic imagery is less likely to prevent two cars from crashing but can, for example, convey the essence of that experience to someone who was not present at the time. So it is not breadth of scope for its own sake, the mere accumulation of exemplars, that is significant but breadth of scope for the surprising fact that so many different actions, objects, behaviors, in so many different contexts, all appear to operate in a similar fashion, that warrants attention.

Breadth of scope has come to be accepted as one of the hallmarks of semiotics. Although the original brief definitions permit this same breadth, it may not have been immediately evident. Multiple lists abound; let me quote just one further author on the topic, Hawkes:

> Human beings emerge from any account of semiotic structures as inveterate and promiscuous producers of signs. . . . Accordingly, nothing in the human world can be *merely* utilitarian. . . . All five senses, smell, touch, taste, hearing, sight, can function in the process of *semiosis*: that is, as sign-producers or sign-receivers. . . . Conceivably there is a *langue* of cooking, of which each meal is a *parole*, and in connection with which *taste* is the sense most exploited, although *sight* and *smell* also have their role. Equally, there is no doubt a *langue* of perfume and, as Barthes has demonstrated at length (with complications in his *Système de la Mode*) of ''fashion'' and of writing about fashion at large. (Hawkes, 1977, p. 134)

The new vocabulary words here, *langue* and *parole* (the French words for *language* and *speech*), are adopted from Saussure's writings. They refer to the distinction normally made by linguists between an entire *langue* or language (understood to include every possible word and sentence utterable in that language) and any one example of *parole* or speech (a particular instance of someone uttering a word or sentence or longer stretch of talk). This quote also demonstrates the way in which language generally serves as a metaphor for other systems of communication; here, cooking and clothing are assumed to follow the model of language in that both exist at one and the same time as a single *langue*, or presumed system, as well as through various examples of *parole*, or immediately available exemplars. As with language, we can never ''see'' or study the entire *langue*, but assume its existence from the evidence of *parole*.

An example of *langue* is all of the food you ever ate at your parents' house as a child. It would of course be impossible to prepare a complete listing of every item of food and every menu from every meal that you ate in your parents' house. For this reason, *langue*, by its nature, exists theoretically rather than concretely. That does not imply a lack of significance but only a certain ephemeral quality. You know what you ate as a child, but it would be hard for you to make me know it in the same way unless I too had participated in all those meals. *Parole* is used to refer to the particular meal you ate last night for dinner. It would be relatively easy to describe this, and so *parole* is understood to be quite concrete.

Part of what is interesting about restaurant food is that many of the items prepared are not regularly part of the *langue* of food eaten by the customers when they are not present. So, in fact, it sometimes becomes a marker of status if the restaurant serves food customers have only read about (e.g., fiddleheads—the top of the ostrich fern cut just before it opens in the spring, considered a delicacy when included in a salad in Wisconsin), in addition or instead of food they know how to prepare and regularly eat.

As this example demonstrates, it is helpful to have words available to describe the distinction between the realm of what one normally experiences and considers possible, and one's actual experience on a particular occasion. Such words permit us to explain just what is special about expensive restaurants as well as to describe such things as the differences in family experiences between spouses raised in different parts of the country or different countries altogether. It is not that one intends to fuss about the food served for dinner by the other, just that it might not have been expected.

As compiled by Umberto Eco, an Italian semiotician and one of the major figures in the field, the classic list of what is to be included in the study of semiotics is some five pages long. Among other areas named, those most directly of interest to communication researchers include various channels of nonverbal communication as well as mass communication and rhetoric (Eco, 1976, pp. 9–14). Lists do not convey the breadth of the field half so well as particular examples, however. The following abbreviated version of a quote from a newspaper article by Pines explaining semiotics to a lay audience, uncommonly concise and vivid in its imagery, serves well as an introduction:

> Everything we do sends messages about us in a variety of codes, semioticians contend. We are also on the receiving end of innumerable messages encoded in music, gestures, foods, rituals, books, movies or advertisements. Yet we seldom realize that we have received or sent such messages, and would have trouble explaining the rules under which they operate. . . .
>
> Nothing seems too trivial or too complicated for semioticians to analyze. Take the matter of cowboy boots, for instance. A New Yorker who buys such boots is actually responding to well-established myths about the cowboy in our culture, and also to the new power of the oil millionaires and ranchers who support the Reagan Administration, says Dr. Marshall Blonsky. . . .
>
> "In both myths, the wearer of cowboy boots handles the world masterfully," says Dr. Blonsky. "He is virile, self-reliant, free to roam over the wide-open spaces that New Yorkers lack, and has or supplies virtually limitless energy." Nobody cares that real cowboys often lead humdrum lives, he points out. New Yorkers don't want real cowboy boots—just the *idea* of cowboy boots. So they buy boots made of lizard or snake that serve as symbols or signs of cowboy boots, in which they can roam the city with a feeling of power, but wouldn't be much good for rounding up cattle. . . .
>
> The method of semiotics is, first, to separate an act, called "the signifier," from its meaning, called "the signified." When a man offers a woman a red rose, for instance, the signifier is the act of giving the rose, but the signified is romance. The rose itself has little importance. (Pines, 1982, pp. C1, C6)

In bringing together cowboy boots, advertisements, and films, Pines accurately represented semiotics as the broad field it generally intends to be. By saying that semiotics studies even the trivial, she did not denigrate the field but pointed out that even minor details convey information and are worthy of serious study. The example of cowboy boots conveys an appropriate impression of what semiotic analysis might look like, here specifically limited to the study of the myths attached to objects. The new vocabulary words, *signifier* and *signified*, are critical terms in semiotics. Every sign has two components: the visible part, or signifier, and the absent part, or signified. (Dividing a sign into parts has traditionally been a major subject of discussion within semiotics and is addressed in greater detail in chapter 2.)

The statement that "the rose itself has little importance," though overly cute, is basically correct: The *rose itself* conveys less information than the *use of the rose* by a particular person within a particular context, in this case a man giving a woman a red rose. There is nothing about the color red or the type of flower that has to convey the message romance, though by tradition many people have come to expect that red roses do convey that message. But even with this assumption in place, a red rose growing in my garden does not by itself and in that situation convey romance; only when my husband cuts it and hands it to me does it acquire the implication of romance.

The complete version of Pines's article summarizes a famous comment where Eco defined semiotics as the study of lies. The original quote elaborates on the idea. As one of the more novel presentations of what constitutes semiotics, it is quoted at length here:

> Semiotics is concerned with everything that can be taken as a sign. A sign is everything which can be taken as significantly substituting for something else. This something else does not necessarily have to exist or to actually be somewhere at the moment in which a sign stands for it. Thus semiotics is in principle the discipline studying everything which can be used in order to lie. If something cannot be used to tell a lie, conversely it cannot be used to tell the truth; it cannot in fact be used "to tell" at all. I think that the definition of a "theory of the lie" should be taken as a pretty comprehensive program for a general semiotics. (Eco, 1976, p. 7)

Linguists have suggested the ability to lie as one of the defining characteristics of language.[8] Lying as used here is to be understood in the broadest possible sense, that is, "the ability to describe things not currently existing," rather than the narrower, more common meaning of "telling untruths." As such, it supplies a critical component of our ability to analyze and change the current world. By studying how we lie, we study as well how we bring about change. We cannot change the world until we understand it, so the more we come to understand it, the more we recognize the multiple connections between factors seemingly unconnected, the better our chances of changing it. The social world has an ecology, just as the natural one does, and it is just as easy to bring about an imbalance inadvertently, despite good intentions. Thus, semioticians might be described as ecologists of the social world: They study interconnections, seeking to understand the system in its entirety, not any one part alone.

The notion of a sign as "substituting for something else" proposed by Eco merits clarification. Signs work through their ability as pointers; that is, they serve as a kind of shorthand, pointing or referring to something absent. This explains why even trivial details can function as signs: They point to larger, more abstract concepts. We move from the present physical detail (a rose) to the absent but invoked abstraction (a particular notion of romantic love) without effort and take the move so much for granted it is essentially lost. We *see* a rose, but *interpret* romance, moving so quickly from one to the other that we often fail to realize that a visible instance of romance itself was not presented. A large part of semiotic analysis consists of learning how to notice shifts of this sort. If as participants we generally we see A but interpret Z, with all the steps between invisible but obvious, then as semioticians we make explicit all the invisible but essential steps moving us from what we see to what we interpret.

Having presented these explanations, it becomes possible to elaborate upon the previous brief definition of semiotics as the study of signs. There have been many complicated definitions proposed, each attempting to meet a specific need. One useful rephrasing (adapted, obviously, from Saussure's original proposal of "the life of signs within society") has been put forth by Ungar and McGraw, suggesting that semiotics takes as its subject matter "the material practices, forms, and institutions of signs in culture" (1989, p. xii). Their wording shifts focus from *society* to *culture*, that is, from institutions and structures to behaviors and activities, appropriate given today's understanding of these terms.[9] Another definition, by Tobin, suggests that semiotics is "a general philosophical theory dealing with the production of signs and symbols as part of code systems which are used to communicate information" (1990, p. 6), shifting the focus from *individual signs* to their combination in *code systems*, in larger sets or groupings of signs, a point that is important later. Tobin here separated symbols from signs, though not everyone does. Symbols are one type of sign, a minor distinction in this chapter, though a primary topic of discussion in chapter 2.

For the purposes of this book, the formal definition of semiotics adopted is the original, most straightforward one ("the study of signs"), but it should be understood to imply at least the following assumptions:

1. We begin with an interest in discrete signs. (Specifically, we are interested in how signs function, which can be known, rather than in how people come to create them, which is considerably more difficult to discover.)
2. We are interested in how signs are organized into and operate within larger groups (which are termed codes).
3. We are interested in how these code systems operate together and in still larger groups (which are termed cultures).
4. We are interested in how codes within different cultures are related and interact in subtle and complex ways.

Through the study of semiotics, we can learn more about ourselves and others, how we make and convey meanings, how we understand what happens in the world; by identifying with the study of semiotics, we identify ourselves as interested in understanding such issues.

## CONTRIBUTION OF SEMIOTICS

As with every field, there is a related set of important underlying questions: Why study semiotics? What does it have to offer? Why do we need it? What can it help us as researchers do that we cannot do so easily without it? Part of the answer to these questions has just been provided: It helps us learn about ourselves and others and how we make and convey meanings, surely a worthy topic of study.[10] More of the answer lies in a quote from Eco, who said: *"Every act of communication to or between human beings*—or any other intelligent biological or mechanical apparatus—*presupposes a signification system as its necessary condition"* (1976, p. 9). Semiotics has the potential to serve a significant support role in the study of communication. The logical steps are as follows:

1. Communication researchers study communication.
2. Communication, in order to occur, presupposes a common signification system.
3. Semiotics is the study of signification systems.
4. Therefore, those who study communication may find it useful to also study semiotics.

As part of a very different argument (critiquing semioticians for spending too much time discussing jargon and too little time actually studying human behavior—an appropriate critique), David Sless wrote: "Semiotics is far too important an enterprise to be left to semioticians" (1986, preface). Anyone interested in how people create meaning for themselves and others can put semiotic theory to good use. If some who self-identify as semioticians become more interested in arcane discussions of jargon than in human behavior, that is a problem of where they choose to direct their energy, not a problem inherent in the theory, that theory remains available for others to adapt and use for their own purposes.[11] If this sounds like a potentially large group, it is.

The transdisciplinary nature of semiotics is often stressed. This has led to some pretentious statements about the role of semiotics as the one overarching discipline.[12] One of the less provocative versions comes from a major figure in French semiotics, A. J. Greimas:

> The problem of signification is at the center of the preoccupations of our time. . . .
> The human world as it appears to us is defined essentially as the world of signification. The world can only be called "human" to the extent that it means something. Thus it is in research dealing with signification that the human sciences can find their common denominator. (Greimas, 1983, p. 3)

With Sless, Greimas thought the study of the meaning that results from semiosis (here termed *signification*, a common alternative) must be the focus of semiotics, returning the emphasis to human activities and the world as people make sense of it, as it subsequently appears to them.[13]

It may not yet be clear that semiotics primarily studies *relationships*, rather than individual facts, texts, or objects. No one fact, text, or object exists alone in a universe unto itself; therefore, one cannot properly study it devoid of context. That context is most appropriately made up of other similar facts, texts, or objects, gathered together in what is sometimes termed a *system of relations* (Culler, 1981, p. 26). This is the reason for expanding the definition to include codes (the more technical term for systems of relations) and then to look at those codes in relation to each other. This point is critical to the basic position taken in this volume; it is elaborated upon in detail in chapter 7.

An emphasis on the centrality of signs and their use in human communication has led some authors to create a new label for people stressing their ability to create signs as the critical component in what defines humanity (parallel to the technical term for humans, *homo sapiens*, or "man the thinker," more generally "people who think"). No one term has come to be accepted, though several have been offered: (a) *homo symbolicus*, literally translated as "man the symbol-maker," more generally understood as "humans are those who make symbols";[14] (b) *homo significans*, "humans are those who signify";[15] and (c) *animal symbolicum*, "[humans as] the animal who makes symbols."[16] These terms share an emphasis on the centrality of signs (symbols being one type of sign) to human behavior. As Deely phrased it, "Indeed, at the heart of semiotics is the realization that the whole of human experience, without exception, is an interpretive structure mediated and sustained by signs" (1990, p. 5). This, then, provides the final answer to the question of the value of semiotics: If we as researchers wish to understand human behavior and how humans communicate with one another, a large part of what we must study is the creation and use of signs; because that is precisely what semiotics studies, semiotic theory, by definition, provides a good starting point.

## LINGUISTICS AS A MODEL FOR SEMIOTICS

Largely due to Saussure's role as a linguist, his early statements about semiotics are generally understood to imply that language be taken as the model for other semiotic systems and that linguistics (the formal study of language) serves as the model for how to study all semiotic systems. In Roman Jakobson's words, it is generally assumed that "the basic, the primary, the most important semiotic system is language; language really is the foundation of culture" (1971b, p. 557).[17] There has been considerable discussion recently about the appropriateness of this presumptive role of language as the preeminent semiotic system and whether linguistics always serves as the best model for semiotic analysis.[18] Such discussion, though it will influence the future, does not change the fact that language has, to date, served as the model for much work within semiotics.[19]

Eco demonstrated the value of language as a productive model in the following:

> I am speaking to you. You are understanding me, because I am following the rules of a precise code (the English language), so precise that it also allows me to make use of it with a lot of phonetic and grammatical variations. Its strong underlying structure in some way acts like a lodestone which magnetizes and attracts my deviations from the norm. You understand me because there exists a code (a sort of inner competence shared by you and me) and there exist possible messages, performed as concrete utterances and interpretable as a set of propositions. (Eco, 1973b, p. 57)

This is the sense in which I see language performing valuable service as the model for semiotic analysis; at the very least, it provides an effective starting point. Clearly, it is not the only resource, but as it presents a good beginning, we should not ignore it; at the same time, we must not permit the beginning point to become the final goal. It is already well known that language works because its speakers share particular signs (words, after all, are signs) and share a code (each language combines words through grammatical structures) as well as sharing understandings of how to use that code to convey meaning (norms of use of that particular language). Language works as a model for semiotic analysis insofar as linguistics presents language as potentially analyzable in terms of a hierarchy of meanings: sounds (which have no meaning) combined into words (which have many meanings) combined into utterances (which make clear which word meanings are relevant and which can convey subtle shadings of difference). All signs are integrated into progressively larger systems, comparable to language. Not all sign systems need be as complexly structured as language for this general model to remain valid. This proposal of hierarchy is not intended to imply unnecessary rigidity or to encourage an emphasis on structure to the exclusion of process.

At the very least, there are some valuable lessons to be learned from linguistics; we should be wary of casually tossing it aside as our model before we have learned all we can from it. Julia Kristeva, noted French semiotician and linguist, pointed to part of the reason why the study of language has loomed over semiotics: Linguistics was the first of the human sciences to develop a "scientific method" of its own (1989, p. 298).[20] She proposed that the other human sciences can learn from the model provided by linguistics by treating other aspects of human behavior as languages and put forth semiotics as the umbrella term for the set of human sciences because they all study meaning and sign systems. In addition to the reasons that linguistics serves as the key to understanding human behavior for a variety of fields, it remains central to semiotic theory due to the added historical connection, via Saussure and his followers.[21]

## CULTURE, COMMUNICATION, SEMIOTICS

Two concepts essential to an understanding of semiotics are *culture* and *communication*. Definitions of both abound because they are central to the understanding and study of human behavior. The subject matter of semiotics is often described as being communication, as evident in some of the quotations supplied previously. Thomas Sebeok, the dean of semiotics in the United States, made this absolutely explicit:

> The subject matter of semiotics, it is often credited, is the exchange of any messages whatsoever, in a word, *communication*. To this must at once be added that semiotics is also focally concerned with the study of *signification*. Semiotics is therefore classifiable as that pivotal branch of an integrated science of communication to which its character as a methodical inquiry into the nature and constitution of codes provides an indispensable counterpoint. (Sebeok, 1986a, p. 36)

If Sebeok is correct that the subject matter of semiotics is communication, and he should know, then the connection between the two fields is established.[22]

Just as consideration of several definitions of semiotics grounded discussion of the critical points, similar discussion here of communication definitions may demonstrate the connections between the fields.[23] Ray Birdwhistell suggested an early definition of communication as "a structural system of significant symbols (from all the sensorily based modalities) which permit ordered human interaction" (1970b, p. 95), pointing to the importance of *symbols*, to their combination in systems, and to the essential service provided by signification to human interaction. A revision of this definition was presented by Worth and Gross, who saw communication as "a social process within a context, in which signs are produced and transmitted, perceived and treated as messages from which meaning can be inferred" (1974, p. 30). What they added is an emphasis on the context within which signification occurs. I add but one more definition to these, that of James Carey, who proposed that *"Communication is a symbolic process whereby reality is produced, maintained, repaired, and transformed"* (1975, p. 10) also stressing symbols (and the more active form, symbolization) as the core of communication and naming the social construction (here elaborated to include production, maintenance, repair, and transformation) of reality as a central issue.[24]

From these definitions come several ideas: (a) Communication involves the use of a particular type of signs, symbols; (b) it involves the combination of symbols into codes; (c) it uses symbols and codes as a way to socially construct (produce, maintain, repair, transform) reality; and (d) it permits ordered human interaction. Connections to the definition of semiotics presented earlier are obvious.

These connections between semiotics and communication will not surprise anyone familiar with the history of the study of nonverbal communication. In 1964, Margaret Mead, summing up her impressions of the Conference on Linguistics,

Nonverbal Communication and Semiotics, pointed out, "If we had a word for patterned communication in all modalities, it would be useful. I am not enough of a specialist in this field to know what word to use, but many people here, who have looked as if they were on opposite sides of the fence, have used the word 'semiotics' " (see Sebeok, Hayes, & Bateson, 1964, p. 275). In response, Birdwhistell pointed out that for him the word *communication* served adequately as the name for the larger whole (patterned communication, in Mead's terms). Mead responded it already had been corrupted, and she thought a new name would be valuable (see Sebeok et al., 1964, p. 276). It is important that, as recently as 1964, *the two fields of study were deemed to be so close that the names were viewed as interchangeable.*[25] Others since have documented the connections between nonverbal communication and linguistics, with linguistics, the older field, serving as the clear model for study.[26] At the same time, the study of nonverbal communication has sufficiently "stretched" the concept of language that it now routinely includes paralanguage, if not kinesics and proxemics.

Once the connections between semiotics and communication have been documented, only *culture* remains to be drawn into the circle of key terms. Traditionally, the definition of culture stressed patterns of learned behavior, as David Schneider mockingly described it: "that Tylorian inventory of pots, pans, rocks, and crocks which must of necessity end with the phrase 'et cetera,' thereby constituting a list of all those things with which man is not born but which he somehow creates or learns" (1976, p. 203; Tylor [1871/1958] presented the first definition of culture, and it was a list).[27] The now widely quoted definition of culture Schneider proposed as a replacement, "a system of symbols and meanings" (1976, p. 197), has made its way into the communication literature in slightly revised form as "an ordered though contradictory and heterogeneous system of symbols" (Carey, 1989, p. 51).

There are two divergent views of culture, summarized nicely by Michael Schudson as the hegemony view that "cultural objects are seen as enormously powerful in shaping human action," and the tool-kit view that "Culture is not a set of ideas imposed but a set of ideas and symbols available for use . . . [but] a resource for social action more than a structure to limit social action" (1989, p. 155). His attempt to mesh these two views, which are both at least partially correct though seemingly contradictory, is to suggest that "The study of culture is the study of what meanings are available for use in a given society from the wider range of possible meanings; the study of culture is equally the study of what meanings people choose and use from available meanings" (1989, p. 156).

Lotman and Uspensky focused on a different level, emphasizing the connections between culture and texts; they proposed a view of "culture as a mechanism creating an aggregate of texts and texts as the realization of culture" (1978, p. 218). They provide the rationale for studying small segments of cultural behavior, seeing each as a way in to understanding the larger whole.

Parallel to the understanding of communication reached previously, the pertinent understanding of culture includes the following notions:

1.  Culture is composed of symbols and other signs; these provide a structure for social actors, limiting possible choices to those culturally available.
2.  These symbols and signs are the tools people use to convey meaning; these are the resource materials from which people choose to convey what meanings they wish.
3.  These symbols and signs are combined into systems (or codes).
4.  Researchers study particular texts in order to understand how the larger entity, culture, operates.

Despite the impossibility of getting everyone to agree on specific definitions of culture, communication, and semiotics, it is possible at least to be explicit about which definitions are useful for which purposes. For my purposes here, the definition of *culture as a set of systems or codes of symbols and meanings*, of *communication as human symbolic activity*, and of *semiotics as the study of signs and sign systems* are fruitful, especially when the elaborations entailed, as presented previously, are borne in mind. Obviously the study of communication and the study of culture are interrelated and overlapping with each other and with semiotics (Kress, 1988b; Leeds-Hurwitz, 1989).[28] Some authors have stated this strongly, as when Eco suggested putting all three terms together: "To communicate is to use the entire world as a semiotic apparatus. I believe that culture is that, and nothing else" (1973b, p. 57). My purpose is not to conflate all three fields of study (difficult anyway, given a historical reality in which they have taken separate paths through the academic world) but rather to ensure that they be considered jointly, in light of what they have to offer one another.[29]

## NOTES

1.  In that spirit, it may be helpful to briefly summarize the research by others in communication presenting semiotics. For various reasons, the majority of attention appears within general theoretical introductions, the most explicit being John Fiske (1982), who applied semiotics to the study of mass media. He subverted the common emphasis on communication as a process to communication as the generation of meanings, with a secondary emphasis on structure. His definition of communication, seen from semiotics, is "the generation of meaning in messages," stressing meaning as an active process negotiated between individuals.

    John Stewart has also explicitly discussed what semiotics has to offer communication, though assuming a definition of communication as limited to language. As did Fiske, he provided a basic introduction to semiotics (though biased toward Peirce, whereas Fiske's bias is to Saussure). Stewart additionally emphasized social constructionism, stating that "human language ability includes not only the capacity to craft and utilize signs and symbols but also the power to reveal or constitute world *in talk*" (1986, p. 55; see also 1991, in press).

Gary Cronkhite's (1986) article proposing the definition of communication as human symbolic activity has already been mentioned. Unlike Fiske and Stewart, Cronkhite did not specify a connection between communication and semiotics, a surprising omission given his implication that we should absorb it in the name of consolidating our own field. It may in fact "redound to our benefit" to be known as the field that studies human symbolic behavior as he argued, but territorial acquisition may not be viewed so positively by the territory's current occupants. I would rather establish metaphorical trade routes, learning what we can through cooperation, rather than simply moving in as the new owners, claiming someone else's turf for our own purposes.

Klaus Krippendorff (1990) argued that semioticians too often establish themselves as objectivists, when they should be constructivists, suggesting this bias is inherent in the very terminology of semiotics (sign, code, etc.). I argue that such bias is not essential to the vocabulary but depends on the use made of that vocabulary by the analyst; obviously I assume it is possible to escape some of the problems he pointed out without abandoning semiotics entirely. Similarly, Eco (1990) argued that taking a structural approach to semiotics has traditionally resulted in studies of a single point in time, preventing studies of changes over time. I argue that the building blocks presented in chapters 2 and 3, though clearly structural in nature, do not by design limit us to structural concerns nor to a single point in time.

Authors within a few specific subfields in communication have at least occasionally discussed semiotic theory, including organizational communication (Fiol, 1989; Goodall, 1990; Hall, 1991); marketing (Umiker-Sebeok, 1987); rhetoric (Cherwitz, 1981; Hattenhauer, 1984; Lyne, 1981a, 1981b; Switzer, Fry, & Miller, 1990; Warnick, 1979); feminist theory (Schwichtenberg, 1989); mass communication (Fiske, 1985, 1987, 1988; Fry & Fry, 1986; Gottdiener, 1985; Heller, 1982; Porter, 1983; Robinson & Straw, 1984); more rarely, interpersonal (Hankiss, 1980; Sigman, 1987, pp. 56–66); and nonverbal (Harris & Owens, 1990). This is not a very long list (and it is close to complete). Current evidence of increased interest in semiotics within communication is available as reflected in seminars and panels at professional meetings, but such informal presentations hardly constitute a major emphasis within the field.

Aside from the general comments cited from Fiske (1982) about the shift from communication as a process to communication as the generation of meaning, only a few of the authors named here offer specific explanations of what exactly semiotics has to contribute to communication. Robinson and Straw (1984) are an exception, however the majority of their comments focused solely on mass media. They offered one important generalization, that the key lies in the notion of *text*, a term currently used to refer to a stretch of interaction available for analysis (a poem, a dance, or a greeting are all texts). A similar emphasis was proposed by Kress (1988b, pp. xi–xii). Clearly, there has been considerable influence not only of anthropology (via Geertz, who influenced Carey's view of cultural studies), where ethnography is now considered one of many possible texts open to analysis rather than itself being the presentation of a closed analysis, but also of literature (via Derrida), where the idea of the written text metaphorically expands to include unwritten texts (spoken language and material culture, among other possibilities).

The recent argument by Switzer et al. (1990) that semiotics has much to offer communication scholars would at first seem to be quite similar to the position taken by this volume, however, there is a substantial difference between the aspects of semiotic theory they recommend as valuable and those recommended here. They have been most primarily influenced by Peirce, by way of Sebeok, and argued for a return to quite old rhetorical traditions; whereas I have been influenced by Saussure and argue for a revitalization of his ideas as a semiotics of culture and thus of communication. It is my impression that those who study actual behavior will learn more of value from Saussure; those preferring to discuss terminology will utilize Peirce.

Richard Lanigan (1972, 1979, 1983, 1986, 1990), probably the most voluble proponent for the study of semiotics within communication, has been caught in the velvet trap of semiotics, particularly Peircian semiotics: Spending so much time and effort discussing theory, it never seems time to apply that theory to concrete behavior.

2. Within the semiotic literature, Sebeok (1976) provided a good brief historical introduction and Innis (1985) wrote a good introductory anthology. The basic reference sources are Sebeok (1986b) and Nöth (1990).

3. A nice summary of the historical context for each of these approaches to semiotic theory is provided by Silverman (1983, pp. 3-53).

4. The existence of two names, *semiotics* and *semiology*, for what is essentially the same field is a potential stumbling block. This volume follows what has become current practice in choosing the name semiotics. In contemporary writing, authors who use the term semiology are generally understood to be identifying with the European tradition of scholarship (as opposed to the American) or with an emphasis on language as the dominant system (as opposed to either nonverbal or nonhuman systems or as opposed to the more abstract idea of logic as a system), although far more slippage occurs between terms than is implied here. The classic exposition of semiology is Guiraud (1975); a more accessible introduction is Eco (1973b). Many of the basic early readings in both semiotics and semiology may be found in D. S. Clarke (1990). More subtly, those who have identified with the Saussurean school focus their energy on applying the basic ideas to particular aspects of human behavior rather than on discussing theoretical issues (what semiology is and should be), perhaps due to the limited theoretical guidance Saussure himself provided (Barthes, 1967/1983). What comments he did supply emphasize the relations between fields then existing (primarily psychology and linguistics), the gap he perceived between them, and the need for a new subject, semiology, to fill that gap.

   Traditionally, those who use semiotics to describe their study identify with the American school, with philosophy, or with logic specifically (those who use semiotic are by implication sticklers for detail). More subtly, those who identify with Peirce are likely to devote considerable energy to discussions of theory and especially vocabulary, in part due to the very real need to sort out the distinctions proposed as relevant by Peirce himself. His emphasis was never on actual behavior (such as the linguists and psychologists discussed by Saussure studied) but on concepts and their implications as studied by the philosophers and logicians he assumed to be his audience. He was more interested in abstractions than in concrete phenomena, a focus maintained by his followers.

5. Peirce is influential whether followed (as in Cherwitz, 1981; Lanigan, 1972, 1983; Lyne, 1980, 1981a); or argued against (as in J. Stewart, 1991).

6. Obviously, in attempting to address a communication audience, this volume crystallizes semiotic theory into a particular form that is not seen as obvious by all who call themselves semioticians, though I imagine most would be unhappy with what is left out rather than with what is included.

7. Because the translation of one of the major works of this group, Uspensky's *A Poetics of Composition* (1973), was undertaken in part by a graduate student in the Department of Rhetoric at the University of California, Berkeley (Valentina Zavarin), the value of this research to communication scholars apparently was recognized by at least a few scholars nearly 20 years ago.

8. See Hockett (1968) for discussion. Originally thought not to be a characteristic of animal forms of communication, it now seems a few animals are capable of lying as well (Page, 1988; Thorpe, 1988).

9. A move from structure to action is particularly appropriate for communication researchers given the substantial influence of Giddens' notion of structuration on our field to date (Giddens, 1984).

10. It was Gregory Bateson who pointed out that "any study which throws light on the nature of 'order' or 'pattern' in the universe is surely nontrivial" (1972, p. xvi). For me, semiotics helps throw light on the nature of order in the universe and, as such, is valuable.

11. Others have also pointed out that most semioticians, at least in the United States today, are primarily interested in theory for its own sake, rather than applying theory to original investigations. Middendorf quoted Sebeok as saying that "semioticians do not *do* research, they think and write about what people in other fields have done or are doing" (1990, p. 305). For me, this is a problem. Theory does not stand alone; it goes hand in hand with research.

12. For example: "Among the human sciences, semiotics is unique in being a study concerned with the matrix of all the sciences, and in revealing the centrality of history to the enterprise of understanding in its totality" (Deely, 1990, p. 81). See also Deely, Williams, and Kruse, where the authors concluded the argument by suggesting that semiotics will provide "a new superstructure for the humanities and the so-called hard or natural sciences alike" that others have only dreamed of (1986, p. xv). My favorite image from discussions of the centrality of semiotics is that provided by MacCannell and MacCannell, who suggested viewing semiotics as an all-terrain vehicle conveying important issues across the various scientific and humanistic fields (1982, p. 14).

13. There is, within the larger field of semiotics, some concern for animals (*zoosemiosis*) and plants (*phytosemiosis*) as well as humans (termed, in this classification, *anthroposemiosis*), though only human meanings are of interest in my volume. (See Deely, 1990, for a clear explanation of these ideas and the justification for including them in semiotics.)

14. Bailey, Matejka, and Steiner (1978, p. vii).

15. Hassan (1987, p. 93).

16. Steiner (1978, p. 99); originally from Cassirer (1944).

17. For discussion of linguistics as a model for various aspects of culture, see Basso and Selby (1976); Silverstein (1976); Threadgold (1986). Jakobson's emphasis was paralleled by other Russian Formalists who, beginning as they did with an interest in language and literature, often casually refered to the different social codes as "languages" (as in Uspensky, Ivanov, Toporov, Piatigorskij, & Lotman, 1973, p. 1).

18. See Tobin (1990) for the most elaborate discussion of this (from the viewpoint of history of linguistics). Comments by other linguists may be found in Rauch and Carr (1980); comments from the perspective of semiotics may be found in Deely (1990, pp. 1–8), Deely et al. (1986), M. L. Foster (1990b), Hervey (1982, pp. 1–8), Innis (1985, pp. 24–27, 292–293); in anthropology, see McCracken (1988, pp. 57–70); in communication, see Corcoran (1981).

McCracken is the most unhappy with the continued used of linguistics as a model for the study of material culture, pointing out, "What was once a lively and illuminating suggestion of similarity is more and more a statement of apparent fact...It now dulls our critical senses as it once stimulated our imaginative faculties" (1988, p. 62). We must attend to his warning, but I would disagree that the implication is to reject the model entirely.

19. See Barthes (1967/1983) and Metz (1974) for two very different uses of linguistics as a model, the first for an analysis of fashion and the second for an analysis of film.

20. See also Levi-Strauss, who pointed out that linguistics "is not merely a social science like the others, but, rather, the one in which by far the greatest progress has been made. It is probably the only one which can truly claim to be a science and which has achieved both the formulation of an empirical method and an understanding of the nature of the data submitted to its analysis" (1963, p. 31). For discussion of linguistics as a model in the development of the study of nonverbal communication, see Leeds-Hurwitz (1990b).

21. The Russian Formalists and Czech Structuralists in particular used linguistics as a more dominant model than other semioticians, in large part because their original interests were in language and literary analysis. The names taken by the two major informal groupings of scholars known today as formalists and structuralists appropriately reflect this: Moscow Linguistic Circle and Prague Linguistic Circle.

22. The use of the term communication within the semiotic canon is not limited to Sebeok. A wide range of authors have demonstrated clear agreement: "Semiosis is the process by which empirical subjects communicate, communication processes being made possible by the organization of signification systems" (Eco, 1976, p. 316); and "Semiotics is concerned with signs in general, and as signs are the stuff out of which messages are made it seems almost inevitable that an interest in communication will lead to semiotics" (Sless, 1986, p. 10).

23. Obviously there are many definitions of communication available, and I am selecting particular ones for what they contribute to the discussion here. I make no excuse for the bias inherent in

my choices; everyone who chooses a particular definition of communication demonstrates comparable bias.

24. For further discussion of the issues implied by social constructionism, see Lannamann (1992), Leeds-Hurwitz (1992a), and Steier (1991).

25. See Rey (1978) for related comments. Lanigan reversed the direction of influence described so far, speaking as he did from communication rather than semiotics: "all communication is semiotic by force of being constituted and regulated by systems of signs" (1982, p. 63). Grossberg (1982) expanded the discussion to what he termed "*cultural semiotics*"; Hodge and Kress (1988) and Sigman (1990) moved in a different direction with a related term, *social semiotics*. For further discussion of the distinction between "formal" and "social" semiotics, see Thibault (1991).

26. See Steiner (1978); Kendon (1990, pp. 15-50); Leeds-Hurwitz (1987, 1990b). When Part II of this volume argues for the need to study food, clothing, and objects as simultaneous aspects of nonverbal communication and semiotic behaviors, the discussion should be understood as a clear outgrowth of the original connection between semiotics and linguistics.

27. For further discussion of this understanding of culture and the overlap with communication to which it points, see Leeds-Hurwitz (1989, pp. 62-65).

28. This is not the place for detailed discussion, but there has been extensive consideration of semiotics within anthropology, starting with Levi-Strauss' comment in 1960 that anthropology would henceforth devote itself to the study of signs and symbols, in short to semiotics (Levi-Strauss, 1976, pp. 9-10; see M. Singer, 1984, p. 39, for discussion). The key names in symbolic and semiotic anthropology in addition to Levi-Strauss are Clifford Geertz, Raymond Firth, Edmund Leach, Rodney Needham, David Schneider, and Victor Turner. For summary discussion, see Schwimmer (1977); Singer (1984); Parmentier (1985).

29. There are additional related fields of study such as the study of semiotics within sociology, but these are not essential to the current discussion (see Robinson & Straw, 1984, p. 107, for useful comments; Zito (1984) provided an introduction to semiotics intended for sociologists). Semiotics has been most influential within literature—Culler (1981, 1988) and Hawkes (1977) are good introductions—but as a separate tradition with surprisingly little overlap to communication (with the notable exception of the Russian Formalists/Czech Structuralists, as described previously).

# Chapter 2

# Signs

A definition of semiotics as "the study of signs" points to signs as worthy of considerable attention. In the majority of semiotic writings signs are central; typically, Sebeok named them the "pivotal notion" of the field (1986a, p. 39). They have been proposed as a concept equally central for related fields as well, often in grandiose terms. The following quote comes from Charles Morris, noted American semiotician, but the sentiment is not his alone: "Indeed, it does not seem fantastic to believe that the concept of sign may prove as fundamental to the sciences of man as the concept of atom has been for the physical sciences or the concept of cell for the biological sciences" (1938, p. 42). The sign is thus presented as a building block, comparable to these other building blocks in other fields.[1]

This assumption of the significance of signs by semioticians has definitely *not* been echoed by those in communication, who eschew the term, preferring to write of *symbols*. On the rare occasions communication researchers write of signs, they consistently use the word as a synonym for symbols.[2] Aune stated a generally accepted position in suggesting the only distinction between the two words may be one of implication, sign being the more currently "fashionable" (1983, p. 256). His position obscures the two different meanings currently available and used in semiotics and occasionally in other fields. If the two words are used as synonyms within communication, it cannot be due to lack of available differentiation. In this volume (following Firth, 1973b, among others), sign is used as the general category, with the term symbol reserved for one particular variety of sign.

In chapter 1, a sign was defined as "everything that, on the grounds of a previously established social convention, can be taken as something standing for something else" (Eco, 1976, p. 16). This was sufficient for a chapter introducing semiotics, but further details are useful when signs themselves move to the forefront. Traditionally, there have been two main interpretations of signs: either that they consist of a dichotomy (a two-part relationship) or a trichotomy (a more elaborate three-part relationship).

Consider the dichotomy first: As outlined originally by Saussure, each sign comprises a duality, such that it can be understood to have two parts; these he termed the *signifier* and the *signified*.[3] The signifier is visible or in some way present (such as a flag); the signified is invisible but referred to (the country to which the flag belongs and which it represents). In other words, the signifier is the explicit aspect of a sign, present during the interaction, a material presence of some sort; the signified is the tacit element of a sign, what might be termed an "immaterial" presence, something literally absent yet functionally present because it has been invoked.[4]

Peirce divided signs differently, proposing a triad: the *sign* or *representatum*, the *object*, and the *interpretant*. (For clarity's sake, I will use representatum rather than sign here, though the latter has become the term of choice. Logically, no element of a classification system should be both the name of a set and an element within that set.) In this scheme, the representatum is parallel to Saussure's signifier, identifying the present part of the sign; but Peirce divided Saussure's signified into two: the object (that to which the representatum refers) and the interpretant (the meaning conveyed by the representatum about the object whatever was not previously known about that object but here conveyed).[5] These two schemes should not be viewed as contradictory; Peirce was simply slightly more explicit than Saussure. Because they were writing independently, neither knowing the other's work, they cannot be expected to have come up with identical conceptions; that their views of the matter fit together so nicely should be the surprise.[6] In keeping with my assertion that Peirce's scheme serves as an elaboration of Saussure's, making Saussure's the more basic and essential, in the following pages signifier and signified are the terms of choice.

In addition to designating the component parts of any sign, semioticians commonly sort the class of signs into different groups or types. Peirce actually identified 66 potential varieties of signs, 3 of which have gained wide acceptance: the concepts of *icon, index,* and *symbol.* In each case, the relationship between the signifier and signified serves as focus of attention: An icon has the relationship of similarity or resemblance; an index has the relationship of contiguity or connection; a symbol has the relationship of arbitrariness. That is, any sign displaying a similarity between the present and the absent components is termed an icon; any sign using a part of something to stand for the whole is an index; and any sign using an arbitrary connection between the present and absent components is a symbol. A photograph of a bride is an icon; it resembles her. The top of the wedding cake kept for the first anniversary celebration is an index; it formed a piece of the original event. The bride's white dress is traditionally a symbol of virginity, standing for something it neither resembles nor was taken from.[7]

Religious relics provide a fascinating example of an index. Relics of saints have
no intrinsic value; in fact, parts of dead bodies were (and are) normally considered undesirable, a source of contamination. However, for the religious of
medieval Europe, "relics *were* the saints, continuing to live among men" and were
"immediate sources of supernatural power for good or for ill, and close contact
with them or possession of them was a means of participating in that power"
(Geary, 1986, p. 176). Relics gain their power by virtue of being indices. They
were once literally a part of the saint, and if the saint had power, similar power
may reside in every body part; thus anyone possessing any body part was assumed
to gain part of the original power. Relics were traditionally placed in elaborate
reliquaries, containers specifically designed to hold them, often made of precious
materials such as silver. Sometimes the reliquary was made in the shape of the
body part from which the relic had come, as when a finger bone was placed in
a container designed in the shape of a hand. Others become sculptures, artistic
creations in their own right, as in the illustration provided here (see Fig. 2.1).

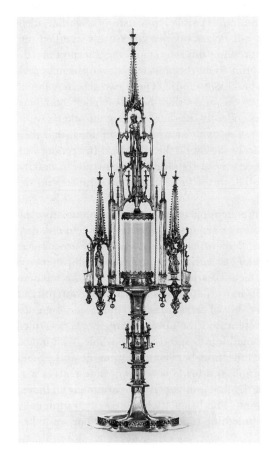

FIG. 2.1. Large reliquary, Ger-
man, circa 1480. Photo courtesy of
Milwaukee Art Museum, Gift of
Richard and Erna Flagg.

The reliquary should never be confused with the relic: the reliquary is not itself an index but only the container of one.

Just to complicate matters, some signs make use of more than one type of relationship in combination (e.g., flags are symbols but occasionally incorporate icons). In practice such combinations cause no real problems, for only analysts make these distinctions, not social actors. In addition, the same sign can serve as symbol, icon, and index simultaneously or in different contexts. A gold wedding band, for example, is a symbol of a relationship; it is an index to the wedding ceremony, having been physically a part of the original event; and it can be an icon (either literally, for example, if it is similar to your mother's ring or metaphorically, in that it is similar in form to everyone else's wedding bands).[8] In the example of relics earlier, they not only are indices but also symbols (of a particular religious belief system, for only a believer would consider a part of a particular dead body a source of power).

Ioan Lewis, an anthropologist, stressed the need to consider the emotional meanings of symbols, in addition to the more commonly considered cognitive meanings. "By 'symbols' we mean, of course, something more than signs. Unlike the latter which may be so, symbols are in principle never fully self-explanatory, self-sufficient or fully autonomous" (Lewis, 1977, p. 1). Symbols convey meaning largely through the connections implied with other symbols. This, then, provides another distinction between symbols and other sorts of signs: Icons and indices carry emotional freight less often. Thus, the current trend in major United States cities of using black for the bridal party's clothing as a symbol of sophistication causes enormous comment, being seen as a deliberately provocative choice because black, the traditional Western color for funerals, is widely accepted as a symbol of grief, an emotion equally widely assumed to be inappropriate at a wedding.

Communication scholars have often considered signs and symbols to be synonyms for an obvious reason: *Symbols are the type of sign most often of interest within communication.* This is true throughout this volume, as for the field.[9] Given that some symbols incorporate elements of indices or icons, I use the more general term sign for the remainder of the volume unless specifically calling attention to the distinction. In fact, the majority of the time the topic of discussion is symbols.

## COGNATE TERMS

Although I fully intend to avoid the detailed discussions of terminology commonly found in books on semiotics, a small set of words used to describe particular aspects of signs in common usage comes in quite handy.[10] Only the most valuable of these (valuable in the sense of what they permit one to do analytically) are described.

*Motivation* or *constraint* (the words are virtual synonyms, with motivation being

the more common, constraint the more obvious) refers to the degree to which
the signified determines the signifier. When the signified closely determines the
signifier, one describes the sign as being highly motivated or highly constrained.
An example is a photograph, for it is commonly assumed the image should closely resemble the person indicated. An example of a sign having low motivation
or constraint is a political cartoon, where the resemblance to the person indicated
need not be so close. This concept is particularly useful because it cuts across
the categories of signs just presented (icon, index, symbol) and can thus be used
to characterize any (and every) sign.

Gold wedding bands as symbols of relationship status have low motivation as
currently used, though some older rings, depicting two clasped hands, have higher
motivation. That is, the two clasped hands more obviously stand for a relationship by demonstrating a connection between two people than does a gold ring
in and of itself. The use of flowers at a wedding has high motivation, insofar as
they are assumed to indicate new life and a new beginning, clearly what a wedding ceremony represents. Red roses have low motivation as a signifier of romance
and love; there is no logical reason why yellow daffodils could not serve equally
well, though tradition may argue otherwise.

*Convention* refers to the degree of tradition or habit associated with a particular
sign. For example, in the United States, conventional stick figures are understood to characterize female and male, commonly found on bathroom doors among
other places. The convention has been taken for granted for so long that we forget not everyone can interpret it correctly: This conventional image of a woman
wears a dress, and the man wears pants, but these clothing norms are not universal (nor are they even consistent standards in the modern United States). Becoming accustomed to a particular sign apparently causes most people to "forget"
or at least to "overlook" the role tradition, rather than logic, plays in providing
the link between signifier and signified. Convention is often particularly valuable
in discussions of symbols, where there is greatest choice of signifier.

Despite the variation in motivation, both gold bands and flowers at a wedding
are high in convention: In the United States we have used them as symbols in
weddings for a long time, and they are expected; thus, they are effective in communicating particular information. Equally, insofar as red roses are conventionally accepted as a symbol of romance, yellow daffodils are incapable of conveying
the same message without an accompanying verbal explanation or contextual frame
(couples with a personal history associating daffodils with their actual courtship
can use them to indicate romance at their own wedding without having to make
the connection explicit, at least for themselves).

*Denotation* refers to the explicit, obvious, straightforward, first meaning of a
sign; the related term *connotation* refers to the implicit, conventional, second meaning of a sign, imposed by a specific culture. A wedding cake denotes food to eat,
but connotes such factors as time (spent decorating the cake), money (some varieties being more expensive than others), or adherence to tradition, ethnicity, and

so forth. Eco gave a good explanation of the difference between denotation and connotation, using as his example the word *torch*:

> It means a piece of wood soaked in some substance which enables it to burn slowly and give off light. This is the denotative meaning of the word. But in our culture the torch has assumed a connotative meaning of liberty. So if a painting or a movie depicts a man with a torch, it is a sign used for its own connotative power, because I know that in a certain culture a torch represents the idea of liberty. I could look at a primitive painting of a man with a torch, to which I could attribute the meaning of liberty and I could be wrong because a torch did not have that meaning within the code of that civilization. (Eco, quoted in Balducci, 1976, p. 37)

This quote calls attention to the culture-specific nature of connotation, something that may not otherwise be immediately apparent and that is one of the reasons denotation and connotation merit considerable attention: Denotation often crosses cultural boundaries; connotation almost never does.

To continue with the example of yellow daffodils, the couple having previous experience with them as an indication of romance may choose to include them in their own wedding, but only some of the guests will understand the connotation without accompanying explicit verbal comments. Couples can use the subtlety and exclusivity of connotation to multiply the meaning of their own wedding ceremony in a variety of ways: A bride who chooses to wear the dress her mother wore at her wedding does so for the implications of continuity and family tradition, but rarely does every single guest know the story and understand the connotations.

Semiotics has accepted all of the previous terms as useful and significant. Hodge and Kress recently proposed a provocative newcomer to the list, *metasign*, adapted from Gregory Bateson's concept of *metacommunication*. Though new, this term is potentially powerful and therefore worthy of inclusion here. A metasign conveys information about how to interpret other information, specifically other signs. Hodge and Kress suggested that "Metasigns are sets of markers of social allegiance (solidarity, group identity and ideology) which permeate the majority of texts" (1988, p. 80). Examples of metasigns include styles and accents, among other possibilities (a Southern accent marks geographic origin; clothing styles are often granted, though sometimes inappropriately, the ability to mark social status). In such cases, a single sign conveys the framework within which information yet to come should be interpreted, and so it is granted a distinctive label. Birdwhistell (1970a) described Southerners smiling more frequently than Northerners, despite intent to display the same degree of friendliness. Someone knowing this and hearing a Southern accent would correctly frame the smile when it appeared. The concept of metasign organizes signs into a hierarchy: It designates some as broader and more general than others (metasigns, being general, tell us how to interpret other, more specific signs that might otherwise be equally likely to convey any

one of several interpretations). Metasigns of group identity are the most numerous and are particularly intriguing.

Holding a wedding that follows traditional norms in many respects (with the
bride in a long white gown, the groom in a tuxedo, with bridesmaids and grooms-
men, flowers and rings) but in an uncommon setting is an example of a metasign: a wedding held on a football field at halftime, on a baseball field before the
game starts, or in a bowling alley. Alternatively, if the bride and groom met
through a chorus to which they both belong and decide to have their wedding
ceremony in song in the middle of a public performance, or if they are both clowns
and wear clown costumes, or if they have a cowboy theme running through the
entire wedding with everyone wearing elaborate Western clothes and boots, these
are all examples of metasigns.[11] Though the remainder of the event may progress
in a fairly normal fashion, the single change alters the way in which the participants
interpret what occurs. Thus, the word metasign demonstrates that some signs
are "more equal" than others.

## SYMBOLS

Symbols have been the type of sign most thoroughly investigated by communication scholars, but it would be incorrect to assume the nature of symbols has been
a frequent topic of discussion. In fact, symbols have been so readily regarded as
a traditional focus of attention in communication that they have often been taken
for granted with details of definition, function, and use left uninvestigated. Most
influential has been Kenneth Burke, who took the concept of symbol as the cor-
nerstone of his work (see especially Burke, 1968, 1989).[12]

Communication and semiotics are not alone in considering symbols central
to their concerns: Sociology (particularly symbolic interactionism),[13] anthropology (specifically symbolic and more recently semiotic anthropology),[14] folklore,[15]
philosophy,[16] and psychology[17] have at various times made similar claims. (A listing of disciplines such as this obscures the considerable cross-disciplinary interest
generated by the concept.[18]) It is interesting that the colloquial usage of symbol
has much the same meaning. In describing a conflict between the University of
Louisville mascot and the Martin Luther King, Jr. holiday, for example, a newspaper article reported "Fans like Mr. Senn take their symbols very seriously in this
city. . . .But a clash of symbols has erupted. . . ." (Marriott, 1990, p. Y16).

Rather than examining the differences between the approaches to symbols followed by each of the previously named disciplines, it is more useful to consider
a series of questions any of them must answer. (In what follows, the term symbol
is used because the individual authors quoted have used it and because it is the
particular variety of sign under discussion. In other disciplines, as in communication, symbol has often been used when referring to the larger class, technically
designated in this volume as signs.)

*Is Symbol-Using a Defining Characteristic of Humans?*    The use of symbols has been commonly named as part of what distinguishes humans from animals.[19] Of such references, Burke has been the most influential within communication, particularly through his definition of man.

Man is
the symbol-using (symbol-making, symbol-misusing) animal
inventor of the negative (or moralized by the negative)
separated from his natural condition by instruments of his own making
goaded by the spirit of hierarchy (or moved by the sense of order)
and rotten with perfection. (Burke, 1968, p. 16)

Note how he named the characteristic of symbol usage as the first aspect of humanity worthy of attention. Note also his elaboration of the concept: People not only use symbols, they make them, and they can misuse them.

Others besides researchers in communication consider symbol usage a defining characteristic of humans: Archaeologists and physical anthropologists commonly cite evidence of symbol usage as one way of dating early humans.[20] Ethologists have described chimps, for example, as clearly capable of *using* human symbols (such as plastic letters or shapes) after sufficient training; presumably they can misuse them as well, but there is no evidence yet that they *make* symbols. Remembering that a symbol involves an arbitrary connection between the signifier and the signified, this is not terribly surprising.

Ernst Cassirer, noted philosopher, also named the ability to create and use symbols the quintessential human characteristic (1944, pp. 24–25). He pointed out that symbols can serve to shield people from reality. People use symbols not only as a way of communicating information to others, but as a way of communicating with themselves; thus as researchers we must recognize symbols as a critical component in the ability to construct an image of reality.[21]

*What Serves as a Sign or Symbol?*    The fact that anything can be a sign if we so wish it indicates the essential role of signs in social life. As Peter Bogatyrev put it, "any item of nature, technology, or everyday use can become a sign whenever it acquires meaning beyond the bounds of its individual existence as a thing in and of itself" (1936/1976a, p. 14). His example is a stone, an object from nature when it lies on the ground, but when someone paints it white and uses it to mark the border between two plots of ground, it acquires social meaning, becoming a sign. Eco carried this general point even further:

Human beings emerge from any account of semiotic structures as inveterate and promiscuous producers of signs. As the work of Levi-Strauss and others indicates, any aspect of human activity carries the potential for serving as, or becoming a sign; we only have to "activate" it in accordance with something like the above processes. (Cited in Hawkes, 1977, p. 134)

This implies that although most of us do not generally think of ourselves as "promiscuous producers of signs," nonetheless we all are. It follows that researchers into symbolic behavior must be alert to the continual creation of new signs, and must not assume documentation and understanding of all the important ones has been completed. It follows further that, as with signs, anything can serve as a symbol since symbols are but one type of sign.[22]

Few people might think of taking a hammer and smashing a ring as a symbol of anything in particular, but a new tradition is developing of doing exactly that after a divorce, with the destruction of the ring symbolizing the end of the relationship. As divorce is often difficult and as wedding bands are the traditional symbol of the relationship of marriage, we can recognize a peculiar appropriateness to this new symbol. Equally, when after a spouse's death a widow chooses to have the diamond from her engagement ring removed and used in a new piece of jewelry (a dinner ring or a pendant are common choices), this serves as an appropriate symbol of both continuing memories of the spouse and the need to go on with one's life.

Though it may be accurate to say that "anything" can serve as a symbol, this vague answer may not always be terribly useful. Generally, the short list of what can be used as a symbol includes *objects* (ranging from small ones like rings to large ones like buildings, from manufactured to found objects), *behaviors* (ranging from individual actions to elaborate community rituals), *texts* (in the sense of discourse, ranging from individual words to story cycles), *ideas* (concepts, images), and *people* (whether real or imaginary).

***How Do People Acquire Symbols?***    That is, how does one come to understand what they mean? This question arises from realizing that symbols are a part of culture. Different cultures use different symbols, so we know people are not born with the knowledge of what they are and how to interpret them. In brief, the answer is that people are gradually exposed to symbols as children and gradually come to understand them through their presentation in a series of contexts, learning over time what they mean to the adults around them (Shotwell, Wolf, & Gardner, 1980).[23] Some authors even speak of children being "inducted" into the appropriate use of symbols within their own culture, though this implies more coercion than most assume (Frank, 1966, p. 7).

Symbols are presented to children both implicitly and explicitly. Implicitly, the process is so constant as to appear to operate through osmosis—that is, simply by being presented with a world full of symbols, children "pick up" their meanings over time and through repetition, with no one deliberately teaching the meanings. One part of why this is possible is because symbols are such basic parts of the social world; whether or not adults attend to the matter consciously, children are exposed to the symbols of their culture every time they observe or participate in any sort of formal or informal event, and they can hardly help figuring out that symbols are important.[24]

Explicitly, adults often formally describe the meanings (whether religious or family or political) of symbols to the future generations, their children and grandchildren.[25] Symbols are a form of shorthand; encapsulating cultural knowledge in particular ways, they serve a valuable role in the deliberate passing on of traditions. This explicit effort is aided by the fact that so many symbols are immediately, materially present, physically intruding in a way that more elusive ideas and concepts simply cannot do. "Artifacts regularly carry the past into the present," as Gailey (1989, p. 149) put it, and symbols not only encourage but are the primary vehicle permitting continuity of the past into the present.[26] To date there has been little attention paid to the acquisition of nonlinguistic symbolic understandings, whether through primary socialization as children or through secondary socialization as adults in a new context or new culture.[27]

***How Does One Recognize Symbols in Everyday Life?*** In a sense, this is a foolish question, for social actors certainly don't ask themselves this, having no problems in discerning what constitutes a symbol and what does not. However, as a practical matter, how a researcher becomes alerted to a potential symbol worthy of study can become an issue. The best answer to this revised question is provided by Eco, who suggested:

> when in a Zen story the Master, asked about the meaning of life, answers by raising his stick, the interpreter smells an abnormal implicature, whose interpretant keys lie outside pre-existing frames. This gesture means not only that the Master refuses to answer, but also that his (gestural) answer has a still uncoded meaning, and maybe more than one. The textual implicature signaling the appearance of the symbolic mode depends on the presentation of a sentence, of a word, of an object, of an action that, according to the precoded narrative or discursive frames, the acknowledged rhetorical rules, or the most common linguistic usages, *should not* have the relevance it acquires within that context.
>
> The standard reaction to the instantiation of the symbolic mode should be a sort of uneasiness felt by the interpreter when witnessing an inexplicable move on the part of the text, the feeling that a certain word, sentence, fact, or object should not have been introduced in the discourse or at least not have acquired such an importance. The interpreter feels a *surplus* of signification since he guesses that the maxims of relevance, manner, or quantity have not been violated by chance or by mistake. On the contrary, they are not only flouted, but—so to speak—flouted dramatically. (Eco, 1986, pp. 175–176)

In the Zen Buddhist tradition, a Zen Master sometimes teaches his disciples through incomplete utterances and actions, leaving them to establish meaning. Although most people would be unlikely to describe the activity of locating symbols in Eco's precise phrase as "smelling an abnormal implicature," that is a good description of what analysts in fact do. Something implied in the use of a word or object or behavior carries more than the usual weight, appears to be out of place, or makes us vaguely uneasy, thus prompting investigation. This revised question brings up a related issue.

***Do All Symbols Carry Equal Weight in a Culture?***   This in turn should lead to the question: Are all symbols equally worthy of study? The short answer to both is, predictably, no. The long answer brings up the issue of *key symbols*, studied explicitly by anthropologists, implicitly by nearly everyone else. Key symbols (or depending on authorial preference, master symbols, dominant symbols, core symbols) carry greatest weight within a culture. They are the source of greatest discussion, elaboration, and attention from social actors and therefore later from researchers (Ortner, 1973; Turner, 1967).

At Thanksgiving the turkey is the key symbol; at Christmas it is the tree. Preparing a Thanksgiving dinner without including a turkey feels incomplete on the rare occasions anyone does it. Having a Christmas celebration bereft of a tree is a classic mark of hardship. Not only do objects serve as key symbols but also people, ideas, texts, or behaviors. In the 1992 Los Angeles riots, the key symbol clearly was Rodney King, and his name was linked to the riots in virtually every news story. At their most powerful, key symbols "enshrine the major hopes and aspirations of an entire society" (Wolf, 1972, p. 150) or fears and concerns, as with the example of King; they are "highly evocative, and multivocal; they are used in a variety of contexts and convey multiple meanings" (Parman, 1990, p. 295).[28] Surely key symbols warrant the special attention they have attracted across several disciplines.

Despite the minimal explicit attention paid to the concept of key symbols within the communication literature (Katriel, 1987, being one exception), virtually every study of symbols within communication to date, particularly but not uniquely within rhetoric, has in fact focused on key symbols.[29] This correctly implies that to date only minimal attention has been paid to the lesser symbols of everyday life. Such attention is long overdue, not for reasons of some sort of theoretical equality but because of their considerable theoretical interest: attention to everyday symbols rewards study.[30]

Mary Catherine Bateson pointed out that each human life is best conceived of as a composition, "a continual reimagining of the future and reinterpretation of the past to give meaning to the present" (1990, p. 29). To me, one of the implications of this statement is that researchers can study how social actors weave together fragments of interaction to form a coherent image for themselves and others. This is an activity best described as continuous, best studied in its mundane aspects. Important as it may be to study major life cycle events, rituals, ceremonies, or dramas, these are but infrequent occurrences in most lives. Thus, it is equally critical to study how people assume and convey meaning the remainder of their lives: When they eat breakfast, choose a new couch, or go for a walk around the neighborhood.

People assume coherence, creating it even where there is none, out of only the most fragmentary and imperfect materials.

> To understand the meaning of artifacts in the broadest sense, we need to focus on the imaginative act by which people fuse their surroundings into a meaningful whole. It is an act more prosaic, but more ambitious, than that of making the most perfect basket or the cleverest tale, because its scope is so great. Yet because every person performs it constantly, it receives less attention and no romantic celebration. (Upton, 1991, pp. 158–159)

People make coherence all of the time, thus few of us notice what an accomplishment it is, how difficult the task we set ourselves. This is a topic worthy of study in and of itself. People make a world of meanings, thus making the world meaningful for themselves and others. Everyday life is not a physical phenomenon, like the trees or the birds; it is a social creation, made by people, for people, available for study by these or other people. People create the world anew when interacting with others and then recreate the world yet again a moment later. Neither as participants nor as actors can we freeze it, hold it in our hands, for it simply does not exist in physical form. Neither does it exist within any one person's imagination, for the social world is a joint creation, existing through the mutual cooperation of a community of creators.

With Goffman (1959, 1983) and Birdwhistell (1970a), I have argued that it is largely through the small behaviors of everyday life that people convey information to one another (Leeds-Hurwitz, 1989). This approach implies that *all* symbols, not only key symbols, are worthy of study. Certainly I would not suggest ignoring key symbols, but there is little danger of that because they generally gain more than their share of research attention. Rather, I argue for reserving a little effort for seemingly insignificant symbols that reward investigation equally. As Carey put it, sometimes it is appropriate to "make large claims from small matters" (1989, p. 190); one cannot do this without paying attention to the small matters.[31]

***What Do Symbols Do That is Valuable?***   Through symbols people create a social reality for themselves, an overlay of meaning laid across the natural world. Von Bertalanffy suggested, "Except in the immediate satisfaction of biological needs, man lives in a world not of things, but of symbols" (1965, p. 26). By implication people do not live primarily in the natural world, which they had no hand in making, but rather in the social world, a separate and later human creation. Carey took this concept a step further, stating, "We first produce the world by symbolic work and then take up residence in the world we have produced" (1989, p. 30). By extension we are prone to forgetting our own role in creating the social world, forgetting equally that we have the power to change it.

Other uses of symbols require a slightly rephrased question: *What is the function of symbols?* Two basic answers are traditionally given.[32] One focuses on symbols as a way of making sense of the world (Geertz, 1966); this is the answer assumed in any discussion of symbols as creating social reality. Symbols serve *reflexively*, as a way for us to tell ourselves a story about ourselves (Gusfield, 1989). This function of symbols implies a vision of symbols as storage containers (Firth, 1973a, p. 79): People use symbols as a way of conveying considerable amounts of information in a small space or short time. They also serve as a way to convey information over time and across generations, as with the symbols used in writing.

The second answer points to the function of symbols as tools for changing the world. This also implies the metaphor of symbols as storage containers but to a different end. Rather than serving as a way of communicating with our later selves or future generations, symbols here serve as a way to communicate our views to potential competitors or even antagonists. Carey elaborated upon the potential of symbols as sites of conflict:

> Reality is, above all, a scarce resource. Like any scarce resource it is there to be struggled over, allocated to various purposes and projects, endowed with given meanings and potentials, spent and conserved, rationalized and distributed. The fundamental form of power is the power to define, allocate, and display this resource. Once the blank canvas of the world is portrayed and featured, it is also preempted and restricted. Therefore, the site where artists paint, writers write, speakers speak, filmmakers film, broadcasters broadcast is simultaneously the site of social conflict over the real. It is not a conflict over technology. It is not a conflict over social relations. It is a conflict over the simultaneous codetermination of ideas, technique, and social relations. It is above all a conflict not over the effects of communication but of the acts and practices that are themselves the effects. (Carey, 1989, p. 87)

According to this view, then, symbols are one vital component of a power struggle over whose ideas, whose constructions of reality, whose interpretations, will come to be accepted as the norm.[33]

Symbols depend for their value on shared meanings, thus, they can be accurately described as one result of social interaction. As Franks warned us, "the invisible and intangible nature of the symbolic component (of experience) should not lead to a diminished appreciation of its power" (1985, p. 34). When we take symbolic meanings for granted, we miss a large part of the picture. We must discover whose meanings we are accepting, and whose we have rejected.

An extension of this function is the recognition that symbols can serve as markers of identity (Berger, 1984c). Displaying symbols is one way of announcing a particular identity or affiliation with a particular group, whether that be national, occupational, corporate, religious, or gender based. (This obviously involves the concept of metasigns described earlier.[34]) As Jacques Maquet pointed out, "By means of cultural performances and emblems, each segment of a contemporary city tells to itself and the other segments who their members are and from whom they are separated'' (1982, p. 10).[35] He assumed a city as his environment because large numbers of members of different communities converge in cities. It is easiest to consider symbols in their positive function as markers of group identity (who we are); yet it is also the case that markers of identity simultaneously serve a negative function, making who we are not, thus defining group boundaries.

Symbols certainly indicate more than identity, though that is a commonly described function; they also indicate characteristics such as status. Status is an even more complex notion than identity, if that is possible, involving a hierarchy of identities within a particular group.[36] As with individual identity, social status is either *ascribed* (socially inherited) or *achieved* (acquired through individual performance). In other words, some forms of status parents are able to pass on to their children; others have to be earned. If nothing else, however, parents pass on assumptions about how to indicate a particular social status: Whether children choose to adopt theirs or to move away from it, their assumptions are framed first at home (subject to later modification by friends, the mass media, and so forth).

In the cases of both identity and status, there is an underlying reason for the fine distinctions made: ''One of the basic conditions of social life is knowing whom one is dealing with and, therefore, being able to recognize individual and group identity'' (Guiraud, 1975, p. 84). Although he did not apply his comments to status, I would, for status is nothing if not an aspect of identity. Whatever people learn about those with whom they interact is taken into account in the interaction, whether consciously or unconsciously. Symbols are one vehicle for displaying information about ourselves to others, friends and strangers alike, and to ourselves as well.

**Why Study Symbols?**   Because symbols are important to social actors, they must be important to researchers. People cannot see into one another's heads to understand motivation or behavior, but symbols are readily available for observation. ''Symbols are the directly observable data of sociation, and, since it is impossible to use symbols without using them in some kind of structure or form, we cannot discourse about society with any degree of precision unless we discourse about the forms social relationships assume in communication'' (Duncan, 1962, pp. 2-3). In sum, if the goal is to understand human behavior, one must study symbols, for they provide one of the best ways to gain such understanding.

## INTERPRETATION AND MEANING

Implicit in the previous discussion are the twin problems of *interpretation* and *meaning*.[37] It is time to confront them directly. In both cases I specifically refer to symbols rather than signs, for indices and icons, with their obvious connections between signifier and signified, only rarely call issues of divergent interpretations and multiple meanings into question.[38]

Interpretation as a term has been used widely in the humanities over a long period of time: Literary critics interpret the work of the authors they study, just as art critics interpret the work of the artists they study. In this usage, the term was not at all controversial, being accepted as obvious. More recently, the term has been applied to the social (and, less often in practice but just as appropriate theoretically, behavioral) sciences in a usage that has proved controversial.[39] Basically, the position taken is that for studies of human behavior such as conversations and rituals, as for human products such as art and literature, the researcher (read "critic") interprets what occurs. Despite the fact that it has been a controversial stance, it is no more than a logical extension of the understanding of reality described previously. *If it is the case that people live in a social world rather than a natural one and if they perceive what occurs through their own understanding of reality, then researchers are no more able to directly observe objective reality than is anyone else.* Simply saying so won't make it so, as researchers we might as well admit that we study subjective reality rather than the objective reality we thought we were studying.

In communication, the interpretive approach became most noticeable with the publication of Putnam and Pacanowsky (1983) and has now come to be accepted as one among many theoretical approaches. As James Anderson has recently suggested, "For the interpretive social scientist . . . the business of inquiry is not to reveal the world to us but to create some part of the world for us. Inquiry is the professional practice of the social creation of reality" (1990, p. 14). Specifically, the interpretive approach argues that all research creates a view, a picture, an interpretation, of one part of the world, despite the explicit intent to reveal the world as experienced by others.[40]

Most literally, interpretation simply means "understanding, on the basis of some previous decoding, the general sense of a vast portion of discourse" (Eco, 1976, p. 131), and the text taken for study is not always vast. Generally, however, there is an additional implication: Interpretation "suggests an imposition upon raw data of a meaning not inherent in them" (Fish, 1979, p. 244). This is the colloquial understanding of interpretation: there is reality, and there is your interpretation of reality, and there is mine; the interpretations can differ, but we resolve them by checking them against what we understand to be objective reality. But as Fish went on to point out, a more adequate understanding of reality requires the realization that the text may not exist separately from our interpretations of it; even if it does, we cannot perceive it apart from our interpretations of it. This, then, is the warrant for interpretive social science, as it is the warrant for an interpretive approach to communication. The job of a researcher is accordingly redefined: it is not his or her job to report objective reality, which may turn out to be an impossible task, so much as to discuss the various interpretations placed upon that reality by various social actors. Despite the initial hesitation of many, this task is proving to be challenging enough by itself.

Implied here is the issue of potential multiple interpretations, multiple realities. The term *polysemy* refers to the fact that the same signifier can have several signifieds (the ring I wear may indicate wealth or style to you, but family connections to me).[41] It is equally true that every signified can be indicated by multiple signifiers (the concept of liberty is indicated both by the United States flag and the Statue of Liberty. In D. M. Schneider's graceful phrase, "every symbol can have a number of different meanings and . . . every meaning can have a number of different symbols" (1976, p. 214).

There has been considerable discussion to date about whether symbols can be indefinitely polysemic with the general conclusion that they can, at least theoretically (in other words, a symbol can potentially mean an infinite number of things to an infinite number of people). Though possible theoretically, this would be rare if not impossible in practice, for a symbol loses its power if it never means the same thing to different people (Fernandez, 1982).

An example of polysemy is a hope chest, a wooden storage box traditionally associated with a young girl preparing for marriage. The same object can alternatively be viewed as a storage container, as a seat, as a marker of wealth, as an indication of hopes and expectations, as a statement about a woman's proper role in life, as a place to store objects related to the wedding once it is over, even as a toy chest after children are born. These different implications of a hope chest can be held by the same person at different times or by different people at the same time.[42] In either case, there is polysemy: a single sign conveying multiple meanings.

It is generally accepted that some interpretations are dominant over others and more likely to hold for a larger number of people (Grossberg, 1989). This has occasionally led to discussion of whether one single correct interpretation exists for each symbol, a position uniformly rejected, partially for its totalitarian implications and partially because the use of symbols clearly contradicts it. To resolve the issue of single interpretations, it has been suggested that the word *meaning* be assumed to be plural every time it occurs (O'Sullivan, Hartley, Saunders, & Fiske, 1983, p. 132). This approach would stop many problems before they arise because if researchers always assume there is more than one meaning for a symbol, they are less likely to attempt to privilege the one they find most appealing personally.

Eco (1976) popularized the idea of referring to texts as either *open*, where the complexity of a text can only be understood when multiple interpretations are considered, or *closed*, where one reading is strongly preferred over the others. Generally, researchers view open texts as a more interesting focus of study than closed texts with their limited possibilities, but it is possible to play with these concepts. Sometimes the search to understand what clearly were intended as closed messages becomes a sort of game.

For example, consider the elaborate beading on Sarah Ferguson's wedding gown when she married Prince Andrew in 1986. Everyone could be expected to know that the hearts included in beadwork on the train indicated romance, for that is widely understood, thus an open reading. Many people figured out that the anchors and waves stood for Prince Andrew's role as sailor. But the bumblebees and thistles beaded on the bodice of her dress were more obscure, coming from her family's coat of arms, a closed reading known to a limited circle of family and friends; closed, that is, until the newspapers published the information, so everyone could feel included in that circle (Menkes, 1986, p. 5).[43] It is worth noting that an explanation of the decorations on the wedding dress was printed by *The [London] Times* the day after the wedding; that is, as soon as the symbols were displayed, they needed to be explained.

Within 2 hours after the royal wedding, copies of the dress were already on sale for other brides and apparently in great demand ("Shops Quick", 1986). What is fascinating about this, aside from the astonishing speed, is that the symbols appropriate for Sarah Ferguson's wedding dress cannot be assumed to be correct for anyone else. Why would these others want to display inappropriate symbols? Apparently any reference to the royal wedding was sufficiently widely understood that it was viewed as more correct to copy the original completely than to adapt it to the owner of the imitation. This, then, is another type of closed reading, even more subtle than the first: here one not only has to know that bees and thistles refer to Sarah Ferguson's family crest and are to be expected on her wedding dress, one has to know that the symbols from her family crest incorporated in someone else's wedding dress are to be understood as reference to the royal wedding, rather than as a statement about the family background of the bride displaying them.

Presumably only the legacy of the physical sciences, where it is assumed that the focus of study is objective reality, leads to the assumption that there should be one and only one right interpretation of human behavior.[44] (Today, there are those who question even the assumption that it is possible to describe an objective reality in the physical sciences when human perception serves as one of the research tools.) Communication researchers, as with others, now generally acknowledge this one-to-one ratio of reality to interpretation as oversimplification and are gradually coming to be less interested in achieving the patently impossible goal of discovering the single correct interpretation of symbols than in coming to understand the range of interpretations that exist and the implications of such variety for social actors.

Occasionally a related type of polysemy is useful. In the previous description, it was assumed that each symbol could mean something different to each different person; it is also possible for a single symbol to mean one thing to a person at one time and another thing to the same person at a later time. Thus, a photograph of someone takes on new meaning after their death. This is no more than an expansion of the fact that context bears upon interpretation of symbols and, as such, it should be taken for granted that meanings will change. It would be much stranger if symbols never changed, always bearing identical implications for people. Hassan, noted literary critic, suggested, *"Briefly put, nothing has intrinsic sense: a strong sense must be made of everything"* (1987, p. 198). Interpretation, or sense-making, comes from the people who see symbols, *not* from within the symbol; thus, there can be considerable change over time, across space, even from person to person at the same time and place.

Although analysts may appreciate the existence of multiple interpretations for any symbol, social actors do not generally grant these equal value.[45] Cultural Studies, in particular, has sparked investigations of whose interpretations come to be valued and how these dominant readings come to be subverted by various social groups.[46] Relying upon this literature, Fiske (1982, pp. 113–114) referred to three major ways of reading any text: the *dominant* reading, conveying the dominant group's values; the *subordinate* reading, where a nondominant group accepts the basic structure of power relations in the society, aspiring only to a higher standing within that structure; and the *oppositional* reading, where a nondominant group calls the entire existing social structure into question, requesting not a higher status but a tearing down of the entire structure in order to begin anew.

As an example, these concepts can be applied to honeymoons. A dominant reading of a honeymoon implies a several week stay at a distant location, preferably some representation of paradise, typically one or more islands (thus Hawaii or the Caribbean are popular destinations). A subordinate reading implies a desire for that dominant possibility, admitting its value, yet settling for a lesser version (a week in Florida or at Niagara Falls serving as a common alternative). In both cases the ideals of the couple getting away together to spend "quality" time and establish the marriage on a good base are accepted; in both cases the couple often spends as much as they can readily afford, if not quite a bit more, to indicate the importance of this event. An oppositional reading, however, denies the significance of the honeymoon as starting point, considering it a flagrant waste of money that could be better spent (so some couples choose to spend the same amount on a down payment on a house or on a car, rather than on a vacation they can ill afford). Logic says that this is a perfectly reasonable thing to do, but tradition is surprised, and often insulted as well, at the flaunting of the norm.

*Meaning* has not yet been discussed separately from interpretation. Just as interpretation has the colloquial implication of "my (possibly skewed) understanding of what you intended," so meaning has the colloquial implication of "what you really intended, whether or not I understood it." Todorov (1982) clearly linked meaning with sender and interpretation with recipient, although this suggestion relies upon an outdated vision of communication as involving separable senders, receivers, and messages and does not sufficiently account for the actual complexity of social interaction.[47] It is more appropriate to assume the concepts symbol, interpretation, and meaning are intertwined in various ways. Otherwise, researchers might (incorrectly) assume it appropriate to characterize meanings as either right or wrong, a choice explored in detail by Burke:

> Meaning, when used in the sense of "correct meaning," leads to an either–or approach. "New York City is in Iowa" could, by the either–or principles, promptly be ruled out. The either–or test would represent the semantic ideal. But I am sorry to have to admit that, by the poetic ideal, "New York City is in Iowa" could *not* be ruled out.
>
> Has one ever stood, for instance, in some little outlying town, on the edge of the wilderness, and watched a train go by? Has one perhaps suddenly felt that the train, and its tracks were a kind of arm of the city, reaching out across the continent, quite as though it were simply Broadway itself extended? It is in such a sense that New York City can be found all over the country—and I submit that one would miss very important meanings, meanings that have much to do with the conduct of our inhabitants, were he to proceed here by the either–or kind of test.
>
> "New York City is in Iowa" is "poetically" true. As a metaphor, it provides valid insight. To have ruled it out, by strict semantic authority, would have been vandalism. (Burke, 1989, p. 90)

As with interpretations, then, we must understanding meanings to be multiple and varied, not less but more valuable for the lack of clear-cut "correctness." Meanings are multiple, and they are fluid (Guss, 1989, p. 162). As with interpretation, meaning eventually leads to issues of politics and the distribution of power (the power to introduce new meanings or to assert the priority of one's meanings over someone else's) (Kress, 1988a).

Meaning can be discussed not only in its relationship to interpretation but also in its relationship to signs. Sless pointed out that " 'Sign' and 'meaning' are inextricable; to identify something as a sign is in the next breath to interrogate its meaning, for it is in the nature of signs (or so it would seem) to have meaning" (1986, p. 88). Yet accepting meaning as a property of signs does not aid the effort to understand it.

The specific connection between symbols and meaning might be questioned, though it appears superficially obvious: Symbols "mean" something to somebody. Simply saying "the central problem of symbolism is meaning" (Foster & Brandes, 1980, p. xiv) conveys little. It helps a little more to say symbols are taken as the "locus of meaning" by anthropologists (Ortner, 1984), that is, they are an appropriate starting point if the intention is to study cultural meanings (and authors such as Carey, 1989, have said that should indeed be our intention). When perceived as appropriate points of entry into a meaning system, signs are rarely studied individually and granted individual value, as is the case in semiotics (and communication) but instead as a means to an end, that end being the desired understanding of a particular culture as a whole system.

A more elaborate definition of meaning, provided by Roland Barthes, introduces a new concept: "any kind of intertextual or extratextual correlation, that is, every feature of the narrative which refers to another moment within it or to another locus of the culture required in order to read it'' (as presented and translated in Lydon with Woodruff & Warren, 1989, p. 41). Ultimately, people attribute meaning to actions by sifting current events through the filter of memories of past events. It is only when we recognize a behavior as fitting with or contradicting a past norm that we are able to assign meaning.[48] The concept of *intertextuality*, taken from Kristeva's presentation of Mikhail Bakhtin's writings, is understood to describe the ability of any one text to make reference to another or to several others.[49] Kristeva (1969) proposed that much of the meaning gained from a text is brought to it through intertextuality: Texts "resonate" with meaning when they refer to previous texts, perhaps because they do not require as much work to decide how to interpret them. If nothing else, intertextual quotations provide the "point of departure" here described by Barthes.

There are actually three uses of the term intertextuality. First, a direct quotation of one text within another.[50] For example, in the film *True Love*, the bride decided to have the mashed potatoes at her reception dyed sky blue to match one of the colors of her bridesmaids' dresses, an uncommon choice, one the groom did not particularly appreciate. If a bride in real life were to dye her mashed potatoes blue, it would no longer have the same meaning of simply breaking traditional expectations but could be understood additionally to be a reference to that particular film (even though the blue mashed potatoes are only referred to, never actually shown). Incidentally, this example demonstrates that intertextual quotation is limited neither by genre constraints nor by the boundary between art and reality (Morgan, 1985, p. 34).

Valentin Voloshinov's writings on reported speech contribute to an understanding of this type of intertextuality.[51] He pointed out that "Reported speech is regarded by the speaker as a message belonging to *someone else*, a message that was originally totally independent, complete in its construction, and lying outside the given context" (1930/1971, p. 149). This leads in two directions. First, as there would be no attempt to quote a segment of text from another interaction unless it had value in its original form, as actors we try to maintain what is quoted exactly as it appeared in its original context; at the same time, it is unlikely to fit a new context quite perfectly if held to its original form, and so we change it according to new requirements. As researchers, then, we focus on the critical balance between maintenance and revision.

Bakhtin further described reported speech as being "double voiced," simultaneously presenting someone else's voice and one's own (1929/1971, p. 187). This is the power of intertextuality: one multiplies one's voice, and consequently, multiplies the meanings.[52] Every bride who chooses to wear a long white dress with train and veil, to hold flowers, and to walk down the aisle invokes images of every other bride who has ever made the same choices. These images may be of actual prior brides from weddings personally attended or of media brides from film or television portrayals. The meaning taken from the scene is magnified through this resonance with multiple past experiences.

Second, there is a more recent use of the term intertextuality that relies on implicit knowledge of a culture. This use assumes that "any one text is necessarily read in relationship to others and that a range of textual knowledges is brought to bear upon it. These relationships do not take the form of specific allusions from one text to another and there is no need for readers to be familiar with specific or the same texts to read intertextually" (Fiske, 1987, p. 108). In this second sense of the word, participants draw upon popular culture myths and images, though not always explicit characterizations, to convey meanings. There are entire genres of literature (mysteries, westerns, science fiction) made comprehensible only by assuming knowledge of the basic tradition, but no *one* particular book must be read to understand the reference. All members of the class share enough characteristics that basic allusions are clear.

We can deliberately foreground a particular aspect of an event so as to multiply meanings for ourselves or others. Choosing to wear the same lucky sweater each time when going bowling, because I once got a high score wearing that sweater, relies on intertextuality. Doing so, I hope to recall exactly how I felt and played on that prior occasion, by wearing a part of the outfit (an index) worn then. Each time I get another high score wearing that sweater multiples the effect and makes it seem appropriate to continue the behavior. The first time I wear the sweater, there may be no relevant intertextuality.[53] The second time I wear it, there is intertextuality in its strongest sense: a clear reference to the time I got a high score wearing the sweater. The third, fourth, and tenth times, however, there is intertextuality in the weaker sense: a reference to previous bowling attempts and continued efforts to maintain a high score.

The third use of intertextuality is the most general, most implicit. All conversation, all interaction, is ultimately intertextual in this limited sense: sharing the same vocabulary and the same actions, one cannot help but to repeat choices made previously by others, thus borrowing and playing upon their meanings, intentionally or not. "Our everyday speech is full of other people's words: with some of them our voice is completely merged, and we forget whose words they were; we use others that have authority, in our view, to substantiate our own words; and in yet others we implant our different, even antagonistic intentions" (Bakhtin, 1929/1971, p. 187). For obvious reasons, the first use of intertextuality is the most studied, the second is just beginning to have an impact, and the third is still a new topic. This last, most subtle use of intertextuality may prove the most important to the study of social interaction, being the most prevalent.[54]

Most commentators appear surprised at the frequency with which intertextual references can be located in various literary and/or social texts. However, perhaps they should rather be impressed that there is so much rampant creativity, so much that is new. It is far easier, and more predictable, and faster to simply make use of the past in a new way, whether this is by express citation or by more subtle allusion. Thus researchers should take note not only of what is repetitive but of what is original.

***How Does One Arrive at the Meaning of a Sign?*** Gronbeck stated that a particular form "depends for its meaningfulness upon 1) a stock of knowledge, possessed in common by both the communicator and the viewer, and upon 2) a set of signs or markers which invoke that stock of knowledge" (1983, p. 241). Intertextuality relies upon the sharing of a common stock of knowledge for the conveyance of meaning. In other words, if a particular symbol evokes past symbols for me but not for you, you will of necessity miss much of what is conveyed to me. For this reason, intertextuality is not a universal phenomenon but requires a cultural context to be effective. If you come from a culture where brides wear red instead of white and where white is a symbol of grief associated with funerals, as in China, then the sight of a bride in white will conjure up memories of funerals instead of weddings. The pleasant effect of multiple ghost images, of prior brides standing behind the current bride as she maintains tradition, will be perverted.

***Where Does Meaning Reside?*** It has sometimes been assumed that meaning resides within the sign itself, despite the fact that this is contrary to the current understanding of meaning residing in the context, in the social actor(s), or best of all in the combination of all three—the sign, the context, and the social actors.

Since at least Alfred Schutz and George Herbert Mead, it has been widely accepted that "it is misleading to say that experiences *have* meaning. Meaning does not lie *in* the experience. Rather, those experiences are meaningful which are grasped reflectively" (Schutz, 1967, p. 69). In other words, meaning is not present in a sign or an experience until a particular individual contributes it. But even this is not broad enough, for "Significance belongs to things in their relations to individuals. It does not lie in mental processes which are enclosed within individuals" (G. H. Mead, 1922, p. 163). Thus, meaning resides neither in an object nor in a particular individual but in social relations. A good summary of this position is provided by Coutu, who suggested, "Since meaning is not an entity, it has no locus; it is something that occurs rather than exists" (1962, p. 64). It is a mistake to characterize meaning as an entity, whether one posits it as existing within an individual's mind or independently in the text.[55]

Because the term meaning is consistently the term of choice in a wide range of fields, it is futile to advocate rejecting it altogether (much as this would simplify matters). Presumably this discussion has at least clarified the matter: Meaning cannot be found residing in any individual sign, not being an independent creation. Here the metaphor of sign as storage box betrays us, for what one puts into a storage box, by implication, should be available to another for removal at a later time. We turn for help to the metaphor of sign as shorthand, with its suggestion that signs serve as reminders of complex totalities and relationships only hinted at. Someone else reading my shorthand would find it idiosyncratic, uninterpretable; just so, he or she must either share or take time to learn my signification system to understand what my symbols convey to me.

Implied in the previous discussion is an understanding of how symbols change over time: The meanings people give them change. "For all their apparent solidity, meanings remain mutable products of use and, as usages change, meanings shift" (Sless, 1986, p. 114). Structures only appear stable; actually they change constantly. People ascribe meanings to symbols dependent upon their usage in particular contexts; over time, as these contexts change, the meanings ascribed to symbols change as well. It has even been suggested that the appropriate object of study is not symbols but meanings, for meaning is "the constitutive and organizing power in cultural life" (Wagner, 1986, p. ix; he went on to reverse the general order: Rather than studing symbols through their meanings, he proposed studying meaning through its symbols). Because meaning changes, it has been described as "imperceptible."[56] Far from being problematic, this vagueness, this openness of symbols to a variety of meanings, has been suggested as their primary value (Eco, 1986, p. 153). People manipulate them, thus, their extreme flexibility is a benefit.

Hodge and Kress proposed the use of the term *social semiotics* for the part of the field of semiotics specifically studying change in meanings, emphasizing process over structure:

> Traditional semiotics likes to assume that the relevant meanings are frozen and fixed in the text itself, to be extracted and decoded by the analyst by reference to a coding system that is impersonal and neutral, and universal for users of the code. Social semiotics cannot assume that texts produce exactly the meanings and effects that their authors hope for: it is precisely the struggles and their uncertain outcomes that must be studied at the level of social action, and their effects in the production of meaning. (Hodge & Kress, 1988, p. 12)

In some ways, this requires communication studies to step back and begin again at an earlier point: If we as researchers cannot assume meanings are consistent and taken for granted, we must begin by understanding which meanings have become sufficiently important to gain their own symbols. In this usage, social semiotics with its focus on meaning is contrasted against formal semiotics, the study of definitions for theory's sake (Thibault, 1991).

Accompanying the acceptance of interpretive approaches to the study of human behavior is the assumption that discovering the meanings others attribute to their behavior is the appropriate goal.[57] That many scholars have made such an assumption is clear from a variety of fields. Meaning has been described as the proper subject of anthropology because, "The study of culture necessarily entails the study of meaning" (Basso & Selby, 1976, p. 3). Meaning also has been defined as the proper subject of sociology, holding "the problem of meaning" at "the core of sociological observation" (Gusfield, 1989, p. 5).[58] In addition to these areas, the study of meaning is now put forth as the goal of communication: Carey suggested researchers "conceive of communication as a cultural science whose objective is the elucidation of meaning" (1989, p. 181).[59]

It is important that the search for meaning and the reinterpretation of the field of communication as emphasizing that search not be overly narrow. In the past, the study of meaning has often been taken to imply the appropriateness of freezing social interaction in order to study a single symbol or a single text, without equal attention paid to the context in which that symbol occurs and the people for whom that symbol has meaning. Hodge and Kress spoke also to this:

> We see communication essentially as a process, not as a disembodied set of meanings or texts. Meaning is produced and reproduced under specific social conditions, through specific material forms and agencies. It exists in relationship to concrete subjects and objects, and is inexplicable except in terms of this set of relationships. (Hodge & Kress, 1988, p. viii)

As described earlier, the tension is between the investigation of process and the investigation of structure. Tempting though it might be to privilege one over the other, it is most valuable to investigate the tension between the two, using them as two ways to approach the same phenomenon, that being communication.

As with interpretation, meaning leads to *polysemy* with its related implications of power and politics, of whose meanings shall be dominant and whose ignored. Researchers must remember to study the context as well as the text, the people who make meaning as well as the meanings made. Clearly, we must expand our focus beyond the individual sign as sufficient topic. But how are we to do this in practice? Whict part of context must we attend to? Where do we draw the line between what must be included as relevant and what may safely be left outside that line for others to study? These questions lead to the concept of codes, the topic of the following chapter.[60]

## NOTES

1. The anthropologist Victor Turner pointed out that a symbol is the "smallest portion to which a ritual sequence or dynamic total can be reduced by subdivision without losing its semantic structural identity" (1969, p. 8). Minus his particular attention only to symbols and rituals, this explanation demonstrates how a building block serves as the perfect metaphor for understanding how signs function: They are the smallest unit to which behavior can be divided without losing meaning.

2. Cherry (1980, p. 251); see the longer list of offenders in O'Sullivan, Hartley, Saunders, and Fiske (1983, p. 234). As Culler (1981) pointed out, Saussure used the term sign in discussing what are now widely called symbols, adding to the confusion.

3. Good resources for discussion of signifier and signified are Barthes (1964/1967); Hawkes (1977); Nöth (1990); for a rare reference specifically within communication, see S. Glynn (1986).

4. This distinction has been put particularly well by Eco:

> We have a sign every time we have a material presence—perhaps a sound, an image, an object—which refers to something which is not there but which is accorded recognition by a human being on the basis of certain cultural conventions of an experiential nature. For example, let's consider a round sign that says "DETOUR"—we look at the sign and we realize that something will occur, say, two miles ahead. A physical presence refers us to a situation we cannot detect. Therefore, whether the sign describes a real situation or not, a *sign relationship* has been established, nevertheless. We react: we make a detour. Semiotics, then, studies the laws governing this kind of relationship. (Eco in Balducci, 1976, p. 36)

  Dan Sperber pointed out that "the most interesting cultural knowledge is tacit knowledge—that is to say, that which is not made explicit" (1974, p. x). Ultimately the relationship between the two, the tacit and the explicit, the signified and the signifier, may be the most interesting of all.

5. For further information on Peirce's comments, see Peirce (1985); Sebeok (1986a); Nöth (1990).

6. There are many other authors who have discussed signs in detail, often dividing them up differently from either Saussure or Peirce. The best source for discussion of these variations on the theme is Nöth (1990).

7. Hawkes (1977, p. 129) gave the following example, useful for its combination of all three types of signs: A leaf from a tree is an index of that tree (it was originally part of it); a sketch of that tree is an icon (the sketch looks like or in some way is modelled after the tree); the word *tree* is a symbol for it (the word is an arbitrary choice, as demonstrated by the fact that other languages than English have chosen other words to stand for the same object).

8. Sigman (1991, pp. 115–116) discussed wedding band as symbol and index: It serves to mark a continuing relationship when both parties are not present.

9. For an up-to-date consideration of the concept of symbol within communication, see J. Stewart (in press).

10. These are most clearly understood through a combined reading of Barthes (1964/1967) and Fiske (1982); this discussion is in no way intended to obviate the need to read original sources.

11. These are not hypothetical examples. The Milwaukee Skyline Women's Barbershop Chorus presented a night of music and romance entitled "The Honor of Your Presence," on February 15, 1992, culminating in the marriage of two barbershoppers. The examples of the clown and Western weddings are based on brief descriptions of actual weddings presented by my students in Spring 1992.

12. Later publications have frequently been oriented to the study of language, that most significant system of symbols (J. Stewart, 1972), rhetoric (Brummett, 1979, 1980; Logue & Patton, 1982, are typical examples; Katriel, 1987, is atypical in that she applied rhetoric not to speech but to fire inscriptions), even nonverbal communication (Haiman, 1982; Merriam, 1975), and mass communication (Rothenbuhler, 1989). Most of these authors shared a common unspoken assumption that symbols are the obvious focus of attention, a point perhaps justified by the existence and widespread knowledge of Burke's prior research even when it is not explicitly cited. More general theoretical considerations have appeared, though rarely. There has been, for example, a recent special issue of a major communication journal devoted solely to consideration of symbols (see Osborn, 1983; within that issue, see in particular Aune, 1983, and the response it sparked by S. Glynn, 1986). It was in a deliberate attempt to build upon these and the many other existing references that Cronkhite proposed "human symbolic activity" as the central concern of the discipline (1986). That his suggestion is appropriate has been demonstrated through its quiet acceptance by others (most recently, Friedrich & Boileau, 1990).

13. Within sociology as a whole, the early work by G. H. Mead (1922, 1974) is useful; for the connections between social interactionism and communication, see Littlejohn (1977); Maines and Couch (1988); Nwankwo (1973).

14. Anthropology has gone through at least three major stages in its concern for the symbol; in all of these symbols were viewed as basic "building blocks" (Werbner, 1989, p. 11). The first stage was structural anthropology, most closely identified with Levi-Strauss (see 1966c, p. 114 for his famous comment that "Men communicate by means of symbols and signs; for anthropology, which is a conversation of man with man, everything is symbol and sign, when it acts as intermediary between two subjects"). The second stage was symbolic anthropology, identified with Turner (1967, 1977); M. Douglas (1970); Geertz (1973); Firth (1973b); Leach (1976); Ortner (1973); and Dolgin, Kemnitzer and Schneider (1977b). The third stage was semiotic anthropology, most clearly influenced by M. Singer (1978, 1984), extended in Mertz and Parmentier (1985). Ortner (1984) provided a different division, together with an extremely useful insider's history of the concept of symbol within anthropology.

15. See, for example, H. R. E. Davidson (1977).

16. Within philosophy, the standard references are Whitehead (1927/1959), Langer (1967), and Cassirer (1944); see also Bryson, Finkelstein, MacIver, and McKeon (1964). Langer summed up this point of view nicely when she said "The concept of meaning, in all its varieties, is the dominant philosophical concept of our time. Sign, symbol, denotation, signification, communication—these notions are our stock in trade" (1967, p. 549).

17. Within psychology Royce (1965) and White (1962) are old but particularly useful.

18. Bryson et al. (1964) provided evidence of this cross-disciplinary interest. It is noteworthy that their book contains several articles by researchers in communication (such as Lasswell and de Sola Pool).

19. See Morgan, Frost, and Pondy, 1983; Von Bertalanffy, 1965; White, 1962.

20. Kitahara-Frisch (1980), for example, specifically cited technology and language as two early functions of the symbol process.

21. See also Whitehead (1927/1959, p. 62). White, an anthropologist, felt strongly that the ability to use symbols was a defining characteristic of humans. He invented a new word to call attention to this faculty: "There is, then a kind of behavior which is peculiar to an animal species, *Homo sapiens*. It consists of originating and bestowing meanings upon things and events and in comprehending these meanings. This kind of behavior should have a name. We propose the term *symboling*. A human being *symbols*, just as it performs any other function of which it is capable" (White, 1962, p. 313). Although the verb *symboling* has not come into wide usage since he proposed it 30 years ago, that does not speak to its potential usefulness. I am not proposing that it be added to the vocabulary now, only that researchers bear in mind the significance of the activity, whatever name has it.

22. M. Foster (1990a) elaborated on this, specifically describing symbols now, with examples:

> It can be said—although some may argue—that anything that is used culturally is a symbol. Thus an apple is a symbol in our culture because it is integrated into our food system as something to be eaten when prepared with other ingredients as the ending to a meal (apple pie, apple pan dowdy, etc.), by itself between meals, as a main dish accompaniment for pork (applesauce), or spread on bread (apple jelly). When cultural rules are devised into which particular objects are integrated, those objects become part of the system of symbolic representation of that culture: "As American as apple pie"; "An apple a day keeps the doctor away"; the Apple computer—for "apple" connotes a healthy, familiar item, which would excel in "user friendliness" (p. 83).

Foster showed here how an everyday item, such as an apple, moves from its mundane denotative meanings (apple pies are made from apples) to more enticing connotative meanings (apple pie as symbol of America). She then extended this study of connotations to the use of apples in advertizing, showing how a particular computer company successfully implies user-friendliness through its display of a particularly weighted symbol such as the apple.

23. Halliday (1978) rephrased the question slightly, though his answer was the same with his concern for how children "learn how to mean"; his interest, however, was solely linguistic.

24. As Stephen Foster put it, "it is by expressing themselves through symbols that people view their society, manage and communicate about their relationships, and chart their courses through social and personal relationships" (1988, p. xiv).

25. Hufford, Hunt, and Zeitlin (1989) presented an expansion of this, considering the role grandparents play in teaching traditions to their grandchildren.

26. David Unruh (1983) presented fascinating insights into how, before death, people ensure that particular portions of their identities will be remembered and possibly continued by those who survive, largely through the presentation of both verbal and material forms (ranging from personal narratives to the presentation of artifacts to survivors).

27. There is, of course, an enormous literature on the acquisition of language, one particular system of symbols, but that is not the focus of my discussion here. A few rare exceptions specifically focus on how children learn semiotic understandings and the extent to which they are active participants in the process: Hodge and Kress (1988, chap. 8); Regan (1984); Worth and Gross (1974).

28. " 'Key' or dominant symbols are selected out of the webs of interrelated cultural expressions because they are felt to provide a focus for crucial activities, like rituals, and again, because they supply a metaphorical framework which relates a variety of cultural concerns" (Rosaldo & Atkinson, 1975, p. 44).

29. To name only a few that self-identify as studies of symbols: Brummett (1979, 1980); Logue and Patton (1982); Rothenbuhler (1989).

30. This argument is comparable to that provided in *Secular Ritual*, where the authors suggested even nonreligious rituals are significant and worthy of study (Moore & Myerhoff, 1977).

31. An informant of Stephen Foster's put this beautifully: "Knowing a whole lot of very specific things adds up to a whole way of life" (1988, p. 194). This is what Warren Roberts (1988) called "looking at the overlooked."

32. See Kitahara-Frisch (1980, p. 219) for a clear statement of these and for some elaboration, though she did not originate these ideas.

33. See also Sless (1986, particularly chap. 9) and all of the British Cultural Studies research (beginning with Hebdige, 1979).

34. The use of symbols as markers of identity becomes more theoretically interesting when it is expanded to include the ways in which an organized system of symbols (termed an *ideology*) can transform identity (Stromberg, 1990). For a related article within communication, see Brown (1978).

35. This is actually his summary of Milton Singer (1982), but it is a more concise statement of Singer's ideas than any available in the original article.

36. Walter Goldschmidt expanded upon this: "The essence of any symbol does not lie in the symbol itself, but in what it stands for; status symbols demonstrate that the possessor has achieved merit, is a worthy person, due the respect of the community. The symbol is not entirely arbitrary, for it is representative of something that the community as a whole cherishes" (1990, p. 38).

37. For a technical discussion of the various theories of meaning assumed by communication scholars, see John Stewart (1972), an article strong on the philosophical underpinnings of communication theories that view language as a system of symbols (which of course it is). The theory of communication centered most clearly on meaning is the Coordinated Management of Meaning (Cronen, Pearce, & Harris, 1982; Pearce & Cronen, 1980).

38. Peirce's interpretant would seem to be the obvious starting point for discussion because as he described that term, it refers to the meaning a representatum grants an object, yet oddly enough this point is rarely brought to discussions of either interpretation or meaning.

39. Rabinow and Sullivan (1979) is the landmark collection.

40. For discussion of the issue in general, see Steier (1991); for application to interpersonal communication specifically, see Leeds-Hurwitz (1992b).

41. Turner (1969, p. 8) used *multivocality* to mean roughly the same as what I intend by *polysemy*; others have used *multivalency* to convey approximately the same meaning (Musello, 1992, p. 55; Young, 1991, p. 161).

42. Because hope chests are not now so common as they once were, presumably due in large part to the opening up of roles available to women, ads for them have changed and now emphasize the role of storage container for a student at college, toy chest for a child, or a place to store a winter comforter at the foot of the bed, at least as often as a place to store objects that will later be used in establishing a new home. It is incidental, but important, that hope chests are tradition- ally given by parents to their children in support of the role(s) they see as appropriate for them.

43. There are statements here to be made about the way in which closed readings, if known to exist, imply a challenge that many people wish to pursue and about the interest in discovering what lies behind closed readings particularly for royalty. Such ideas are enticing but not essential to this discussion at this point.

44. "The 'proper' interpretation of symbols is a pursuit long practiced in the West. . . . But the mere idea that there is or can be a 'proper' interpretation for symbols is itself normative, when in most societies individuals are left fairly free to interpret symbols as they please" (Sperber, 1985, p. 71).

45. The implications of this approach have been put especially well by Henrietta Moore, in her dis- cussion of Ricoeur's work: "In human societies, it is simply not true to say that all those who can read may provide interpretations. Interpretation—as Ricoeur himself argues—always has symbolic significance, and often it may have economic and political consequences as well. In- terpretation is always bound up with social inequality and with domination" (1990, p. 116).

46. See especially Hall, Hobson, Lowe, and Willis (1980) for an introduction to this idea.

47. Oddly enough, this is the understanding of communication most commonly assumed as appropriate in what semiotic literature does consider the matter.

48. Wieder (1974/1988, pp. 168–170) provided a good example of the various meanings conveyed by a single phrase, "You know I won't snitch," depending upon the degree of knowledge brought to the utterance by various speakers.

49. For further discussion of the concept of intertextuality, see Culler (1981); Fiske (1987, 1989); Neusner (1990); and especially Morgan (1985). The initial translation from the Russian seems to be taken from Kristeva (1969) as a way of presenting the concepts of *dialogism* and *heteroglossia* in Bakhtin's work (1981); see Wertsch (1985) and Todorov (1984) for discussion of Bakhtin's original comments.

50. See Morawski (1970) for an expansion of the functions of quotations.

51. There has been considerable debate about whether work published by Voloshinov was actually written in part or entirely by Bakhtin (Todorov, 1984, pp. xi–xii). I follow Todorov's lead in using the names that appear on the publications.

52. Obviously this volume, in its attempt to integrate the words of others with my own, can be ap- propriately described as making considerable use of intertextuality.

53. There can be lots of irrelevant intertextuality, however: the sweater can, for example, be the same color as a dress I once had or made of the same yarn as a sweater a friend once had, etc.

54. Fiske quoted Barthes as saying that "intertextual relations are so pervasive that our culture con- sists of a complex web of intertextuality, in which all texts refer finally to each other and not to reality" (1987, p. 115).

55. For this reason, Culler proposed to substitute the concept of sense-making:

> Indeed, the semiotic program may be better expressed by the concepts of "sense" and "making sense" than by the concept of "meaning," for while "meaning" suggests a property of a text (a text "has" meaning), and thus encourages one to distinguish an in- trinsic (though perhaps ungraspable) meaning from the interpretations of readers, "sense" links the qualities of a test to the operations one performs upon it. A text can make sense and someone can make sense of a text. If a text which at first did not make sense comes to make sense, it is because someone has made sense of it. (Culler, 1981, p. 50)

Culler's argument is persuasive, though it has not yet held sway. Though technical usage still relies on meaning, it would clearly be better to consign this usage to colloquial discussion only, substituting sense-making for all technical uses. It appropriately highlights the active role played by the people who create meaning rather than leaving the active role to be played by the text (whether that be words, actions, ideas, foods, clothing, etc.). Texts, after all, are not animate and cannot have their own agendas. They are human creations having only the meanings humans give them.

56. Petitot-Concorda (1985, p. 273); see discussion of this in Greimas (1987). In a way, it is this problem of the imperceptibility of meaning that has led me to study social codes immediately available to the senses: The food, clothing, and objects studied in later chapters have a satisfying solidity to them, deceptive though it may be. See Ackerman (1990) for a detailed consideration of the senses and their influence on daily life.

57. Schwartz and Merten (1971); Basso and Selby (1976); Mertz and Parmentier (1985).

58. Symbolic interactionism, one sociological approach, is all about meanings (Blumer, 1969).

59. See also Littlejohn (1977) and Lincourt (1978). Mumby specifically cited the rise of interpretive approaches as responsible for the increased attention paid to the investigation of meaning (1989, p. 291).

60. There is actually less of a gap between the content of chapters 2 and 3 than appears evident. In order to streamline the presentation, Turner's suggestion that symbols are found in clusters (smaller groupings than entire social codes) has been omitted (1969, p. 19). An example of analysis at the level of a cluster of symbols is provided by Ames (1978), a history of hall furnishings in Victorian America.

# Chapter 3

# Codes

The last chapter presented signs as entities unto themselves, yet signs do not occur singly; they occur in groups. Technically, semioticians term a group or set of signs a *code*. As used here, code is synonymous with system, pattern, network, and grid (all of which are also used to designate groups of signs).[1] Placement of signs into appropriate groupings stresses that *meaning arises not solely, not even primarily, from the relationship of signifier to signified but from relations between signs*. Probably it always will be easiest to investigate signs singly, narrowing the field, ignoring all signs but the one of current interest; it is certainly always more adequate to place each sign in its proper context, that being the larger set of signs in which it is embedded.

Yet the concept of code implies more than ''groupness''; it also includes rules for the organization of individual signs. To limit the definition of code to ''set of signs'' implies simply gathering items together into appropriate sets as a sufficient and worthy goal. Expanding the definition of code to ''set of signs and rules for their use'' encourages investigation of how people actually use signs to create and exchange meanings. Previously it has been pointed out that meaning resides neither in the signifier nor the signified but in the relation between them that together comprise the sign; in expansion of that, it can now be stated that meaning resides not in the sign alone but more diffusely in the code as a whole.

Implicit in this is the question *Why does one need to study codes rather than signs?* The answer has been implied as well: To study a single sign means studying an incomplete entity; signs occur within codes, taking their meaning from the codes of which they are but one component. Therefore, as researchers we expand our study to include not only individual signs but the larger codes that they jointly comprise. Limiting our study to individual signs implies researching one advertisement at a time, one gesture at a time, one food, one item of clothing. Expanding our study to the more encompassing category of codes implies studying a sequence of advertisements, a set of gestures, a food system, clothing styles. "Semiology is thus based on the assumption that insofar as human actions or productions convey meaning, insofar as they function as signs, there must be an underlying system of conventions and distinctions which make this meaning possible. *Where there are signs there is system*" (Culler, 1977, p. 91). If a sign takes its meaning from the system or code, obviously limiting analysis to individual signs is inappropriate; much meaning unintentionally will be missed. We will learn part of what we might, but we will miss more.

Discussing this problem, Edmund Leach used the metaphor of the alphabet: One sign, considered in isolation, is "as meaningless as isolated letters of the alphabet" (Leach, 1976, p. 1). No one has ever suggested that it is appropriate to discover meaning in language from individual letters of the alphabet, of course, nor even from individual words considered out of context. Words are presented embedded in layers of context (at the first level, a sentence or utterance; at the second, the larger text or discourse). We may be able to understand some of the meanings conveyed by a sign considering it alone, as we can understand some of the potential meanings of a word by looking it up in a dictionary, but the dictionary cannot indicate which meaning a speaker intended when choosing that word over other possibilities. Equally, analysis of one sign alone cannot accurately conclude the appropriateness of any of the potential meanings. "To speak of *a* symbol, or of the meaning of *a symbol*, is misleading, for no symbol exists or has meaning except in relation to a network of other symbols. Symbolic representation implies configuration" (M. L. Foster, 1980, p. 371). Logic requires the study of signs in codes, as they actually occur, rather than as hypothetically discrete items, though the latter is easier to examine.[2]

Language most often serves as the model code, for it is the code originally of greatest interest to Saussure. Clearly language includes more than a vocabulary list; the rules for combining individual items, termed grammar, form a critical part of the same package. As with the code of language, so with others: Codes are always assumed to include not only sets of related signs but also rules for the usage of those signs.[3]

Unfortunately, too literal a use of language as the model code and linguistics as the model field of study has drawbacks.[4] Four of these are presented. First, researchers often assume *descriptive* linguistics (focusing almost entirely on the text, including but little context for it) as the particular aspect of linguistics utilized as model, whereas *sociolinguistics* (the study of speech in use) might be a more appropriate choice. Among other distinctions between the two, sociolinguistics takes a larger context for understanding discourse into consideration.[5]

Second, language is a *digital* code (with signs, words in this case, clearly distinguishable from each other); many other codes are *analogic* (that is, individual signs run together, as in kinesics or proxemics, being separated only by the analyst for the purpose of interpretation). Digital codes are easier to understand and easier to analyze than analogic codes; thus, too literal a use of them as model misleads.[6]

Third, developing exact correlations of grammatical rules is probably impossible for most communication codes, despite the fact that in keeping with the model of linguistics, this has often been set as the goal. Other times, researchers have assumed a goal of establishing a set of rules to explain past and predict future behavior. In fact, the proper goal may not be anything so rigid. Researchers need to think about what goals are appropriate to the study rather than adopting them wholesale from another endeavor.

Fourth, and perhaps most significant, using linguistics as the model implies that linguistic communication is somehow primary, that words come before actions or other aspects of nonverbal communication. This assumption underlies much research in communication, though rarely explicitly stated. It can be attributed to the traditional emphasis on the study of verbal behavior rather than a deliberate decision that such emphasis is theoretically appropriate.

None of these arguments is sufficient to prevent the limited use of language as a model code and linguistics as a model of analysis. Recognizing that there are some drawbacks, however, encourages us to move cautiously. (Nothing here is unique to the use of linguistics, of course. Any model chosen has some drawbacks; that is the nature of models.) Researchers must choose which aspects of language and linguistics to use as models rather than assuming what has been done previously will continue to be appropriate. Shifting focus from linguistics and the study of language to the broader study of communication may have subtle implications; these need to be searched out, and our assumptions modified accordingly.

## CHARACTERISTICS OF CODES

All codes share the same set of characteristics. A reasonable list proposed by O'Sullivan et al. (1983) serves as the basis for elaboration here:[7]

1. Codes have a number of units arranged in paradigms from which one is chosen.
2. These chosen units are combined syntagmatically into a message or text.
3. Codes convey meaning derived from the agreement among and shared cultural experience of their users.
4. Codes are transmittable by their appropriate media of communication.
5. Codes can be a way of classifying, organizing, and understanding material as well as of transmitting or communicating it.
6. Codes are, by their very nature, full of gaps and inconsistencies and subject to constant change. (pp. 36–37)

Deceptively brief, this list is rich in implication. Some implications of these brief comments are laid out as follows, taking each characteristic in turn.

### 1. Codes Have a Number of Units Arranged in Paradigms From Which One Is Chosen.
The first characteristic introduces a central concept into the discussion, that of *paradigm*, a term bequeathed by Saussure; though old, it continues to be useful. Briefly, a paradigm is a set of signs or units from which social actors choose only one for display. In the clothing code, all shirts taken together form a single paradigm; all pairs of shoes are another; all jackets a third. Constituent elements of a paradigm are generally *mutually exclusive* in their use: Each person normally wears only one shirt, one pair of shoes, or one jacket at a time. This feature can be contradicted, in which case the duplication itself becomes noteworthy. The "layered look" in clothing exemplifies this, with designers suggesting several shirts, sweaters, or vests be worn simultaneously.

Codes, by definition, always include a group of signs from which at least one is chosen to convey particular information. Staying with the example of clothing, the choice of a down jacket may convey information about the weather, whereas hiking boots may convey information about an intended or preferred activity. Within a paradigm, the differences *among* elements determine meaning: An observer mentally compares a down jacket to a suede jacket with fringes or one made of fox fur or a nylon windbreaker, all very real alternatives; each is understood to entail some meanings the others do not. The items making up a paradigm must have something in common in order to be placed together. For example, all objects to wear on the feet are placed into a single paradigm, despite obvious differences in their appearance, because all serve the same function.

Sometimes one discovers individual signs that are new, never previously considered potential members of the paradigm. In *Steel Magnolias*, much is made of a groom's cake shaped like an armadillo, a red cake (representing blood and flesh) covered by gray icing (representing skin; see Fig. 3.1). This example shares just enough characteristics with past examples (groom's cakes are usually dark rather than light, as are bride's cakes; it is presented within the appropriate context and labeled with the appropriate name by participants) that wedding guests are forced to recognize it as one possible member of the class, though it conflicts with enough other characteristics (the deliberate reference to blood and skin, neither of which one would expect to be forced to consider while contemplating a cake, and the unappetizing color of the icing) that guests may be made uncomfortable by it. The film makes much of the questionable nature of the image (the person who baked the cake is a relative of the groom, who must be tolerated for that alone; extensive joking by the bride's family and friends surrounds the presence of the cake before and during its appearance at the wedding reception). Knowing that this example (armadillo cake) is a marginal member of its class (the paradigm of all possible groom's cakes) helps viewers of the film to understand why that joking is both necessary and funny.[8]

**2.  Units Chosen From Paradigms Are Combined Syntagmatically into a Message or Text.**   The term paradigm is generally used in conjunction with another term, also bequeathed by Saussure, *syntagm*. A syntagm is that new set resulting from the combination of elements drawn from different paradigms. All clothing worn by one person at one time forms a syntagm, composed of items taken from various paradigms. This, then, is the second characteristic of codes: not only does a single code include numerous paradigms, individual items selected from these various paradigms normally appear neither together (within their original paradigms) nor alone (one sign at a time) but rather in combinations, in newly formed sets termed syntagms. This is important because meaning is primarily located at the level of syntagm. Conceivably I am going hiking if you see me wearing hiking boots, but you actually evaluate this interpretation's viability by viewing the rest of my clothing in context. Thus, when someone from Alaska wears hiking boots while going clothes shopping in the "lower forty-eight," he or she conveys a statement about origins and interests rather than immediate activity, a statement potentially capable of being understood by the majority of viewers. Whether or not there is *intention* to convey that message is irrelevant; those who observe the behavior interpret it based on their knowledge of what constitutes appropriate clothing for various activities.

One implication of the previous discussion is that paradigms are abstract, existing only in the heads of people, whereas syntagms are concrete, having physical existence.[9] In other words, one does not normally have access to all of the shoes in someone's closet, seeing only the pair chosen for display today. The other pairs of shoes exist individually; they are potentially viable (presumably they could have been chosen) yet not having been chosen, they are not brought out for

FIG. 3.1.   Armadillo groom's cake from *Steel Magnolias*. Photo taken from the videotape; permission courtesy of Tri-Star Pictures.

observation. Remaining unchosen, whatever meanings they might have conveyed remain unavailable. On the other hand, the entire syntagm (say, all of the clothing worn by a person at one time) is available for whatever interpretation one chooses to make. Ben-Amos pointed out that syntagms and paradigms are simply two sorts of order imposed on social and cultural reality (1977, p. 46).[10]

To continue with another example from *Steel Magnolias*, Annelle arrives in town shortly before Shelby's marriage. She is invited to the wedding but protests she has nothing appropriate to wear and no time to acquire something new. Shelby insists that should not bar her from the celebration, offering her own closet as resource. The viewers are then shown Annelle in an awkward combination of her own items integrated with those borrowed from Shelby: Her own cat-eye glasses and dark leather purse, both long out of date, are combined with a chic dress of Shelby's and short lace gloves (see Fig. 3.2). The humor not only is due to the incongruous combination of these elements into an inappropriate syntagm but to the inappropriate use of the separate items: Annelle eats finger food while wearing the lace gloves and constantly tugs at the low-cut dress to make it cover her. The result is to quickly demonstrate Annelle's lack of sophistication; anyone used to such a dress and such gloves would know better. The audience may wonder what Annelle would have chosen from her own closet, though the film implies she would have had nothing appropriate and might have avoided the event altogether rather than admit to such a lack.

The description of paradigm and syntagm presented so far relies heavily on

FIG. 3.2. Darryl Hannah as Annelle in *Steel Magnolias*. Photo courtesy of Tri-Star Pictures and Darryl Hannah.

Saussure's distinction between *langue* (language) and *parole* (speech). As explained in chapter 1, *langue* refers to a complete language, existing only in potentiality: No one can ever write down every possible utterance in a given language. *Parole* refers to particular utterances actually occurring, each but one possible realization drawn from the larger set of infinite potentialities. Just as analysts infer *langue* from *parole*, so they infer paradigms (the potential resource sets) from syntagms (the actual combinations).[11]

There are actually several levels of *langue*, perhaps best viewed as concentric circles. Taking food for an example, the set of all possible meals within my culture can be drawn as an extremely large *langue*; forming a smaller set of choices, contained entirely within the first, is the set of meals I have ever eaten, still described as a *langue*, but a smaller subset of the original circle. The particular meal on the table in front of me tonight appropriately can be described as an example of *parole*. Here language serves well as model: The particular utterance I make (*parole*) is drawn from the set of possible utterances using the vocabulary I know (*langue*), in turn a subset of all possible utterances in my language (*langue* as well but a different, larger, more complete version) (see Fig. 3.3).

*Competence* and *performance*, related terms, contribute to our understanding of *langue* and *parole*. *Competence* refers to the abilities of a person, something that researchers cannot fully discover, for they are never completely displayed (e.g., the exact extent of anyone's knowledge of a language is quite difficult to ascertain). *Performance* refers to what someone actually does, drawing upon the full set of competencies. Researchers have access to performance but not competence and, therefore, performance alone can be studied (to continue the same example, language testing checks a particular subsection of vocabulary and grammar, making assumptions about what else someone knows from the partial knowledge demonstrated). Each example of *parole* presents a particular performance, hinting at one's

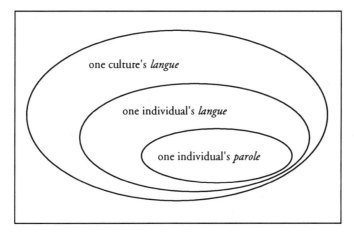

FIG. 3.3.   The relationship between *langue* and *parole*.

underlying competency with the relevant *langue*. Of the two sets of terms, per-formance/competence is the more active and *parole/langue* the more passive (Hymes, 1974, p. 130).[12]

A single example used to explain all three sets of terms may clarify their rela-tionship. In the example given previously, Annelle wore a particular outfit to Shel-by's wedding. Each part of her outfit (the lace gloves, the low-cut dress, the glasses, the purse) is a single element, each is drawn from a set of possibilities called a paradigm. (Thus, all the gloves she has access to, all the dresses, all the styles of glasses and purses, each set is termed a paradigm). What she actually chose to wear, taken together, is a syntagm, a particular combination of elements into a coherent whole. The *langue* available to her was extremely limited, so she bor-rowed elements from Shelby's larger *langue*. The particular outfit she wore is an example of *parole* when contrasted to the larger set of possible combinations, though it is called syntagm when the point is to refer to it as a new combination of dis-parate elements. In the process of combining elements into a whole, she displayed a particular performance, demonstrating her knowledge of appropriately dress-ing for a wedding. One assumes her competence in this area by what she demon-strated, though there is no way of actually measuring it. By the standard of the other guests at the wedding, the audience discovers that her performance does not display a great deal of competence (what she wears and how she wears it show her inexperience in these matters). For the purposes of the film, the audience is encouraged to make assumptions about her past experience and knowledge (her competence) based on her current choices (her performance), in order to discover her relative naiveté.

Together, paradigm and syntagm demonstrate how each sign creates and con-veys meaning through two possible relationships with other signs:

1.  separation of the similar, where members of a set are distinguished from one another even though they are basically similar (through paradigms); and
2.  unification of the different, where members of a set are joined together though basically dissimilar (through syntagms).

For example, all of the shoes owned by one person perform essentially the same function, protecting the feet, and thus are similar; however they are quite differ-ent in implication from one another (say, the difference between turquoise and pink surf walkers and black leather pumps). In this case, social actors create dis-tinctions between what are actually quite similar signs in function, conveying subtle differences in information. When the shoes combine with additional articles of clothing to make up a single outfit, the outfit as a whole creates meaning rather than each of the elements separately, though they function in diverse ways (the combination of a white silk blouse and gray wool suit with the black pumps con-veys a single message, one quite different from that implied by combining the same blouse and suit with the surf walkers). Meanings emerge through unification of different elements into a particular whole and through a mental matching of the resulting set with other potential sets remaining unchosen.

In both cases, something new is learned by understanding codes to be the locus of meaning. This is really not so different from the study of individual signs as it may at first appear: Those who study individual signs or symbols often find it necessary to incorporate descriptions of at least some related signs, thus speaking of the larger codes involved, taking for granted the appropriateness of doing so. However, it is useful to make this largely tacit assumption of the need to provide some context for the interpretations of signs clearly explicit, so it may be taken into account in all examples.

*3. Codes Convey Meaning Derived From the Agreement among and Shared Cultural Experience of Their Users.* The third characteristic points out that codes have no existence apart from the humans who use them. Although individual signs have physical existence, the full set of potential signs and the rules for their use do not exist outside of someone's head. "Indeed the connection between symbol and object exists *only* in the minds of those who belong to a social group. A community of minds is the condition of *any* signification, and not only of the signification requiring the knowledge of a conventional code" (Maquet, 1982, p. 9). Researchers locate codes in "a community of minds," as Maquet phrased it here, rather than in the physical world, due to the fact that codes are implicit. In no one physical place are all possible shoes worn by members of a particular group present (though the variety of shoes displayed in a shoe store comes close), thus, a code is not a physical reality. Yet such a set exists in the minds of the members of the community, so it is most certainly a social reality.[13] Social realities are just as legitimate as physical realities, though a little harder to study. A reasonable facsimile of the set of all possible shoes exists in the minds of the members of the community (*not* in the head of any *one* individual, but in the *combined* minds of the group). Together we know what is possible; alone we each know only a portion of the range. Because the set does not exist in the head of any individual, neither can meaning be assumed to reside in the head of any one individual, arising instead from that same "community of minds."

By implication codes are culture-bound and context-specific. The rules for their use are not self-evident, not readily available to everyone presented with a particular sign.[14] Not all people are party to the same codes: There must be a group available to support the particular agreements of any code, this group being what is generally called members of a culture. Only a legitimate member of the group using the code has the knowledge to appropriately interpret the meanings of any sign.

This is why the wearing of gang colors can be dangerous in today's inner cities for the uninitiated, who know neither the meanings associated with particular items of clothing nor the boundaries of the communities through which they pass, yet their innocence of intent is no protection from retaliation: They are treated as if they intended to convey what they are understood to have conveyed to the initiated.

Group membership permits predictability: One is able to reasonably interpret the behavior of others if, and only if, enough of the same assumptions and background knowledge are shared. "Meaning is a product of coding, and coding is a form of behavior that is learned and shared by the members of a communication group. . . . Coding is learned and shared, and any behavior that is learned and shared is cultural" (Smith, 1966, pp. 6–7). Thus, we are returned to the concept of culture and must reconsider the connections among the communication, culture, and semiotics. One relevant definition of communication emphasizes the "negotiation and exchange of meaning, in which messages, people-in-cultures and 'reality' interact so as to enable meaning to be produced or understanding to occur" (O'Sullivan et al., 1983, p. 42). This definition attends particularly to the following series of constituent elements: (a) the message or text, (b) the person who created the text, (c) the people interpreting the text, and (d) the external reality to which both text and people refer. Some authors emphasize the text (linguists such as Saussure); others emphasize the connection between the text and its creator (the majority of communication studies), the connection between the text and its readers (literary critics such as Jacques Derrida), or the connection between the text and external reality (philosophers such as Peirce). Wherever emphasis is placed, ultimately meaning arises from the *combination* of the text, its creator, its audience, and the external world.

**4. Codes Are Transmittable by Their Appropriate Media of Communication.** The fourth characteristic of codes assumes an interest in and focus on mass media such as television and film. The implication is simple: One learns to interpret codes in part through these media. Because assumptions about behavior are not always conscious, directors, photographers, and others incorporate them unconsciously into the media. From our media products, others come to accept similar assumptions, also unconsciously. For example, when television characters eat junk food rather than regular meals, it is a minor part of the story but, repeated often enough, it influences viewers' assumptions about the appropriateness of various eating habits (Webb, 1990). When children see violence often enough on television, it has an impact on their assumptions as to the appropriateness of violence in a variety of contexts.[15]

The concept of *intertextuality* introduced previously has been applied primarily to the study of film because it is easy to match two films checking for visual quotes in the later of the two.[16] With some effort, the same aspect of intertextuality, "quoting" from one event to another, could be usefully applied to the study of social interaction as well. The combination of the two, that is, intertextual references from the mass media brought into everyday interactions, although not generally studied to date, is likely to be productive as well.

*5. Codes Can Be a Way of Classifying, Organizing, and Understanding Material, as Well as of Transmitting or Communicating It.*    The fifth characteristic is extremely important, implying the question of how codes function: What do they do, and how do they do it? As with signs, codes serve most essentially to mediate understandings of reality.[17] Codes help structure perceptions and help make sense of the enormous amount of information presented in any social interaction. The new is matched against the old, placing each individual sign against the background and into the context of the larger code already known. Codes permit enormous condensation of information. Part of the problem in conveying meaning is the need to convey something complex relatively quickly and easily; codes are one of the means available to us for this purpose, as are signs. Signs are thus one part of how one makes sense of and interprets reality; codes are another. According to Fiske:

> The point is that "reality" is already encoded, or rather the only way we can perceive and make sense of reality is by the codes of our culture. There may be an objective, empiricist reality out there, but there is no universal objective way of perceiving and making sense of it. What passes for reality in any culture is the product of that culture's codes, so "reality" is always already encoded, it is never "raw." (Fiske, 1987, p. 4)

Fiske's use of the term *encoded* is not defined here but should be self-evident. If there is a code, then it is possible to encode (to convey information through that code) and also to *decode* (to interpret information from the code). Some of the early sources for an understanding of coding, particularly the focus on encoding and decoding and on establishing the degree of comparability between them, are found in the early cybernetics literature (Shannon & Weaver, 1949).[18] This has advantages, as it showed the way to some interesting ideas early on, but it has disadvantages as well. The use of a physical metaphor (such as a telegraph) underlying the early cybernetics can sometimes cause problems, just as the use of a linguistic metaphor can cause problems, if one is not careful enough about the distinction between the model utilized for analysis and the behavior to be analyzed.

To give a concrete example: People encode particular information into family history every time they choose to take photographs of some events but not others. In most families, major life-cycle events, such as birthdays, are frequently recorded, but everyday life, such as the organization of a typical evening meal, is generally omitted from the record. In addition, they sometimes deliberately pose for photographs in order to mislead others who will decode the photographs later: Family members who have been fighting may chose to stand near each other and smile, lest the fight be remembered rather than the relationship. Thus, they encode meaning for others (or their later selves) to decode at a future time.

In *Cousins*, Mitch is a rebellious teen-ager recording events at a wedding reception that everyone would rather not have preserved. He films someone vomiting after overindulging, the groom mooning the assembled crowd, teen-agers making-out in a closet, and an adulterous couple leaving in a car together. He shows the resulting videotape at the next major family gathering, but the audience is quite unhappy with the result, partially due to the inappropriate nature of his choices and partially due to the supplemental images incorporated from other events (footage of people starving interleaved with footage of people overeating at the reception, for example). The problem is that he has chosen to encode information that the majority of viewers would rather not have available for later decoding, omitting images they would have preferred to preserve.

At a later wedding, for Dean and Terri, the cousins caught kissing in a closet, Mitch again runs into trouble through his choice of material. As he points his videocamera at the bride and groom during the reception, particularly emphasizing the bride's obvious pregnancy, an older relative Sofia stops him, saying, "No X-rated pictures, you bad boy. Weddings are a joyful occasion." One explanation for her discomfort with recording the pregnancy is that she wishes to withhold information from the future. By preserving the image, Mitch makes it real, whereas if she can deny it long enough, keeping it from the camera's eye, it will not be visible to the future and effectively will not have happened.

A focus on encoding and decoding leads directly to a focus on the people doing the encoding and decoding and often to the degree of match between what the one has encoded with what the other decodes.[19] Obviously, encoders and decoders who share similar codes (and similar cultural experiences) will encode and decode similar meanings in text; those who have learned different codes as a result of different cultural experiences, will not.[20] Essentially, this defines the major topic studied by intercultural communication (although rarely stated quite this way): Intercultural communication seeks to understand problems arising due to an inappropriate fit between encoding and decoding, attributing these problems to differences in cultural knowledge.

The related term *subcode* refers to something less than an entire code, partially but not entirely mutually comprehensible to users of the larger code. Implicit is the related idea that members of a *subculture* (a small group within a larger culture) are the users of a subcode (Krampen, 1986).[21] Implicit also is the assumption that most members of a culture are simultaneous members of several subcultures; as such, they have access to multiple subcodes. The problem is always knowing which subcode is appropriate to which context; learning this takes time. Young children who discuss what are designated family topics in public places are the classic example of incomplete learning. A child who comes out of a public restroom yelling, "I went potty, mommy," embarrasses the parents due to the public context, despite the fact that these same parents may have been encouraging or even requiring similar statements at home as part of toilet training.

Even adults often display what they consider to be appropriate subcultural behavior, only to discover that others, as members of adjoining subcultures, consider their choice inappropriate. To return to *Cousins*, Tish wears an outfit she presumably considers appropriate to Dean and Terri's wedding: a tight black dress with ruffles of white fabric with black polka dots, a long red scarf, red high heels, a red bow in her hair, and black stockings and earrings. Sofia, always the voice of tradition, asks her, "Is that a dress you wear to a wedding?" Tish responds with a smile, "I made it. It's my own design" accepting the question as a compliment. As she walks away, Sofia evaluates the dress more explicitly, saying to Edie, her sister-in-law, "That's a dress you wear to a hooker's wedding." Clearly Tish has encoded the rules of her subculture, but those rules are not the same as Sofia expected, despite the considerable implied overlap in their backgrounds. As a result, what Sofia decodes from the dress is quite different from what Tish thought she was encoding into it.

Related to their basic function of filtering reality, codes serve to indicate group membership. Social practices are learned, serving as identifying *markers* for past experiences, whether related to social class, education, or other factors. As French sociologist Pierre Bourdieu described in detail, tastes can serve as markers of class:

> Tastes (i.e., manifested preferences) are the practical affirmation of an inevitable difference. It is no accident that, when they have to be justified, they are asserted purely negatively, by the refusal of other tastes. In matters of taste, more than anywhere else, all determination is negation; and tastes are perhaps first and foremost distastes, disgust provoked by horror or visceral intolerance ("sick-making") of the tastes of others. There is no accounting for tastes: not because *"tous les gouts sont dans la nature,"* but because each taste feels itself to be natural—and so it almost is, being a habitus—which amounts to rejecting others as unnatural and therefore vicious. Aesthetic intolerance can be terribly violent. Aversion to different life styles is perhaps one of the strongest barriers between the classes: class endogamy is evidence of it. The most intolerable thing for those who regard themselves as the possessors of legitimate culture is the sacrilegious reuniting of tastes which taste dictates shall be separated (Bourdieu, 1980, pp. 253–254)

Thus do we build social barriers where none existed through our differing manipulation of signs and codes. Bourdieu's work especially illuminated the labeling of tastes as due to individual preferences rather than prior experience (Bourdieu, 1984). The connections between social class and expressions of taste are no less important for the fact that they generally remain hidden from their users.

Others have expanded on the gap between encoding and decoding to demonstrate how particular groups change the meanings conveyed by particular signs, even by whole codes, and how some subcultures handle this ability with great facility. Using the following example of the adoption of safety pins by punk groups in Britain for purposes other than their makers intended, Hebdige (1979) made precisely this point:

> These "humble objects" [safety pins] can be magically appropriated; "stolen" by subordinate groups and made to carry "secret" meanings: meanings which ex-

press, in code, a form of resistance to the order which guarantees their continued subordination.

Style in subculture is, then, pregnant with significance. Its transformations go "against nature," interrupting the process of "normalization." As such, they are gestures, movements towards a speech which offends the "silent majority," which challenges the principle of unity and cohesion, which contradicts the myth of consensus. (Hebdige, 1979, p. 18)

As Hebdige made clear, the change of a single sign is not at issue so much as the challenge of entire social codes (in this case, clothing). Through a series of individually minor changes, members of the larger culture have their expected meanings subverted; in this way members of a subculture gain a limited degree of autonomy and even power.

All codes change over time. Few people wear the same clothes as their grandparents, for example. If they do, as with teen-agers who wear bib overalls similar to those worn several generations ago by farmers, the meanings have been subverted (they no longer support the connotations "work clothes" or "farmer") and the details revised (as when one of the straps is left unfastened, a common modification popularized by several musical groups in the 1990s). It actually requires far more effort to prevent social codes from changing over time, as demonstrated by the continued efforts of the Amish needed to keep their children in traditional dress (Enninger, 1984), but this is not to say that anyone ever expects the particular changes that occur.

As Krampen put it, codes are "states of dynamic equilibrium" (1986, p. 128). They maintain a precarious balance between times of stasis, appearing rock solid, and times of rapid change, when it is hard to remember they ever appeared constant. Subcultures are hardly the only locus of change but serve as a particularly useful point from which to observe change (P. Cohen, 1980; Halliday, 1976). This is particularly obvious to most people when the subcultures involved include different generations, because there are several generations in most families who can observe each other's behavior far more closely than that of members of different ethnic groups or different geographic regions.

Examination of a code as it exists at a single point in time is called *synchronic* analysis; examination of a code as it evolves through time is named *diachronic* analysis. Traditionally, it has been more common in semiotics and in linguistics, and certainly in communication, to focus on synchronic analysis; recently diachronic analysis has gained adherents. This is in part due to the inherent appeal of observing changes as they occur and the potential for discovering how and why they come about.[22] A synchronic analysis emphasizes what exists at a particular point in time; a diachronic analysis concentrates on changes over time. To use living room furnishings as an example, a synchronic analysis focuses on such details as the usual distances between couch and chairs and tables and the class connotations of various styles of furniture; a diachronic analysis focuses on the changes in styles of furniture over the last 100 years or the addition of such new features as photographs, plants, and mirrors matched to the simultaneous disappearance of pianos.

Though they are generally distinguished as quite different, it is incorrect to assume synchrony and diachrony are anything but integrally related. Jurij Tynjanov and Roman Jakobson pointed out how synchronic and diachronic analyses are intertwined:

> The opposition between synchrony and diachrony was an opposition between the concept of system and the concept of evolution; thus it loses its importance in principle as soon as we recognize that every system necessarily exists as an evolution, whereas, on the other hand, evolution is inescapably of a systemic nature. (Tynjanov & Jakobson, 1928/1971, p. 80)

The division between synchrony and diachrony is thus seen to have less reality than commonly assumed. It is absurd to think that any synchronic analysis can totally ignore the past and the future, or any diachronic analysis can be presented without substantial detailing of one place, at one time. It is most accurate to view analyses as primarily either synchronic or diachronic in focus but rarely one to the exclusion of the other.

As exemplar, a synchronic analysis of wedding gowns would theoretically emphasize the description of the major design elements in use today. But it is characteristic of wedding gowns that they utilize an enormous array of design details taken from the history of women's clothing over the past 300 years, combined in new and incongruous sets (sleeves from the 1600s matched to a collar of the 1800s, for example). A careful synchronic analysis would thus of necessity incorporate considerable diachronic analysis as well, regardless of the analyst's original focus.

Codes serve as a marker of group membership in part due to the existence of what are termed *restricted codes*. This is another way of referring to particular categories of subcodes that, in the original usage at least, was less than positive. Restricted codes were originally proposed as applying to language and were those with a smaller vocabulary, a simpler syntax, and greater redundancy, relying upon joint prior experience to fill in the frequent gaps between actual utterances and obvious intent. They were originally studied as part of a pair, with *elaborated codes*, the more highly valued, by British linguist Basil Bernstein (1966, 1975). Elaborated codes were defined as the more explicit, with a larger vocabulary and more complex syntax, making meanings available even to listeners who did not share prior experiences, listeners who could not be relied upon to properly interpret vague or incomplete utterances. Bernstein suggested that elaborated codes are acquired only through formal training (higher education), implying those with greater education (generally the middle class) had the ability to use two codes, either restricted or elaborated, as the need arose. Those with less education (generally the working class) had limited access to elaborated codes and so were limited in use to only a single code, the restricted. Bernstein pointed out that restricted codes were just as complicated to use, but implied greater flexibility was significant, so someone with the ability to manage two codes would be more successful than someone with the ability to only manage a mere one. As Bernstein's ideas were generalized through the 1960s and 1970s to imply either distinctions between oral and written forms (restricted codes often are oral, and elaborated codes are often written), or differences in intelligence (elaborated codes appear more complex, leading to their use as a measure of higher ability), they generated heated controversy. Today the terminology has changed. What were once called restricted codes are now called *subcultural styles*. As the more negative implications have generally been avoided, the controversy has abated considerably.[23]

*6. Codes Are, by Their Very Nature, Full of Gaps and Inconsistencies and Subject to Constant Change.*     Codes are human inventions, designed to create order where chaos might otherwise reign. As such they are imperfect, suggestive rather than complete. There is no plenitude (completeness, such that every corner is filled) in a code, though some might wish it. The "gaps, modifications, and inconsistencies" Firth attributed to symbols equally characterize codes (1973b, p. 426). A code is implicit and thus can never be created in its entirety before it is used. That being the case, it can never be finished, and the unfinished inevitably has gaps and holes. Again discussing primarily symbols, Turner suggested: "In no concrete society is 'system' realized. 'On earth the broken arcs, in heaven the perfect round.' But symbols operate among the 'broken arcs' and help to substitute for the 'perfect round' " (1975, p. 146). His comment about the nature of symbols describes equally the nature of codes: in both cases, what exists is incomplete. Any sense of completion is contributed by the individual making use of the symbol or code, not inherent in the sign or code. Codes are only given voice by analysts, and too precise a sense of order or completion must be attributed to the analyst, not assumed to be previously extant in the subject under analysis.

Related to the unfinished nature of codes is another issue: tradition versus innovation. It would be wrong to imply that codes are rigid or that they leave little room for individual creativity. Precisely because of their incomplete nature, they can never be rigid: The many gaps permit ready infiltration of the new and different. Only something quite finished could appropriately be described as rigid. This means one always understands behavior in light of what Jakobson termed two orders: "the traditional canon and the artistic novelty as a deviation from that canon" (1935/1971a, p. 87). One interprets social facts simultaneously by the traditions they preserve and by the innovations they introduce.

Often small innovations open the way to larger, more encompassing changes. In *Fiddler on the Roof*, Tevye breaks with tradition to permit his oldest daughter, Tzeitel, to marry the man she loves, Motel, rather than forcing her to go through with the marriage he previously arranged with Lazar. At their wedding, Perchik dances with the second daughter, Hodel, flaunting the Jewish orthodox tradition requiring women to dance with women and men to dance with men. On the one hand, they are dancing, which is traditional, but on the other, they are dancing across gender lines, which is shocking for that group in that time and place. The event is complicated by the clear implication that the first case of rule-breaking made the second possible.

The six characteristics of codes outlined previously are broadly stated, applying to all codes, in all places, at all times. Together they supply the basic definition of codes and suggest the basic rules governing the functioning of codes. With these six, the list may be taken as (temporarily) complete. But describing the nature of codes is not the only way to learn about them; at the very least one also needs to know which types of codes exist.

## TYPES OF CODES

As with many other fields of study, semiotics lends itself to typologies. The following typology of codes is widely accepted: (a) *logical codes* (the codes used by science), (b) *aesthetic codes* (the codes used by art), and (c) *social codes* (the codes used by society). Examples of logical codes are: mathematics, morse code, the alphabet, braille, the highway code, assembly diagrams. Examples of aesthetic codes are: painting, architecture, photography, sculpture, literature. Examples of social codes are: trademarks, clothing, greetings, food, furniture, objects of any sort, games, and sports.

It is possible to summarize the essential elements of the differences and similarities between the various types of codes in the following chart (see Table 3.1).[24] Taken together, these concepts clearly demonstrate why social codes have the greatest potential interest for researchers in communication. As the majority have been previously introduced, they are only briefly summarized in the following discussion.

TABLE 3.1
Comparison of Codes by Type

| Logical Codes | Aesthetic Codes | Social Codes |
|---|---|---|
| Monosemic | Polysemic | Polysemic |
| Denotative | Connotative | Connotative |
| Digital | Analogic | Analogic |
| Conventional meanings | Conventional or new | Conventional or new |
| Single decoding possible | Aberrant decoding possible | Aberrant decoding possible |
| Decode by explicit agreement | Decode by clues within text | Decode by convention |
| Symbolic | Iconic | Symbolic |
| Social | Individual | Social |
| Stasis as the norm | Change as the norm | Dynamic relation between stasis and change |

Logical codes are *monosemic* (the signifier stands for only one signified), whereas both aesthetic and social codes are *polysemic* (the signifier can stand for more than one signified). Science uses logical codes because the number 4 always stands for the same number of items, whereas my birthday gift to you of a scarf, as part of a social code, implies not only that I remembered your day but equally that I know (or do not know) your preferences in color and fabric.

Logical codes are *denotative* (there is a literal meaning clear to any audience) whereas both aesthetic and social codes are *connotative* (there is a variety of implications available to knowledgeable audience members). Not only does the number 4 always mean four items rather than two or three, but there is never an implication of sadness, happiness, and so forth.

Logical codes are generally *digital* (they can be divided into discrete units) whereas aesthetic and social codes are more often *analogic* (no discrete units). The numbers 3 and 4 do not blend together (even when placed side by side they do not mean "something between 3 and 4," but "34"), whereas it can be difficult to divide a painting or a loaf of bread into component parts.

Logical codes are *conventional* (traditional meanings assumed to be understood by the audience are used), whereas both aesthetic and social codes are either conventional or *new* (the author/artist/social actor draws new connections between signifier and signified never drawn before). The number 4 has meant the same thing for a very long time; therein lies its value. Silk adopts new implications as clothing is made of a washable form of the fabric, thus decreasing its prestige value (yet, in apparent contradiction, only the traditional prestige value of silk accounts for the brisk sales of this new variety, still priced well above other washable fabrics).

Due to all of the previous characteristics, logical codes have a *single possible decoding* (what I intend should always be what you understand), whereas aesthetic and social codes have the possibility of *aberrant coding* (you have a good chance of learning something I never intended, or missing what I considered obvious). With logical codes, there are explicit, deliberate agreements about what the individual signs indicate; with aesthetic codes, the clues for decoding are made available in the text to an insightful interpreter but are rarely explicitly agreed upon; and with social codes, there is conventional use, unwritten expectations based on shared experience, for decoding (Fiske, 1982, pp. 82–87). This explains why only logical codes have a single possible decoding: having explicitly agreed as to the meaning of individual signs, there is little likelihood of confusion. With aesthetic and social codes, the lack of explicit agreement as to the interpretation of signs permits aberrant decoding.

Thus far, aesthetic and social codes appear similar, but there are a few important differences. Aesthetic codes are generally *iconic* (made up of icons, signs with a relation of similarity between the signifier and signified), whereas social and logical codes are generally *symbolic* (made up of symbols, with an arbitrary relation between signifier and signified). And aesthetic codes are more clearly *individual* (the individual artist can create entirely new meanings), whereas logical and social codes are more often *social* (conveying consistent meanings known to the larger society).

Along one dimension, each is unique. Logical codes have *stasis* as their norm (they can change little over time and then only with explicit agreement, or they would lose their value). Even once agreed upon, changes are often slow to take effect. The metric system has been making its way into the American public school system over the past decade at a snail's pace, despite official encouragement; the problem lies in the hesitancy of the present generation to give up the measurements to which they have grown accustomed. The problem is compounded by the fact that as each generation refuses to adopt the metric system, they permit a new generation to grow up unaccustomed to its use, thus delaying change even further. For aesthetic codes *change* is the norm and innovation highly valued (creating a painting exactly the same as that of someone else is called forgery, not art, and the most innovative artists are those most likely to be remembered by the future). Social codes generally have a *dynamic relation between change and stasis* (even if I wear a unique combination of clothes each day, the individual items belong to categories you most likely recognize).

The codes of greatest interest to communication researchers are social codes; for that reason they serve as the focus of the remainder of this chapter and volume. There are so many possible social codes, that it is impossible even to provide a complete list. As Leach pointed out, "*all* the various non-verbal dimensions of culture, such as styles in clothing, village lay-out, architecture, furniture, food, cooking, music, physical gestures, postural attitudes and so on are organised in patterned sets" (Leach, 1976, p. 10). Although not generally put this way within communication, Leach's comment makes sense according to the chart of types given previously: all nonverbal channels of behavior are appropriately labeled social codes, though there are more social codes than just nonverbal channels. Together all social codes make up a large part of a culture (each culture also including logical and aesthetic codes).

The previous comments lead to new questions concerning the connection between culture and code. Just as a single sign does not convey meaning alone but as part of a larger set or system of signs (a code), so a single social code also does not stand alone but functions as one part of a set or system of codes. This larger network or system might best be called a *culture*. Many anthropologists currently define culture as a "system of symbols" (M. L. Foster, 1990b; Ortner, 1975), making no use of codes as the middle level of organization standing between symbols and culture. A system of symbols is properly a code, and a system of codes forms a culture. Describing a culture as a system of symbols omits a critical structural level. This nesting of levels has been stated most clearly in the "Semiotics of culture" approach, originally developed by the Moscow–Tartu School, summarized by Umiker-Sebok as follows: "culture is a universe created by a plurality of mutually interacting and mutually supportive sign systems" (1977, p. 122).

In at least some of its assumptions, the semiotics of culture matches the approach put forth in this volume.[25]

Just as it is easier to study a single sign rather than an entire social code, so too is it easier to study a single social code rather than an entire culture. Here, however, greater justification exists for limiting the boundaries of what is taken into consideration. Individual social codes are already relatively large systems, providing a broad context for understanding the use of a single sign, easily justifiable as sufficient for many purposes. For this reason, chapters 4 through 6 of this volume provide analyses stopping at the level of the code. For a more complete analysis, codes do ultimately need to be set one next to the another, considered as mutually influencing bodies. The same people convey and interpret meanings from several codes simultaneously; it is virtually impossible to have a single code alone (there is little food that does not appear at a table and on a plate, and the plate provides an equally appropriate subject for study, as does the sweater worn by the person eating the food). A thorough study would account for multiple codes simultaneously rather than treating them individually.[26] The largest such grouping coincides with the boundaries of a culture, here redefined as "all of the codes available to a particular community or group of people."[27]

Of course, in today's global village, even this degree of context is not always sufficient. In most cases, political borders are social realities rather than physical barriers with infiltration of foreign meanings arriving in company with foreign objects, words, and persons. In addition, the social boundaries of a culture are no longer concurrent with the political boundaries of a country (if indeed they ever were). Still, for practical purposes, when boundaries need be drawn somewhere, the edges of a single culture provide the standard stopping place.

## NOTES

1. See J. Thomas (1989) for the historical origins of the term code and specifically for discussion of the differences between the terms code and *system*; see also Krampen (1986) and Culler (1977).
2. For further discussion of this issue, see Culler (1981, p. 30); M. Douglas (1970, p. 11); Hodge and Kress (1988, pp. 37–78, 97); Sperber (1974, p. 70); Varenne (1973, p. 229).
3. As the term *code* was originated by a linguist, it is not surprising that one of the disciplines still using the term today is linguistics. For typical use by linguists, see Gumperz and Hymes (1972), especially the chapters by Gumperz, Hymes, Blom and Gumperz and Bernstein. Code has been widely used within the ethnography of communication literature, where it generally means "a way of speaking," something smaller than a language (Bauman & Sherzer, 1974). A related use comes from information theory; see Deutsch (1966) for discussion. Schwimmer attributed much of this application to the influence of Gregory Bateson (1972), for whom "the 'codification system' *is* the culture" (1977, p. 163).

    The term code frequently appears in communication research but is defined and applied inconsistently. Most generally, code has been used as a synonym for language. Although coding has been named "One of the fundamental concerns in the study of communication" in basic introductions to theory (as here in Littlejohn, 1978, p. 80), it is generally taken for granted rather than studied explicitly.

Attention to date has come primarily from three areas: nonverbal communication, intercultural communication, and mass communication. In all three cases, the influence comes by way of considering how best to study social interaction in a variety of contexts. There is also a very recent application of codes to organizational culture growing out of the interpretive approach, where the definition of codes proposed here is followed exactly (Donnellon, 1986; Pilotta, Widman, & Jasko, 1988).

In nonverbal communication, *interaction codes* has been pressed into service as the cover term for all linguistic and nonlinguistic channels of communication (Birdwhistell, 1972, p. 390; Sigman, 1987, p. 110; see Harrison, 1976, for an outline of types of nonverbal codes). In this usage, the term code is a direct borrowing from linguistics with language the model code guiding the study of nonverbal channels (Leeds-Hurwitz, 1987). A particular focus has been on the activities of encoding and decoding and the relationship between messages sent and received (Katz & Katz, 1983b, pp. 205–207). A less frequent focus, but very up-to-date in its concerns, views codes as markers of social identity, as when Ramsey (1976) described the nonverbal codes identifying various subcultural groupings within a prison culture.

Within intercultural communication, the early influence of linguistics on the field has assured only that the term code would be used not that it would go on to become a central research focus (Leeds-Hurwitz, 1990b). Both the early role played by those trained outside the field and the more recent influence of the ethnography of speaking (Carbaugh, 1985, 1988, 1990; Katriel, 1986, 1991; Leeds-Hurwitz, 1990a) have resulted in some attention to codes as the vehicle for cultural knowledge and therefore as an appropriate research site. As Cooley put it: "My first assumption is that the study of codes should be one of the central concerns to the study of communication. . . .My second assumption is that a body of descriptive research centering on codes is sorely needed in the study of communication today" (1983, pp. 241–242). The terminology is the same, as indicated by Cooley's definition of code as "a culturally defined, rule-governed system of shared arbitrary symbols that is used to transmit meaning" (1983, p. 242). His usage of the word *transmit* here implies more deliberate intent than generally assumed appropriate today. Although the influence of linguistics has been sufficient to put codes on the research agenda of intercultural communication, it has not yet been sufficient to move them to the top of the agenda, despite Cooley's emphatic comments. Because codes are culturally based, intercultural communication research must eventually pay attention to codes and how they function.

Within mass communication, there has been some analysis of televised interactions using "interpersonal behavior codes" such as proxemics, kinesics, and paralanguage (Gronbeck, 1983; Meyerowitz, 1979). Clearly this simply adapts research on nonverbal communication codes to mass media; as such linguistics maintains a heavy influence. As with the influence on intercultural communication, this shows the way in which generalizations about interaction follow social actors from setting to setting; whether in face-to-face encounters with members of the same culture, members of a different culture, or on television, the same vehicles serve to convey meanings and often those vehicles are social codes.

Wieder's (1974/1988) work on the convict code was originally cast as a sociological study, particularly as an example of ethnomethodology, but it provides an excellent analysis of a particular behavioral code set into context.

4. As mentioned in chapter 1, McCracken (1988) provided the major theoretical grounds for rejecting the model of linguistics as code. What follows can be considered my continuation and expansion of that argument, for I do agree with part of it. Yet, I think there is probably more value to the metaphor than he grants, especially if descriptive linguistics is not considered the relevant part of linguistics to be used as a model.

5. See Botscharow (1990, p. 65) for an interesting discussion of this issue.

6. For further discussion, see O'Sullivan et al. (1983, p. 37); Corcoran (1981, p. 187).

7. O'Sullivan et al. (1983) restricted the application of these characteristics to what they termed *signifying* codes (comparable to the social codes described later). These same characteristics are applicable to all types of codes and so I have enlarged their discussion accordingly. The sixth characteristic is my own addition.

8. This is but one example of a larger category of ambiguous members of classification systems; the study of ambiguity is an important topic in its own right. M. Douglas (1966) provided extensive discussion of marginal members of classification systems.

9. "Paradigms are virtual rather than realized. . . .A member of a paradigmatic class may become realized by virtue of selection to occupy a before or after slot in an actualized syntagmatic sequence. Only one member of a class may be thus realized" (M. L. Foster, 1980, p. 373).

10. Threadgold (1986, p. 111) argued against the terms synchronic and diachronic, because they, of necessity, overlap.

11. See Culler (1977) for further discussion.

12. Sociolinguistics developed in response to the realization that linguists were studying performance, whereas they had thought they were able to study competence. In fact, it is inordinately difficult to ever study competence, because all researchers ever have access to is a particular performance or, at best, a set of performances.

13. Wieder (1974/1988, p. 36) provided a good summary of the related sociological concept of "social facts." It is the set of social facts that taken together, make up the social reality described here.

14. See Lyne (1981a, p. 203) for discussion.

15. This is why there has been so much research on children and television within communication. See Bryant and Anderson (1983); Salomon (1979); and Gerbner, Gross, Eleey, Jackson-Beeck, Jefferies-Fox, and Signorelli (1977) for an introduction to this literature.

16. See Metz (1974) and De Lauretis (1984).

17.     . . . Groups have symbolic codes, or systems of signs, which give order to the beliefs held by their members, which shape the development of new knowledge in the group at the same time that they tend to insure that old observations will be repeated. . . . these codes, like the conscious codes of individuals, represent a condensation of a complex set of motives, experiences, knowledge, and desire, which they help to shape and express at the same time that they keep so much of it unsaid and below the surface. (Dolgin, Kemnitzer, & Schneider, 1977a, p. 6)

18. Shukman (1978) documented the influence of the early American cybernetics literature on late Soviet semiotics.

19. S. Hall (1980) elaborated on the concepts of encoding/decoding, explaining particularly the inappropriateness of the traditional telegraph model. He also provided a sophisticated discussion of connections to several related pairs of theoretical terms: connotation/denotation, competence/performance, and dominant/subordinate.

20. See O'Sullivan et al. (1983, p. 212) for elaboration. Further discussion of this idea, labeled *aberrant decoding* by Eco (1980), becomes relevant later in the chapter.

21. Subcode has largely replaced the earlier *anti-language*, proposed by Halliday as the language used by an *anti-culture*, now more commonly termed a *subordinate subculture* (Halliday, 1976).

22. Cultural Studies, above all other areas, has given extensive consideration to diachronic analysis and brought it new attention. This research has been influenced in no small part by Raymond Williams (his 1980 collection of essays serves as an easy introduction to his work).

23. For a current adaptation of Bernstein to communication concerns, see Ellis and Hamilton (1985).

24. I have incorporated discussion from Guiraud (1975) and Fiske (1982).

25. See Umiker-Sebeok (1977) for details of the connection between semiotics of culture, symbolic anthropology, interpretive anthropology, comparative symbology, and most recently semiotic anthropology.

26. A complementary new definition of communication, taking the nature and number of codes into account, was assumed by Donnellon when she said, "The human system for interaction is essentially a set of communication codes consisting of elements and rules for the behavioral exchange of information. Among the codes commonly used for communication are language, gestures, physical objects such as street signs or architecture, dance, music, and so on" (1986, p. 138).

27. In 1977, Culler nominated as Saussure's greatest contribution shifting the focus of attention from individual object (here understood as sign) to the structure within which that object is embedded (in this case, code). He pointed out that Saussure has another potential contribution: "To bring us to see social life and culture in general as a series of sign systems which a linguistic model can help us to analyze" (Culler, 1977, p. 129). He argued it was then too soon to determine if this broader goal had been met. Still a valid goal more than a decade later, it is still unclear whether it has been met.

# From Semiotic Theory to Communication Behavior

Part II of this volume supplies examples of particular social codes, intended to ground the theory presented in Part I. It has three chapters, each presenting initial analysis of a separate social code: food, clothing, and objects. Each example of a social code has been chosen for the same reasons and serves the same purposes. First, *all three are basic to human behavior everywhere* (everyone eats, wears some form of clothing or ornamentation, and creates some objects). In all three cases, people could presumably stop with the essential functional role. We could all wear identical clothing designed simply to keep us warm, which would certainly be more efficient than making and buying the current variety of garments. However, and this is a second reason to study these codes, *people do not limit the use of these and other social codes to their primary physical functions but add social functions as overlays*. Clothing has the physical function of protecting our physical bodies, but we use clothing also to mark identity, including such matters as status, gender, and age; we wear clothing that is aesthetically pleasing to ourselves and to others; we indicate mood and expected activities through clothing. (Though incomplete, this list of social functions, all of which clearly move beyond the purely physical function, should make the point.) The fact that people do not limit the function of clothing to protection is theoretically interesting; it is something to study, providing a beginning point in understanding human behavior.

A third reason to study food, clothing, and objects is that *food, clothing, and objects are clearly utilized as forms of communication, thus they are appropriate topics for communication researchers to study*. The majority of the theoretical work in communication explicitly considering semiotics, signs, or codes, analyzes language almost exclusively. However, it is equally possible to apply these concepts to the study of social interaction, incorporating the study of nonverbal behavior with the analysis of language. A parallel to the early study of kinesics, proxemics, and paralanguage can be pointed out.

Today these are understood to be major aspects of a particular part of the field of communication and granted their own label, nonverbal communication, although their potential value remained unrecognized for many years.[1] Food, clothing, and objects are largely new, potentially critical, aspects of the field of communication.

Fourth and finally, *food, clothing, and objects provide tangible vehicles for the study of how reality is socially constructed*. Social facts are made visible in all aspects of material culture. Through manipulation of choices in social codes such as food, clothing, and objects, we jointly create the social world we inhabit. Millen (1992) pointed out that it is easier, and thus more common, to discuss the social construction of reality theoretically than to demonstrate it concretely. Chapters 4, 5, and 6 provide one response to the (valid) critique that communication researchers have traditionally done a better job of asserting social constructionism than demonstrating it.

At the same time, there is a major distinction between the three social codes described here (food, clothing, and objects) and those traditionally understood to be the core of nonverbal communication (kinesics, proxemics, and paralanguage). The three I have chosen are all digital and therefore (deceptively) simple, whereas the early nonverbal communication channels studied are analogic and therefore quite difficult to study. Adding to that difficulty was the early use of linguistics as a model: Attempting to force analogic nonverbal behavior to imitate digital speech posed a major problem for researchers.

For all three social codes presented here, the same basic questions are of central concern:

1. Why should food/clothing/objects be studied as a form of communication?
2. What theory should be used to study food/clothing/objects? and
3. What exactly should be studied?

My answer to Question 1 has essentially been provided by the discussion to this point. They are all basic to human behavior everywhere; they are all given social functions in addition to their primary physical functions; all are arguably forms of communication, yet all have been largely bypassed by current communication studies.

My answer to Question 2 is obviously that semiotics provides the appropriate starting point, else this would have been a different volume. Semiotics is certainly not the only approach to use in studying these or any other social codes, but it is a valid and appropriate one and the one of concern here. Within semiotic theory, I have found particular strands more useful than others and stress these in the following chapters.

My answer to Question 3 is different for each chapter, though there is some overlap. Issues of identity and social change are stressed for food, as exemplars of synchronic and diachronic analysis respectively. Clothing serves well as a locus for study of the meeting point of individual identity and social identity (one way of combining the issues of identity and change) as well as for the connections between public and private displays. Objects particularly exemplify the connections between tradition and creativity and the relationship between parts and wholes. In each case, the topics presented are initial starting points only; each topic could be applied to each of the social codes, and many other topics could be studied for any of them. But these are important themes, thus a reasonable beginning.

As with semiotics itself, food, clothing, and objects are all studied elsewhere in the academic division of the reality pie (especially in folklore, anthropology, sociology, history, and psychology).[2] It is my suggestion that they tell the most about patterns of human communication.[3] As with semiotics, this requires careful thought about which aspects of these areas should be appropriately studied by communication researchers as opposed to other scholars. Rather than attempting to expand the territory merely for the sake of expansion, communication researchers must look for the most productive ways of studying particular aspects of these three subjects.

There is substantial precedent within semiotics, if not within communication, for studying aspects of material culture, specifically within the overlapping traditions labeled Russian Formalism, Czech Structuralism, the Prague School, the Moscow–Tartu School, and most recently Semiotics of Culture.[4] Essentially these authors, beginning from an interest in linguistics, moved to an interest in literature, then to art and theater, and finally to the semiotic aspects of social and cultural behavior.[5] These moves are not apparent in the research of any one scholar nor always carried out completely; this is my summary of the logical progression of the work. One of the most influential authors was Petr Bogatyrev (1937/1971, 1936/1976a, 1936/1976b), primarily through the early influence of his study of clothing on French semiotic theory.[6] Another particularly significant author was Yuri Lotman, whose major interests expanded beyond language to everyday behavior as a semiotic system (1970, 1985, 1990).[7]

Because food, clothing, and objects share so much, they are sometimes grouped together under the same term. Depending on the author, the term of choice is either *folklife* or *material culture*, although material culture is sometimes used in a more restrictive sense to refer only to objects.[8] Whichever term is chosen, the basic assumption that "We are material people . . . constrained . . . to prowl the world of matter" (Ingersoll & Bronitsky, 1987, p. xi) provides the logic underlying continued attention to these topics. Despite their intrinsic interest, very few people are interested in material culture for its own sake (even art historians and archaeologists are moving away from this position); rather, they study it in order to discern how social realities are shaped and given form, how experience is given order.[9]

The physical things people make, whether these are meals, items of clothing, houses, or letter openers, are material manifestations of the social realities understood to be relevant and powerful; therefore they are appropriate topics for analysts who wish to study how reality is socially constructed. The material world is one part of social reality, and as researchers we miss a fine opportunity if we neglect it as a resource. As the social-cultural world is made up of a combination of the immaterial (ideas and words) and the material (things), it is an advantage to study both.[10] Studying material aspects of culture is both easier (because they are so clearly visible) and harder (because they distract, taking away from a consideration of the social into the physical characteristics of whichever material object is the focus) than studying oral aspects of culture.[11]

Material culture codes serve as a particularly oblique means of conveying information, allowing culture "to insinuate its beliefs and assumptions into the very fabric of daily life, there to be appreciated but not observed" (McCracken, 1988, p. 69). Their mundane nature permits food, clothing, and objects to convey messages effectively, yet quietly, without calling undue attention to what has been conveyed. Thus, for example, they function particularly well as status markers when status differences are important to a culture simultaneously espousing a rhetoric of equality, such as modern-day America, where an explicit, linguistic assignment of status would not be tolerated.[12]

Food, clothing, and objects have the added advantage of being codes with low mutual intelligibility: that is, the members of small groups within the larger culture use elaboration in different ways, knowing only how to decode the conventions of their own group. This is particularly the case for age-grading: my son knows how to decode slight distinctions in hair style and clothing combinations that I barely recognize as meaningfully different and cannot interpret. Obviously he has learned to make such distinctions within his peer group and not from his parents. Such minute gradations in meaning, such subtlety, is to the advantage of the children who manipulate the details, for it permits them a realm of their own, away from adults, where they can practice their interpretive skills.

As Bogatyrev pointed out, there is a basic difference between examples of language or verbal art, where words function solely as signs, and examples of material culture, where individual items have a dual existence: They are first concrete objects and second, signs (1936/1976b, p. 31). The result is that the study of material culture requires particular care, lest its physical nature obscure or distract from its social implications. Because the physical characteristics of clothing, food, and objects are self-evident, it is possible to overlook the more important social meanings each conveys. In a way, studying language is far simpler, because there is no distracting physical object but only the sign aspect available for study.

Serving the purposes of this volume, each of the three chapters in Part II provides an exemplar of a single social code. Obviously there are more than three in use, but it is impossible to adequately describe all the potential social codes. At least providing these examples should demonstrate how to apply the theory presented in the first part of the volume. In addition, each chapter specifically illustrates several of the concepts introduced in Part I.

This part of the volume should be easy reading, for it reframes semiotic theory through the use of details of everyday life, minor in and of themselves, but significant in what they reveal to us about ourselves and others. According to Barthes:

> To decipher the world's signs always means to struggle with a certain innocence of objects. We all understand our language so "naturally" that it never occurs to us that it is an extremely complicated system, one anything but "natural" in its signs and rules: in the same way, it requires an incessant shock of observation in order to deal not with the content of messages but with their making: in short, the semiologist, like the linguist, must enter the "kitchen of meaning." (Barthes, 1988, p. 158)

With Barthes, I argue that semiotics can aid the search for meaning in human behavior. Life consists of a multitude of concrete behaviors, each seemingly meaningless or at least insignificant but when combined, they provide meaning in lives. Ultimately, "detail is the essence of the matter" (Leach, 1976, p. 95), and the details will provide illumination. Only by deciding to enter what Barthes termed *the kitchen of meaning*, that place where meaning is prepared or "cooked" and where the recipes themselves are kept, can one interpret behavior.

In keeping with the goal of using semiotics to study everyday behavior, the following chapters make use of a wide range of examples taken from popular literature and newspapers as well as more traditional academic studies. This is a deliberate attempt to insure that the potentially threatening nature of semiotic theory be brought down to size through the use of topical and popular examples. By including them, I hope to widen the scope of what can be done with semiotic theory. Semiotic theory applies equally well to small, informal, yet still patterned activities within culture as to large, formalized events such as rituals. Because traditionally large ritual events have been the major focus of attention, my emphasis here is on the everyday.[13]

In the following chapters, participants are assumed to take an active role in conducting their lives: "making choices and decisions, following strategies, negotiating, and improvising" (Sharman, Theophano, Curtis, & Messer, 1991, p. 6). Before the analyst arrives, the participants establish their own meanings, created for themselves and their friends, not for latecomer analysts. Each person composes his or her own life (M. C. Bateson, 1990). If people create nothing else requiring artistic talent, at least everyone participates in this one creative endeavor. The element of creativity lies primarily in the ways we each choose to recombine old cultural elements into new wholes. It should come as no surprise, then, that semiotics, a theory used to study other creative endeavors such as literature, will prove valuable in studying the creation of social meaning in everyday life.

## NOTES

1. Goodall made a similar argument when he described those aspects of nonverbal behavior figuring in organizational culture but not yet included in the studies of organizational communication. He specifically mentioned clothing, accessories, and manipulations of objects on offices or homes (1990, p. 73).
2. On the whole, references to these areas are given in the chapters that follow. Speaking of the more general interest in material culture described by Rutz and Orlove (1989), economic anthropology currently has considerable interest in consumption leading to detailed studies of food, clothing, and shelter (it is surprising that objects more generally do not find their way into this list). See also Appadurai (1986b); Douglas and Isherwood (1979); Baudrillard (1981). A good general history of the study of material aspects of culture within anthropology is found in Fenton (1974).
3. Various authors have commented on the way in which these material forms serve to communicate; see, Glassie, who used Levi-Strauss to suggest that "a case . . . can be made for the study of culture as the study of communication . . . for culture is patterned ideas that can be comprehended only after behavior" (1973, p. 337). Bronner pointed out that folklorists today actively look at material culture as a form of communication (1985c, p. 145).
4. For an introduction to these areas, see Erlich (1969); Lucid (1977); Matejka and Pomorska (1971); Matejka, Shiskoff, Suino, & Titunik (1977); Matejka and Titunik (1976); Steiner (1978); Striedter (1989); Winner and Winner (1976); Winner and Umiker-Sebeok (1979); Winner (1986); see also the entry under "Culture" in Sebeok (1986b). Although Russian Formalism and Czech Structuralism are generally credited as significant forms of literary critique and occasionally as critique of art, they are not as often acknowledged as presenting valuable insights into the study of culture. In keeping with this, most of the books cited previously treat these groups of scholars as literary critics.

   Semiotics of Culture is a bit different from the other areas, being a modern reincarnation and less clearly limited to literature: It "attends to aspects of all sign systems in culture as they interrelate" (Winner, 1986, p. 183). Francoeur (1985) attempted to combine the semiotics of culture with more traditional formal semiotics, though he was not entirely successful. Shukman (1978) provided a summary of the later Russian semiotic research, although this tends to emphasize literature over other cultural forms.
5. Even though much of the discussion of culture writ large is incomplete, it is no less valuable and should be read. Some useful discussion of the stages described here is provided in Gasparov (1985).
6. Bogatyrev's early work was influential because his interests ranged far beyond Moravian Slovakia as a location and far beyond costume as a subject for analysis. Though his topics were always quite specific, his interests were always general, as is clear from the more abstract comments included in his studies (1936/1976a, 1936/1976b).
7. See also Lotman (1970, 1990); Jan Mukarovsky (1977, 1978); Vladimir Propp (1928/1968); Boris Uspensky (1973); Uspensky et al. (1973); Roman Jakobson (1971c).
8. As aspects of folklife studied by folklorists, all three owe much of their current popularity to Don Yoder's early sponsorship. Yoder (1989) provided a good selection of his work.

   For a summary of the range of what can be included under the rubric material culture, see Bronner (1985a):

   > A craft, a house, a food, that comes from one's hands or heart, one's shared experience with other people in a community, one's learned ideas and symbols, visibly connects persons and groups to society and to the material reality around them. That interconnection is material culture. Material culture is made up of tangible things crafted, shaped, altered, and used across time and across space. It is inherently personal and social, mental and physical. It is art, architecture, food, clothing, and furnishing. But more so, it is the weave of these objects in the everyday lives of individuals and communities. (p. 3)

Hirsch separated out a subset of what might otherwise potentially be included in the category of material culture that he termed *cultural products* or *nonmaterial goods* (1991, p. 315). His distinction between those human creations having an aesthetic or expressive function (such as books, movies, or plays) that he termed cultural products and those with only a utilitarian function (such as food, clothing, and detergents) that he did not label but only excluded from the realm of what he considered is intriguing. However, his system really only makes sense if the multiple functions of what he termed *utilitarian creations* are ignored (that is, if food is assumed to have no aesthetic function, no social function, etc.), a position I find untenable. Thus, food, clothing, and objects (as well as other potential candidates) are equally cultural products.

9. Glassie, here described only buildings, but his sentiment holds true for other material forms as well:

> All things embody their creators and become for the period of their existence active images of their creators' wishes. In this, buildings are like other cultural things and there are no differences among kinds of building. Vernacular, nonvernacular, neovernacular—all are cultural ways to create, orderings of experience, like poems, like rituals. (Glassie, 1987, p. 231)

10. "Culture is not a purely ideational structure tucked away in the privacy of the individual brain, but it is an ongoing, creative endeavor, the reality of which is located in its cutting edge, the artifact" (Richardson, 1987, p. 399). Material culture has been variously called "the vehicle through which social structures and cultural categories achieve existence" (Richardson, 1974, p. 6), and "the product and residue of the thoughts and behavior of its [a society's] members" (Dwyer, 1975, p. 5).

11. Glassie emphasized the value of studying material culture: "The artifact is as direct an expression, as true to the mind, as dear to the soul, as language, and, what is more, it bodies forth feelings, thoughts, and experiences elusive to language" (1991, p. 255).

12. McCracken made a similar point but went on to argue that material culture is exceedingly limited in what it can express, particularly being unable to express "irony, metaphor, skepticism, ambivalence, surprise, reverence, or heartfelt hope" (1988, p. 69). I disagree, suggesting that the problem lies in considering individual signs alone; when the entire code is considered, such complex messages can indeed be conveyed effectively. Witness the ability of a formal business suit slit up the thigh to convey ambivalence (Du Plessix Gray, 1981).

13. This is in keeping with the stated goals of the semiotics of culture that also recognizes these two levels of textual analysis (Winner, 1986, p. 184).

# Chapter 4

# Food as Sign and Code

Food is the most basic of all social codes; basic not in the same sense as language, whose study serves as metaphor for the study of other codes, but basic in the sense of sheer survival utility. Humans use language for their psychological well-being, but they require food for their continued physical existence. Those who live in an industrial society tend to forget that obtaining food traditionally was and for many groups, still is the main goal of a day's work. That many in the modern world are able to take food for granted does not lessen its essential nature. Because of this ultimate significance, the study of food is "as material and pragmatic a field as one can get" (Firth, 1973a, p. 260).[1]

Food functions well as a cross-cultural topic of study due to the characteristic of being a common human requirement. Whereas universals are generally hard to come by in the social world, the sharing of food takes on a universal meaning of friendship and community, for all humans can be assumed to need food.[2] Yet there is a distinction to be drawn between need and preference. Despite the common need for food, a wide range of food preferences exists around the world; what one group values, another considers nonfood. Examples of foods eaten by some that are anathema to others range from insects to rotted wood garnished with honey (Gillen, 1944). As Mary Douglas, an anthropologist known particularly for her investigations of food, pointed out, "If biology were the basis for the selection of human foods, diets around the world would be quite similar. In fact, no human activity more puzzlingly crosses the divide between nature and culture than the selection of food. It is part of the nurture of the body, but it is also very much a social matter" (1979, p. 15).

As with any other category of behavior, nonessential variation encourages the assignment of meaning to variety (Gumperz & Hymes, 1972). To explain: If rice and potatoes are relatively equal in functional terms (both denote a nourishing carbohydrate used as the central food item in a number of cultures), there is room for implication and connotation (they are not used interchangeably in most diets). Brown rice and white rice are even closer functionally but far apart in terms of signification, as reported by Masumoto, who tried to introduce brown rice to his Japanese-American family. They rejected it, teaching him that "such a change disrupted the pattern within the entire meal" (1983, p. 140). As Masumoto explained, it was not the color of the rice so much as the lack of associations customarily attached to white rice that his family found problematic:

> Part of the message contained in white rice was the traditional way it was served by Japanese-American families. At our meals rice was a type of centerpiece. It was not only served with each meal (my dad ate it for breakfast with his eggs); it also sat in the center of the table, my mom serving us our portions in *cha-wan*, a specific bowl we used only for rice. There was also a specific order of serving; my dad was first followed by the male children, then my sister and grandmother and mother last. (Masumoto, 1983, p. 140)

Eventually Masumoto discovered that although his plain brown rice was not an acceptable replacement for white rice served as a side dish, others would eat it as part of a larger package, as when he offered the combination of brown rice and sushi prepared in the traditional way with the sole innovation being the type of rice used. In this case the difference was still noticed but accepted.

Foods are particularly useful as signs because they are separable, easily transported, and adaptive to new environments and technologies; most importantly, it requires minimal training to be able to cook adequately and certainly none to eat (Kalčik, 1985). At the same time, "unlike other material manifestations of social life, which can be built and left to stand, food is perishable, ephemeral, constantly renewed by women in their kitchens" (Kirshenblatt-Gimblett, 1991, p. 77). Food is certainly concrete, but it is not lasting. If one does not study it in use, one cannot study it at all, for it is literally consumed as a result of its physical function, leaving no remains for later analysis of social function.

Because of the unique *incorporative* nature of foods (after all, they are the only signs people actually ingest and physically incorporate into their bodies), they have often been granted an important sacred role (Goode, 1989, p. 187). As Eliot Singer pointed out in his study of Hare Krishna conversions, food as vehicle serves particularly well as symbol. He described in detail the role of *prasadam* (the name Krishna devotees give their foodstuffs, literally, "the leftovers of God"):

> Taking *prasadam* is not just a change in a minor activity; it is a transformation of one of the most meaningful and emotionally charged of all experiences. Instead of stressing meat, Krishna Consciousness forbids it. Instead of emphasizing personal satisfaction, Krishna Consciousness emphasizes detachment. Instead of eating for the self, the devotees eat for Krishna. Instead of seeing food as an end towards which

work is directed, the devotees see food as a means by which liberation is achieved. Thus, as the devotees eat food transformed into *prasadam*, they are themselves transformed into devotees. (E. A. Singer, 1985, p. 212)

In the process of learning the customs and ideas surrounding new foods, converts learn the basic concepts of the religion.[3] In Singer's example, food serves equally as a form of communication within a particular group and as a marker of the boundary between various sorts of groups.[4] Generally both functions are served simultaneously, as is the case here. What joins me to my family or chosen social group separates me from strangers. This is a good example of polysemy as the same food item simultaneously conveys multiple messages.

The list of potential functions of food range from the instrumental (at the most basic level, food prevents starvation) to the aesthetic (the presentation of food can be as important as its taste), and different cultures emphasize different components (the Japanese grant the aesthetic function a major role, whereas Americans generally grant presentation only minimal attention). As a relatively complex system involving several stages, different parts of the food system are available for use in signifying something to someone. Charles Camp, a folklorist who has spent time considering the matter, listed five stages: production or gathering of foodstuffs, distribution of foodstuffs, cooking, distribution of cooked food, and consumption (1989, p. 57). Others have proposed different lists; whichever is followed, it is evident that ample room exists for elaboration and signification.

In part due to the complexity of the system and in part due to the nature of the individual items, food lends itself particularly well to manipulation of various sorts. According to Powers and Powers:

> It can be exchanged, bartered, sold, or given away; it can serve as a medium of exploitation, used for or against people to bring them to a point of capitulation. It can be disguised as an inducement, as entreaty, or a trade-off. Food exists as an ingredient of imperialism, and it can be used profitably against a population as if it were a weapon—paradoxically, one as lethal as starvation. (Powers & Powers, 1984, pp. 57–58)

The particular case study detailed by Powers and Powers involved a Native American food system, but their comments are equally applicable more generally. The exchange of food is a particularly fruitful topic for semiotic research, implying as it does the exchange of meanings.

Within groups, rituals and ceremonies are nearly always marked by food use. For all groups, foods serve to convey social information with some using food as a marker consistently on every occasion of any significance, as the Chinese apparently do.[5] The ubiquitous presence of food makes it valuable to researchers; even if every community does not use food as consistently as the Chinese to convey information, everyone at least uses food in some ways, integral to some events.

## FOOD AS SEMIOTICS

The enormous variety of social practices surrounding food has engendered an array of studies from a wide range of disciplines.[6] Cutting across these are a variety of theoretical approaches, among them semiotics.[7] Food has been one traditional topic of choice in explaining semiotic theory, in large part due to its accessibility. The earliest significant work was by Claude Levi-Strauss, the French anthropologist who almost single-handedly invented structural analysis (closely related to semiotic analysis) as a method. Among his works are three related volumes on mythology using food as a central theme.[8] Levi-Strauss is best known for pointing to the distinction between raw and cooked food as the difference between animals (who eat anything they can digest, raw) and humans (who are far more selective, eating the majority of their food cooked). His stress on the significance of transforming a natural object into a cultural one (as occurs when a naturally growing food item is cooked, in the process being transformed into a culturally produced item) has thoroughly influenced later investigators.[9]

A second major contributor to the understanding of food as potentially semiotic was Roland Barthes. As early as 1961, he published an analysis comparing the consumption of sugar in France and the United States, based on the assumption that "sugar is not just a foodstuff . . . it is, if you will, an 'attitude' " (Barthes, 1961/1979, p. 166).[10] He proposed that food be understood as "a system of communication, a body of images, a protocol of usages, situations, and behavior . . . food sums up and transmits a situation; it constitutes an information; it signifies" (1961/1979, pp. 167–168; see also 1972, 1982b). In introducing semiology to his readers originally, food was one of the first topics Barthes presented (1964/1967, pp. 27–28), although his analyses were more suggestive than thorough. Despite their brevity, his suggestions linger in the mind and thus have been granted a status out of proportion with their length.[11]

In contrast to Barthes, Mary Douglas systematically applied the assumptions of semiotics to food as a social code; her work has been accordingly influential. She began by using food quite literally as the material upon which the basic semiotic strategy is demonstrated. "If food is treated as a code, the messages it encodes will be found in the pattern of social relations being expressed. The message is about different degrees of hierarchy, inclusion and exclusion, boundaries and transactions across the boundaries" (M. Douglas, 1971, p. 61). The terms Douglas and Michael Nicod, her assistant, developed for describing the occasions on which people eat food have come to be widely accepted. The first, and most general, is a *food event*, defined as an occasion when food is taken, without prejudice as to whether it constitutes a meal or not. They also referred to *structured events*, social occasions organized according to rules prescribing time, space, and sequence of actions; *meals*, when food is taken as part of a structured event; and *snacks*, unstructured food events in which one or more self-contained food items are served (M. Douglas, 1982b, pp. 90–91). Their hierarchy provides a flexible list of vocabulary words others can utilize in their descriptions of those occasions when food is integral to an event under study.

Structurally, meals supply a middle stage, larger than individual food items, smaller than the entire social code. Douglas herself never phrased it quite this way, but an understanding of the value of studying entire meals is implicit in and grows out of her work.[12] It makes sense, because we are rarely faced with one individual food, consuming instead sets of foods or meals. It is odd that so few studies focus at the level of meals; most begin and end with a single food. The discrepancy may be attributed to the traditional assumption that the sign is the appropriate level of analysis rather than the social code (or, in this case, an analytic category somewhere between the two in size).

With the strong start in applying semiotic theory to food provided by Levi-Strauss, Barthes, and Douglas, it is surprising that so few publications in semiotics today have maintained this focus (although researchers in a wide variety of fields other than semiotics proper have clearly been influenced by these authors and generally acknowledge the influence specifically). Anthropology, sociology, history, and folklore have largely acquired the topic.[13]

## FOOD AS COMMUNICATION

Food clearly serves as a form of communication, thus, it is an appropriate topic for communication researchers.[14] A communication approach to food adds an emphasis on the context in which the food appears; a recognition of the implications of choices of a particular food over other alternatives; and a focus on how food is employed by social actors as one part of the creation of social identity and social roles, in short, one part of how people we construct and maintain social reality through communicative behavior.[15] Tradition associates particular roles with particular foods such as Chicago police with doughnuts (Johnson & Recktenwald, 1991). People don't drink only to quench their thirst but also to demonstrate a public image, thus ginger ale, widely associated with a bygone age, is not as popular as Pepsi or Coca-Cola or even sparkling water because of the image it is understood to connote (Shapiro, 1992). Whether or not such stereotypes hold true may ultimately be less significant than their existence.

Sometimes it is not so much what someone eats as whom one sits next to while eating that conveys relevant information. In high school cafeterias, where a student sits is determined by who his or her friends are. The most terrifying decision of freshman year can be picking a table to join for lunch, because the choice bears directly on a student's social life. New students often eat with teachers while trying to decide which group to join, but overstaying at the teachers' table is itself problematic (Grossman, 1991, p. 4). Research of this sort may only minimally attend to the particular types of foods eaten, emphasizing instead the social constraints surrounding the use of food.

The following pages demonstrate how the major theoretical concepts presented in the first part of this volume (sign and social code) apply to food, moving
from there to a consideration of two productive topics of research in studies of
food to date: food as marker of identity and food as indicator of social change.
Obviously many other topics have been addressed at length such as asking why
particular foods are taboo in particular groups.[16] This and similar questions are
not discussed here because I am not convinced they are the potentially most valuable topics for communication researchers. By pointing to the issues of identity
and social change as central, I am proposing an agenda for future research in
communication having to do with food.

## FOOD: FROM SIGN TO SOCIAL CODE

Often researchers consider individual foods alone, investigating such topics as the
role of tamales for migrant farm workers (Williams, 1985) or the types of bread
historically available in Philadelphia (Arnott, 1983). These authors analyze one
sign at a time, temporarily ignoring the influence of all others. The general rule
has been to choose a food serving as the key symbol for the group in question,
as with crawfish for Cajuns (Gutierrez, 1985). The following quote comes from
an example of the research on food as sign; it is a study of why a particular food,
shown to be dangerous to particular individuals for health reasons, is deemed essential nonetheless, due to its close identification with a particular community.
According to Joos:

> *Sofki* [corn gruel] is a "cultural superfood" of the Seminoles and is identified as a
> uniquely Seminole food, one which they should eat to stay healthy. . . . Fry bread
> is another Seminole food. It is understandable that [diabetic] patients may not be
> receptive to doctors' and nutritionists' admonitions to eat less of these foods; they
> identify one as a Seminole and are considered to be healthful. (Joos, 1985, p. 232)

Obviously this type of study has implications for health professionals as well as
communication researchers. It is important to understand that for many people,
destructive as this may seem to health professionals, cultural implications carry
more weight than medical consequences. This example is not at all uncommon;
similar stories could be told for many groups.

In numerous examples, as here, the focus of the description is the presence
or absence of a single food item. In this case, the emphasis was on investigating
the connections between medicine and culture, technically a synchronic analysis,
involving the study of a particular behavior at a particular point in time. Other
examples utilize historical methods to study how the uses of a particular food
change over time, a diachronic analysis (e.g., Weaver, 1983). In each of these
cases, a single food, a single sign, serves as the focal point for research.

Though it is generally more appropriate to broaden the scope of study beyond a single sign to the entire social code, that should not be taken as implying studies such as those just described are inadequate. They clearly have taught something. My question, however, is whether they have taught all that might be known: even when it is not emphasized, explicating the use of a single sign requires considerable implicit knowledge of the larger social code. Given what researchers know at present, incorporating elements of a larger system, whether that means expanding the boundaries to a single meal or to an entire food system, will generally lead to a more thorough analysis and a more explicit presentation of what the researcher has learned that the reader may not yet know.

Recently it has become common, and certainly it will generally be appropriate, to put individual foods in context, looking at the meanings provided by the situation as a whole rather than expecting all the meaning to be conveyed by one individual food. For example, researchers tend to overlook drinks, but they convey as much information and in much the same ways as other consumables. "The essentially social nature of drinking is indicated by the fact that solitary drinking is commonly considered to be a problematic symptom. The timing, frequency, and, above all, company of drinkers can tell us a great deal about sociability and shared values" (Barrows & Room, 1991, p. 7). Here, the entire constellation of behaviors surrounding the beverage conveys meaning rather than the presence or absence of a particular liquid: timing, frequency, company, and so forth jointly convey particular meanings.[17] The expansion of scope demonstrated here is an example of the type of analysis implied by a consideration of both context and entire social codes.

As Janet Theophano (1991) showed, the more knowledge a researcher has about a particular food event, the more adequate the interpretation. As part of her study of food in an Italian-American community, she contrasted the wedding meals prepared by a mother for her two daughters, finding meaning to lie precisely in the contrast of the two rather than in either meal individually.[18] For participants, this should present no problem, for they expect to be guests at all relevant events. The problems arise when an outsider, who will undoubtedly miss many of the relevant events, attempts to discover what has occurred and whether new meanings have been introduced into the system (or old meanings expanded upon) in his or her absence.[19] Thus a researcher constantly plays the game of "catch-up," trying to discover all of the data participants already know to take into account, so that the final analysis has a hope of being adequate. This is perhaps the most difficult part of cultural analysis: identifying the connections considered relevant by participants. Perhaps this is another way of saying "intertextuality rules," for meanings are subtle, accumulating over time, gaining resonance from a set of events rather than any single occurrence. Legitimate participants learn what is significant through long-term membership in a culture; a researcher must match this to whatever extent possible.

The best studies often begin with a focus on a single food, moving quickly to expand the amount of information taken into consideration in the analysis of how people used that food. Ralph Hattox, for example, presented an excellent case study of the use of food as the key to social changes within the society at large, using as his starting point a single food item, coffee. Beginning with the question of why drinking coffee was so controversial in the medieval Near East, focusing on the debates of the 16th century, he expanded his scope to the coffeehouse as social institution and finally to a comparison of this one with other social institutions. The answer to his question lies in the larger historical context. Briefly, he concluded the controversy was due to the fact that "the worldly activity of the coffeehouse had come in part to replace scholarly study and contemplation in the mosque" (Hattox, 1985, p. 121).[20] This example nicely demonstrates the value of moving beyond an initial focus at the level of a single food item, a single sign, to the larger social code, even to the incorporation of other related social codes.

It would be overstatement to imply that it is *never* useful to focus on individual signs. However, although some meaning can be gleaned through a focus on individual signs, further meaning requires consideration of the larger social code as well. Thus, Gusfield's (1987) examination of alcohol as marker of the transition from work to play is matched by a similar description of coffee as marker of the inverse, the transition from play to work; Bynum's (1987) focus on fasting behavior (lack of food) is analyzed in relation to a similar focus on feasting behavior (overabundance of food); Mintz's (1985) primary concern is sugar, yet he spends time discussing carbohydrates. In all these cases, a richer, more complex, more adequate analysis results from the consideration of additional details beyond what may have initially appeared essential for understanding of behavior.

As with every sign, foods can be analyzed either synchronically (at one point in time and space) or diachronically (changing over time). As explained previously, synchronic and diachronic analyses are generally viewed as mutually exclusive alternatives, performed by different analysts to answer a different set of research questions but they are actually complementary. Thus, a study moving between them, rather than emphasizing one alone, is more nearly complete. A focus primarily on synchronic analysis leads, among other projects, to a study of the ways in which food functions as a marker of social identity; a focus on diachronic analysis leads to the role played by food in social change. There are (as always) numerous other possible research topics, but these are particularly obvious ones and as such are outlined in some detail in the following section.

## SYNCHRONIC ANALYSIS: FOOD AS IDENTITY MARKER

Food's most significant social function is to serve as an indicator of various sorts of social identity, from region to ethnicity, from class to age or gender. Being concrete, foods serve to objectify relationships between individuals and groups. "Social relationships are developed and maintained by symbols, and thus we tend to *see* groups through their symbols and to identify ourselves through symbols'' (Kalčik, 1985, p. 45). As is the case with other signs and symbols, one sees the food (signifier) and understands the implied relationship (signified) without ever noticing the necessary transition between the two. This characteristic function of foods can be deliberately manipulated. Knowing that particular foods are understood to indicate particular identities, it becomes possible to use their presence or absence to make deliberate statements about identity. For example, eating organic foods can be understood to be a protest against a particular political and economic system that puts profit and convenience ahead of ecology (Kalčik, 1985, p. 54); eating Italian food when living among Mormons in Utah can be understood to recreate ethnic identity, maintain traditional boundaries with the dominant culture, and emphasize familial closeness (Raspa, 1985, p. 193).

Food conveys information about at least the following major categories of identity: ethnicity, regional identity, temporal and geographic identity, social class, and relationship status. Each of these is discussed in some detail. Other potential categories such as age and gender have not generally been studied as marked by differences in food, and so they are not described here, but they are no less real. The popularity of the phrase "Real men don't eat quiche" a few years ago attests to the popular existence of distinctions between conceptions of appropriate "male" and appropriate "female" food. And anyone who has ever watched a child grow from being a "picky eater" to a voracious teenager willing to eat almost anything knows that equally real distinctions relate to age.

## Ethnicity

The majority of research on food and identity conducted to date considers ethnic identity in particular. People share food first within families and it can be said that "ethnicity is kinship writ large" (Van den Berghe, 1984, p. 395). In studying ethnicity researchers study the extension of food sharing from immediate family, to larger kin networks, to entire ethnic groups; food serves equally well to mark the existence of relationship ties in each of these ever widening circles.

It has been assumed that "Traditional ways of eating form a link with the past and help ease the shock of entering a new culture" (Kalčik, 1985, p. 37), thus justifying a frequent research focus on the foods of immigrant groups new to the United States.[21] Recently, there has been a gradual shift away from the study of new immigrants to others. This shift seems to have occurred in stages: where initially it was assumed that individual families were the appropriate focus of study for ethnic identity, later it was noticed that a more loosely defined group of families and friends from the same ethnic background was another possible focus for research. For example, after extensive fieldwork in the Philadelphia Italian-American community, Goode, Curtis, and Theophano concluded, "the social network rather than any geographically defined community was the major social unit for the interhousehold transmission and reinforcement of food norms'' (1984, p. 154). Today other researchers as well assume the social network rather than the ethnic group as an appropriate context for the study of food use. In the modern world, where social-cultural boundaries so rarely match precise geographic boundaries, this is an essential move.

## Regional Identity

Moving away from the family unit has led researchers to consider food as a regional marker or to study the ways in which particular foods change from being ethnic markers to being regional markers. For example, Lockwood and Lockwood (1991) described the ways in which the pasty changed from being an identity marker for Cornish immigrants to Finns and then to Italians, each considering it unique to themselves, until it finally metamorphosed into a broad regional marker for residents of the Upper Peninsula of Michigan (see Fig. 4.1). Similarly, Gutierrez (1985) described the way in which one food, crawfish, serves as both ethnic and regional symbol for Cajuns in Louisiana.

Often representatives of two groups interacting appear superficially to be quite similar; only the presence of a particular food at a particular time marks the wide gap between participants' assumptions. In the following incident, reported by Aldrich, a food ultimately distinguished between Northern and Southern regional identities.

> Milk gravy is one of those dishes that one either dearly loves or just can't tolerate. I happen to love it. In fact, it was my first cause for disillusionment with my future husband, Don.
>
> The wedding invitations already had been sent out when he came to spend the weekend with my family. At the first breakfast, my dad handed the bowl of gravy to our crew-cut northern guest.
>
> "Here, Son. Have some Starter and Grower."
>
> Don stared at the pepper-flecked mixture before him.
>
> "Some what?"
>
> "Starter and Grower, Son. Back home we start younguns on that and keep 'em with it. Don't tell me you've never had gravy?"
>
> "Gravy? Oh, sure. My mom always keeps the drippings from the beef roast. But we always put it on our mashed potatoes."
>
> "Huh! That stuff's not worth being called gravy. That's just sop. You should try this. It's real gravy."
>
> Don placed a scant spoonful on his plate, gulped and gave me a "you-better-appreciate-this" look.
>
> But all I could do was stare back at him. Was this the man I thought I knew well enough to marry? In that moment, I realized we had huge cultural differences. (Aldrich, 1985, p. 27)

Here the differences were not sufficient to cancel the engagement, but in other cases, such extreme responses are evident, demonstrating convincingly the power of even a single food to represent potentially irreconcilable differences in background and assumptions. It is important to remember, however, that the gravy alone conveys but little; it is the presence of gravy at breakfast with the entire family seated around the table that conveys meaning. The relation here is really one of metonymy: The gravy stands for a larger system of family life and what it means to be from the South as opposed to the North. The larger systems of meanings clash in this example, implying that people from different parts of the country may over time discover differences where none appear obvious at first.

Very recently, there have been studies of the ways in which food serves as an identity marker of less permanent groupings, neither ethnically nor regionally bound: "Family, neighborhood, temporary associations, ephemeral interest groups, traditional work environments, and other 'made' communities all create festive events in which food becomes symbolic of identity" (Humphrey & Humphrey, 1988, p. 2). In her exemplary case study, Lin Humphrey (1988) demonstrated the theoretical value of studying nontraditional groupings, describing the development of a new tradition, "soup night," meaningful to a group of friends, rather than the traditional larger ethnic or regional grouping. This is a potentially interesting approach, albeit one little studied to date: to follow the creation of identity within a group having *voluntary membership* (i.e., one that a person is not born into but may choose whether to join) through the uses of food to mark the boundaries of that group. Part of the value of this study lies in its ability to convey a sense of modern realities. In the 1990s people are rarely limited to eating within ethnic groups (or other groups having *involuntary* membership), so an interpretation of group boundaries as always implying ethnic group boundaries begin to appear outdated and inappropriate.

FIG. 4.1.   Cornish pasty. Photo by Kate Owen, University of Wisconsin-Parkside.

**Temporal Identity**

Sometimes foods are valuable for their identification with a time of year in addition to place, an expansion of the concept of regional identity. Just as mint juleps are often associated with hot weather in the Old South, travel writers often describe the foods traditionally associated with a particular place as a guide to later tourists, as Stinchecum (1990) did for the foods traditionally associated with Kyoto, Japan, in the summer.

Food habits even can be identified with particular political events and thus by implication with a particular time period, a point not often considered. Rogov described how when Iraq sent missiles into Israel in 1991, eating habits changed considerably:

> As dining patterns have changed, so has the list of foodstuffs Israelis are buying in their local markets. Since the first missile fell, the sale of chocolate has increased by 37%, the numbers of cookies has almost doubled and the sale of frozen pizzas, instant soups and pre-made hamburger patties has gone up by as much as 80%.
>
> People are eating three times as many eggs as usual, twice as much bread and butter, and four times as many potatoes. . . . For reasons not entirely clear, but to the delight of many children, the sale of broccoli, cauliflower and spinach has also fallen off.
>
> . . . establishments that are normally considered fashionable have been abandoned in favor of places that serve dishes that are warming and comforting. The demand for chicken Tettrazini and sole in herbed cream sauce has been replaced by kreplach soup, beef stew and chicken fricassee. (Rogov, 1991, p. 18)

Traditional foods are apparently most comforting in times of war, replacing others considered more intriguing in the short term but lacking the rich connotations of foods remembered from childhood. In a time of political upheaval and potential danger, attention paid to food preparation takes on added meaning. In part, this example demonstrates the complementary enduring nature of tradition and the fragility of innovation. When the system is stressed, there is no room for experimentation with the new and different (and potentially uncompelling); rather, people return to what they know and can rely on for whatever comfort it can offer.

**Social Class**

In some of the examples given to this point, the sheer presence or absence of a single item of food in a single context conveys information; as it works for other varieties of identity, so it works for social class. Even a single food can be understood as an indicator of wealth. Caviar, for example, "has always symbolized the best in life; it is the single food most clearly identified with wealth, opulence and luxury" (Pepin, 1990, p. 111). With the example of caviar, however, as with other individual signs, knowledge of the appropriate context, even when left implicit, is equally important in permitting a complete analysis. "For the purist, there is only one right way to eat caviar: spooned straight from the container onto waferlike buttered toast or small, yeasty buckwheat pancakes called blinis. . . . The spoon should preferably be mother-of-pearl or crystal—not an oxidizing metal. The *de rigueur* beverage is cold vodka, chilled champagne or both" (Pepin, 1990, p. 112). Thus is the value of a move from the level of a single sign to the larger social code (including rules for the proper use of that sign) demonstrated. The *nouveau riche* may have the money to buy the caviar and may know enough to want to serve it at formal events but are unlikely to also know all the subtle rules governing "proper" consumption of that caviar and so mark themselves as not yet fully members of the class they are trying to emulate. Here, the presence of the single food is both sufficient and insufficient as a marker of social class: it must be integrated properly into a larger social code (how it is eaten, which drink accompanies it) in order to completely convey the message. Eating caviar with the "wrong" drink only conveys the desire to belong to a particular social class not the achievement of that desire.

As with any other form of communication, the particular behavior related to food or drink is polysemic and can be interpreted by various participants in differing ways. Brennan demonstrated this with the following example taken from Old Regime Paris:

> Social drinking in taverns was central to popular culture. It gave substance to the rituals of friendship and social interaction; it was the common denominator of all customers and all activities. A glass of wine, the drink, was an idiom of social exchange. As a gift or as a communion, it bound people together in ties or reciprocity and debt, of friendship and solidarity. Social drinking used the signs and rituals of gifting to cement personal ties and articulate social relations. Such sociability—dense, constant, even political in its concern with neighborhood or professional status and power—is central to the significance of taverns and drink. Drunkenness, by contrast, was the metaphor of a consistent and recurring critique of popular culture by the elites. It summarized the waste of money and time, the idleness and immorality of those in the popular classes who refused to respond to a new ethic of work and self-discipline. Taverns became a symbol of their unrepentant reliance on sociability and public consumption in daily life. Whether seen as social drinking or as drunkenness, drink constituted a battlefield of two conflicting cultures. (Brennan, 1991, pp. 80–81)

Here, the behavior and even the context are consistent; yet two vastly divergent interpretations are possible simultaneously. The same behavior, having alcoholic drinks with friends in a tavern, was alternately envisioned as "social drinking" by one social class, an event essential to the conduct of everyday life with positive connotations; or as a demonstration of "drunkenness," an immoral act wasting precious time having negative connotations, by members of a different social class.[22]

Food's function as an identity marker is particularly significant when expectations and actuality are inappropriately matched (technically, a mismatch between encoding and decoding). Witness the following story by Washington, DC reporter, Maureen Dowd:

> Once I got an invitation from the Bushes to spend an informal evening in the family quarters of the White House. The Friday night event began at 7:30 and was described as "a buffet," with a movie afterward.
>
> When I arrived, I eagerly scanned the scene for some cold chardonnay and steaming silver serving dishes. But to George and Barbara Bush, it turned out, the word "buffet" signifies something very different. The White House buffet consisted of strawberry mousse cake and tea. That's all. Some lemon wedges, some Sweet 'n Low, but really, that's all.
>
> As Jackie Mason once said, WASP's are the only ones who don't have cockroaches, because there's no food in the house. (Dowd, 1991a, p. 1)

As Dowd herself made clear, part of the problem in this case was attributable to a difference between what the hosts considered to be the proper connotations of buffet and what the guests expected given the same term. By their own rules, the hosts did exactly as advertised: they prepared a buffet. And yet that buffet did not fulfill the guests' expectations. The mismatch here can be attributed to both social class and ethnicity and perhaps the subtle implication of temporal influence (does a buffet scheduled for 7:30 imply less abundance of food than one scheduled at 6:00, a more traditional dinner hour in the United States?). However, even here, the same guests brought back on another occasion will know better what to expect and be less liable to surprises. Ever after, the word buffet will be more explicitly polysemous, having multiple connotations, for at least these participants (and readers of the story detailing it, who are vicarious participants).

### Relationship Status

Food also serves as an indicator of the start or end of a relationship. In studying the use of food among the Creek, Amelia Bell concluded, "A Creek woman is fundamentally . . . a cook," thus, preparing a food (*sofki*) that serves as a key symbol (representing Creek identity) is acknowledged as clear evidence of the establishment of a relationship (1990, p. 335). Equally, refusing to continue preparing that same food severs the relationship.[23] Other groups use other foods, though generally in a more informal fashion, as indicators of the start or end of a relationship. The proverb "The way to a man's heart is through his stomach" refers to the role of food in courtship in mainstream American relationships.

Taken together, these examples demonstrate the various ways in which food indicates some form of identity, whether ethnic, regional, temporal, social class, or relationship. Obviously, other means convey identity as well (some of which are considered in later chapters), but food serves this purpose particularly nicely.

## DIACHRONIC ANALYSIS: FOOD AND SOCIAL CHANGE

Related in some cases to the issue of identity, a second major research topic to date has been to study the role of food in social change. Early research asked how it might be possible to deliberately change the foods people preferred to eat, particularly due to shortages during World War II and nutritional concerns about healthy combinations of foods (M. Mead, 1943; see also Cussler & De Give, 1952). Later questions posed include: Why are foods among the last ethnic markers to be abandoned? How are new foods integrated into an already existing system of meanings? What are the implications of one group adopting the foods of another? Do all foods change at the same time, or are some preferences more tightly held? These questions and others appropriate to a study of food as communication are addressed briefly in the following section.

*Why Are Foods Among the Last Identity Markers to Be Abandoned?*    As Kalčik pointed out, "foodways seem particularly resistant to change . . . because the earliest-formed layers of culture, such as foodways, are the last to erode" (1985, p. 39). An example of a food surprisingly consistent over time is the fruitcake. Although frequent jokes are made about how fruitcake is really a terrible gift, some 50 million pounds are sold annually. Essentially, "We're talking about an antique cake in contemporary life, and it's trying to make the transition" (MacVean, 1990, p. D17). A large part of the popularity of fruit cakes is likely due to their presence at past celebrations. If memories of previous Christmases include gifts of fruitcake, people are predisposed to incorporate this anachronous food into their present festivities.

As is well known, when Coca-Cola changed the basic recipe for its cola, it was faced with widespread objections and eventually reintroducing the original recipe, renamed "Classic Coke" (Hirsley, 1985). Because a marketing study initially provoked the change, this is a particularly fascinating example of how little sway logic has over purchases and how much influence is granted tradition and habit. Even though the new recipe was more successful in blind taste tests, it had the disadvantage of being new and different, calling specific attention to itself and its otherness from the original recipe at each taste.

A comparable change in the traditional recipe for Ovaltine prompted the comment: "What have they done to my Ovaltine, I wailed—my restorative, my tranquilizer, my link with childhood? . . . Childhood security symbols should be sacred" (Dorgan, 1986, p. 21), a sentiment most would second. We take it for granted that favorite foods will remain as we knew them in childhood, and a change in recipe surprises us, destroying memories, making us unhappy. Clearly there is a sort of sympathetic magic at work here. If we were happy as children when we drank Ovaltine, then drinking Ovaltine was responsible, so drinking it again as adults can be presumed to have the power to make us happy again. Few adults would explicitly claim this as their logic, for it is clearly illogical, yet it seems to be the best explanation of this behavior.

Food often serves as the focal point of dissension between generations, as demonstrated in a study conducted by Blaxter and Paterson of two generations of Scottish working class women and their connotations for various foods. Despite reality, the older generation continues to believe that "the idea of the 'proper' meal has much to do with the idea of 'proper' family life." A proper meal was described as "a cooked meal, prepared lovingly by the mother, and served by her to a family all seated at one table," despite the fact that historically it was rarely cooked by the mother, and everyone rarely sat down together (Blaxter & Paterson, 1983, p. 102). Other examples confirm the finding that people's assumptions and interpretations do not always keep pace with social changes. When faced with the discrepancy between these assumptions (social facts) and reality (historical facts) people seem to trust the former. Thus, a modern mother in this community is criticized not for failing to adhere to the *actual* standards of a previous generation but for failing to adhere to the *ideals* of that previous generation, a much tougher if not impossible measure.

Despite the preference for continuity, food habits do change over time. Some factors involved in change in the food habits of various immigrant groups are: generation (first generation immigrants hold on to their foodways longer than the second generation), occupation of breadwinner, education of cook, state of family (including such factors as the presence or absence of children), economics (e.g., cost of ethnic foods), availability, convenience, commercialization, urbanization, and status of ethnic foods in the larger community (Kalčik, 1985, pp. 39–40). It can safely be assumed that some of these factors play a role in changes within other types of groups as well.

### How Are New Foods Integrated Into an Already Existing System of Meanings?

This is a particularly interesting research focus, given that individual foods are generally already integrated into larger sets or meals before researchers begin their study. One approach is to study the integration of one or a few new foods into an existing, coherent food system. Thus, Prosterman studied how a kosher caterer "works out the ritually pure combinations of new and unfamiliar foods" (1985, p. 137), concluding that the caterer serves as a *bricoleur*, Levi-Strauss's word for someone combining old elements in innovative, often surprising, ways. Every cook who tries a new ingredient in an old recipe, whether because the old ingredient is unavailable in a new country or simply out of curiosity, plays a comparable role of *bricoleur*.

In their study of the Oglala food system, Powers and Powers (1984) demonstrated how it is sometimes easier to integrate a set of foods into an existing food system rather than single foods one at a time. In this case, as presumably in others, a set of foods already having particular well-established connections (beef, coffee, flour, and sugar) proved easier to acquire than any one would have been individually, in large part because there was no need to design new connections between foods or new recipes to make use of them. This goes against what seems intuitively obvious, for it seems less intrusive to integrate a single food into an existing system.

Thus, the answer to the question of how to integrate new foods varies. Single foods can be added to an existing system, or sets of foods can be acquired jointly. Depending on availability, particular foods are frequently omitted from an existing system (as is the case when populations move from country to country, and formerly common foods become difficult to obtain). In any of these cases, it is important to remember that taste is "culturally shaped and socially controlled" (Mennell, 1985, p. 6). As social circumstances change, so do foods. If people have trouble maintaining access to an old food but are not ready to lose the meaning that food conveyed, they may substitute a new food, keeping the meaning viable. Equally, when the old meaning is outdated, they do not necessarily drop the old food; if it is still readily available and the taste still pleases, they can substitute a new meaning for the old.

***Do All Foods Change at the Same Time, or Are Some Preferences More Tightly Held?*** There are varying degrees of change depending upon whether or not a particular food is part of the *core diet* (foods closely associated with a particular group such as rice in Japan), part of the *secondary core* (where there is more willingness to change), or part of a looser grouping of *peripheral foods*, (the most susceptible to change; Kalčik, 1985, p. 41). Summarizing her investigation of the relationship between changes in diet and other changes in ethnic traditions, Mary Douglas concluded: "The sum of this research is that distinctive ethnic diets disappear at the same time as the other ethnic boundaries disappear" (1984, p. 30). This makes sense, explaining the use (or dropping) of a food as ethnic marker. In terms of other identity markers, the research is not yet available, but it would be reasonable to assume the same holds true. When people no longer want to mark regional identity, they drop the foods that previously served that function; those who change social class concomitantly change foods.

***What Are the Implications of One Group Adopting the Foods of Another?*** Foods serve not only as markers of identity within groups but equally as markers of acceptance between groups. To eat the food of another ethnic group indicates some measure of acceptance of that group. This can be understood as one aspect of what has traditionally been termed the *American melting pot*. There have been several recent articles considering the uncommon degree to which Americans have a wide range of acceptable foods. "By ingesting the foods of each new group, we symbolize the acceptance of each group and its culture" (Kalčik, 1985, p. 61). This same interest in food as marker of acceptance of other groups lies behind the frequency of ethnic festivals in the United States, with food playing a particularly significant role. In a summary consideration of such festivals, Abrahams suggested:

> In going public, a cultural contradiction re-emerges, one which has always resided at the hearth of American life: that in the celebration of the many, a sense of oneness may emerge. Paradoxically, the very act of food preparation and cooking may simultaneously proclaim and undermine ethnicity. The means by which an individual maintains a sense of ethnic continuity and integrity in carrying on the food tradition becomes a way to articulate a social and cultural coming-together, as one kind of food takes its place alongside other ethnic and regional offerings in the festival setting. (Abrahams, 1985, pp. 25–26)

When people eat their own foods, they mark group membership; when they present the same traditional foods to others in a joint celebration of ethnicity, sharing foods across group boundaries, the foods no longer serve as markers of group membership and the concept becomes meaningless. Thus do ethnic festivals work to destroy the very traditions they intend to display: By sharing foods, accepted indicators of group membership, people change the meaning of those foods, for clearly people do not become members of every ethnic group whose food they enjoy at a festival. By sharing the food that stands for one group with others, people effectively convey the message that group boundaries are meaningless after all. The presence of this paradox in the festival setting reflects a larger paradox in modern-day American culture. At one and the same time, there is a traditional assumption of tolerance for multiple ethnic groups in the United States ("we are all different"), together with the tradition of the equality of all ("we are all the same"). Clearly the paradox is more significant for the analyst than for the participants. In reality, group boundaries must have been crossed only superficially, for they are reestablished as readily as they are destroyed, when, after the festival, the groups that have come together separate again quite easily.

### At What Point Is It Appropriate to Say That Significant Social Change Has Occurred?    Sometimes the issue of which level serves as the more appropriate focus, the sign or the social code, is answered with "neither." Using an example of preserving hams, Amy Skillman showed that neither individual foods nor their combination alone determines what is considered appropriate or traditional; sometimes the event itself overrides any of the individual elements:

> So when I headed out to Bud's house on that November day, I expected to find an old smokehouse and a secret cure that had been passed from father to son for generations. What I found, instead, was a highly regimented curing process in a USDA-approved facility where the floor and tables are spotless, the meat is cooled to a specified temperature before curing, and a pre-mixed commercial cure is slightly modified but kept within federal government regulations—but no smoke. It was

then that I began to realize: it is the *event* rather than the technique or cure which has remained traditional in the Gardner family for generations and which serves as an important marker of community identity and values. (Skillman, 1988, p. 126)

In this case, the researcher's expectations were exploded by her informants. The traditional methods of curing, initially assumed to be the focus of the event labeled "preserving hams," were no longer used, yet despite this change the participants treated the event as identical to the one their predecessors engaged in a century ago. If the event maintains a consistent function for the group holding it, who is to say that the participants are wrong to use its old name, despite the change of what appear to be critical elements? It is, ultimately, the whole that matters, not change in any of the parts, and the function an event has for the participants should ultimately count rather than its appearance in the eyes of an outside analyst.

## CONCLUSION

There is no doubt that food is used for communication purposes, just as language is, just as other aspects of nonverbal communication are. As Camp concluded:

What matters is that *ordinary people understand and employ the symbolic and cultural dimensions of food in their everyday affairs.* Food is one of the most, if not the single most, visible badges of identity, pushed to the fore by people who believe their culture to be on the wane, their daughters drifting from their heritage, their sons gone uptown. Ordinary people may not write books about how food means, but they participate in an ongoing—in fact, daily—discourse on the subject more keenly cultural than anything in print. (Camp, 1989, p. 29)

Food is an important topic in the study of communicative behavior, whether at the level of an individual item, a meal, or the larger context of the entire social code; it awaits attention from communication researchers.

## NOTES

1. Considering the individual organism, food clearly is more fundamental even than sex, as put first by Richards (1932) in her pioneering study of food habits, for an organism that cannot find food to stay alive cannot live to reproduce another generation.

2. Food may be symbolic, but it is also as efficacious for feeding as roofs are for shelter, as powerful for including as gates and doors. Added over time, gifts of food are flows of life-giving substance, but long before life-saving is an issue the flows have created the conditions for social life. More effective than flags or red carpets which merely say welcome, food actually delivers good fellowship. (M. Douglas, 1984, p. 12)

   See also Goldschmidt (1990, p. 175) and H. B. Moore (1957) on the significance of food as a universal topic. On the related topic of food sharing see Y. Cohen (1961); Katriel (1991, pp. 151–165); Marshall (1961).

3. Bynum (1987) provided another example of the role of food in religion, considering the food-related practices of medieval women.

4. For a very different example of how food functions within a religious context to both create and signify community, see Sacks (1989).

5.     Chinese use food to mark ethnicity, culture change, calendric and family events, and social transactions. No business deal is complete without a dinner. No family visit is complete without sharing a meal. No major religious event is correctly done without offering up special foods proper to the ritual context. (E. N. Anderson, 1988, p. 199)

   See Chen (1990/1991) for additional comments on the significance of food for the Chinese.

6. Within folklore, see J. A. Anderson (1971); Brown and Musell (1985); Camp (1989); Humphrey and Humphrey (1988); Jones, Guiliano, and Krell (1981); Yoder (1972). Within anthropology, see Arnott (1975); Goody (1982); Messer (1984); see Farb and Armelagos (1980) for a popular version of what anthropologists have to say. Within sociology, see Finkelstein (1989); Mennell (1985); Murcott (1983). Within history, see Fenton and Kisban (1983); Grover (1987); Levenstein (1988), Smith and Christian (1984); Super (1988); Tannahill (1989). For a good general bibliography of early work, see C. S. Wilson (1973).

7. Mennell (1985) presented a good summary.

8. Levi-Strauss (1969, 1973, 1978); see also Levi-Strauss, 1966a, a short but significant article expanding on his analysis of food.

9. See, for example, the comments by Super, who reported having needed a way "to bridge the gap between the social and the biological worlds" in his study of history and who found, "Food was the answer for me" (1988, p. vii). Smith and Christian (1984) made similar comments about the value of food as a focus in their historical research.

10. It is interesting that sugar has repeatedly been a topic of research within the food literature; see also Mintz (1985) and Mechling and Mechling (1983).

11. In his early brief discussion, Barthes pointed to the following attributes of the food system: It includes rules of exclusion (taboos), signifying oppositions of units (savory/ sweet), rules of association (dishes combining elements, meals combining dishes), and rituals of use that can be understood as a rhetoric (1964/1967, pp. 27–28). Later, in the same book, he used food as one of his examples in explaining his terms system (more often called paradigm today) and syntagm (pp. 62–63).

12. M. Douglas has been particularly active in both continuing a research agenda focused on food (1971, 1979, 1982a, 1982b) and encouraging others to investigate food (1984) and later drink, as a correlate to food (1987).

13. Nöth's encyclopedic *Handbook of Semiotics* (1990) includes one single reference to food, but folklorists are holding an entire conference on the subject as I write this in June of 1992 (The Fife Conference: The Folklore of Food). The conference brochure says, "Participants will consider the various ways in which food and culture intersect in such arenas as ethnic tradition, regional identity, social function, symbolic and ritual usage." These are all topics compatible with the analysis presented in this chapter.

14. That researchers in communication have rarely focused their attention on food does not make it any less a device of communication, only an overlooked topic. Within communication research to date, Henderson (1970), a brief, exploratory article, stands alone as an attempt to summarize the importance of studying food as a form of communication. The few later discussions of food in the communication literature include Brummett (1981), analyzing the way foods eaten by the presidential candidates in 1980 functioned as synecdoche; Mechling and Mechling (1983), using Burke in their analysis of the rhetoric surrounding the eating of sugar; Winkin (1983), connecting eating with talk about food; Berger (1984b), describing high versus low status foods in the United States; Goode (1989), presenting a brief overview of the study of food; Katriel (1991, pp. 151–165), presenting a study of ritualized sharing among Israeli children; and Katriel (1991, pp. 71–91) describing the use of picnics as mediation between family and army in Israel. Clearly, food as communication can hardly be identified as a major topic within the mainstream of the field.

15. Goffman distinguished between *social identity* as those broad categories to which an individual can belong (age-grade, sex, class, regiment, and so forth) and *personal identity* as "the unique organic continuity imputed to each individual" (1971, p. 189). Following Goffman, I am interested here in social, not personal, identity.

16. For a beginning into this literature, see Harris (1985); Laderman (1981); Sahlins (1976b); Urban (1981).

17. For other considerations of the significance of drink rather than food, see M. Bell (1983); Cavan (1966); M. Douglas (1987); Gusfield (1963); Spradley (1970).

18. This research was part of a larger study reported in a number of publications, including Theophano (1978, 1982); Goode, Curtis, and Theophano (1984, 1985).

19. Other brief examples of the ways in which food behaviors have been described through the use of a wider context abound, from an example of a boy in the kitchen learning gender role socialization (Hodge & Kress, 1988, pp. 240-244) to a consideration of the adult male role in the American kitchen as related to day of the week (Adler, 1981); from the study of Swedish ritualized behavior centering on how adults convince children to eat the last bit of food on the plate because it is particularly good for them (Bringeus, 1981) to examinations of the terms used in referring to particular foods serve as a quick indicator of someone being a stranger to town (O'Neill, 1989).

20. A parallel discussion of the role of the tea house in Tashkent and its role in social life can be found in Clines (1990), a brief but suggestive article.

21. Historically there were other reasons for the emphasis on recent immigrant populations in the United States, though these are of less concern here than the theoretical justifications. See M. Mead (1943) and other early authors.

22. For another example of the varying interpretations of alcohol, see Herd's description of two dominant yet paradoxical images of alcohol in 19th century America: alcohol the enslaver and man as victim of a powerful tempter, a vision held by African-Americans, contrasted to alcohol the disinhibitor stressing the power of alcohol to release the savage within, a vision held by Whites (Herd, 1991).

23. "When a woman agrees to prepare *sofki* for a man, it marks the preliminary relationship, which may become a marriage. After marriage a woman cooks *sofki* for her husband and children. If a woman ceases to cook *sofki* for her husband, impending termination of the marriage is indicated" (A. R. Bell, 1990, p. 335).

# Chapter 5

# Clothing as Sign and Code

As food is the most basic to survival, clothing is the most omnipresent of the so-cial codes included in this volume. There are very few interactions where cloth-ing (or its noticeable lack) does not play a role. We can be in the company of others without food present, and we can stand or sit on the ground, so as to avoid the use of such taken-for-granted objects such as chairs, but we generally wear clothes. As Alison Lurie put it: "We can lie in the language of dress, or try to tell the truth; but unless we are naked and bald it is impossible to be silent" (1981). She did not take the point far enough. Being naked and bald are also revealing, for even the lack of clothes is noteworthy, also interpreted in light of the larger code. Due to its constant presence as a factor in social interaction, clothing plays a major role in communication.[1]

Clothing often provides the first information we are presented about another person. Before someone opens their mouths to speak, their clothes are available for interpretation.[2] Unlike food, clothing is most often a public matter: What people choose to wear is immediately obvious to anyone passing by on the street, whereas food can be more readily maintained as private.[3] Clothing communi-cates information on mood, status, and role through even minor details. Though it is easy to assume different meanings require different items of dress, social ac-tors need not be so explicit: Messing (1960) described the use of clothing among the Tuareg where even subtle changes in the drape of the cloth are granted sig-nificance by those familiar with the code.

People so thoroughly take the presence of clothes for granted that they are un-comfortable when clothes are removed whether voluntarily, as in a doctor's office, or involuntarily, as in a jail. As Elizabeth Wilson put it, dress "links the biologi-cal body to the social being, and public to private" (1985, p. 2). *Clothing is the outermost layer of the private self put on public display.* For this reason, it sometimes has been termed the *second skin*.[4] People often invest themselves more thoroughly in clothing than in what they eat or in which objects they choose to utilize. People deliberately choose what they wear for the meanings it will convey to others, knowing in advance that others take meaning from the choices. Clothing is a uniquely human product; animals do not wear clothes (the rare exceptions being pets whose owners require it of them).

Clothing is part of a larger, more encompassing topic best described as *ornamentation*, including several related components: what is done with the hair, body ornamentation (from tattoos to scarring to gold teeth), as well as accessories of any and all sorts.[5] Most studies on these peripheral areas have emphasized cultural variation, particularly stressing what appears bizarre and unusual to the eye of the researcher. For the purposes of this chapter, a focus on clothing itself is maintained, defined as materials that may temporarily be put on or added to the body, generally serving the physical function of protecting the body. Clothing is not absolutely universal; ornamentation of some sort is. Ornamentation is worthy of equal study as a part of communication; it simply is not the focus here.

Several terms have been used in the literature as synonyms for clothing; these are actually subsets of the larger category and can usefully be distinguished from it. *Fashion* refers to the clothing dictated by designers as appropriate at any given point in time (as distinguished from which clothing people on the street actually wear that can, in turn, be influenced by fashion).[6] *Costume* refers to the particular clothing worn for particular rituals (including theater presentations), though it also has been used to refer broadly to clothing worn in countries other than the one in which an author lives.[7] Characteristically, costumes change slowly, whereas change is the hallmark of fashion.[8] *Uniform* refers to the clothing required by a particular job or role, whether that of a private-school student, or a waitress, or an army officer.[9] The term uniform also functions metaphorically. When people in a particular social role dress similarly, their clothing is colloquially termed a uniform (the classic example of this sort of informal uniform being the Western business suit).[10] This chapter uses the term *clothing* as the most inclusive category.

As in the case of food, clothing serves both an instrumental function and a communicative one, conveying socially relevant information in addition to protecting from the elements.[11] In his preface to Cordwell and Schwarz, presented as "the first full-scale treatment" of adornment and clothing, Tax made the excellent point that the theory of cultures as "systems of symbols" was necessary before such a book could be written (1979, p. v). Once we as researchers understand culture to be composed of systems of symbols, we ask the related questions: Which systems are there, and what do they reveal? Ornamentation and clothing are obvious systems available for study around the globe and as such are coming of age as research topics.

As Bogatyrev emphasized, clothing is simultaneously materially object and sign

(1938/1976c, p. 33).[12] That is, unlike language and like food, clothing is not limited to a social reality but has a physical reality as well. Sometimes the two functions conflict, as when fashionable clothing does not guarantee warmth in winter. A person's choice between the two (wearing a fashionable but not terribly warm coat in the winter, for example) can thus be understood to convey information (here, granting social realities more importance than physical realities). For research purposes, the social use of clothing is of greatest interest.

Erving Goffman's dramaturgical theory applies particularly easily to the study of clothing, for we recognize the deliberate use of clothes as a vehicle to convey meaning. His theoretical concepts of identity kit (1961, p. 20), impression management and presentation of self (1959) fit the ways people use clothing.[13] As Goffman explicitly put it: "dress carries much of the burden of expressing orientation within a situation" (1963, p. 213). As Bogatyrev pointed out, observers can take note of clothing even against the will of the wearer to determine such details as social position (1936/1976a, p. 15). It is thus reasonable that most of us spend time considering which clothes are most likely to be appropriate before preparing to join a situation. People are far more aware of their own use of clothing and that of others and use it more deliberately than is the case for many other social codes.

As demonstrated by Appleby, an excellent example of the self-conscious use of clothing to convey information is Benjamin Franklin, who wore a leather apron in Philadelphia, fashionable clothing in London, and Quaker dress in France:

> In the London that Franklin moved in, he perceived . . . [that] he would do best if he presented himself as a cosmopolitan, as an urbane, witty, elegant man. And, of course, he was already renowned as a scientist and as a very clever writer and conversationalist, so he created this image of himself, which was one that enabled him to move easily in these different circles in London society. . . .
>
> [In Paris], Franklin *re*-fashioned himself for this new urban culture. And now it was not as an elegant man of fashion that he saw that he could move best in these circles and represent the new United States, but rather as a simple Quaker. And Franklin put aside his elegant clothes, and he acquired a wardrobe of very simple suits. The French, he realized, wanted a hero of the rational mind, of the wit of Voltaire, but they also wanted the primitive virtues that Rousseau had so celebrated. And Franklin also must have been aware that in French theater there was a character, the "simple Quaker.". . . And so, Franklin took this on. He wore plain clothes, he developed a fur hat. . . . He carried a walking stick instead of a sword. And the French went *wild* over this Franklin. (Appleby, 1990, p. 35)

Franklin simply achieved what everyone attempts. He matched his outer appearance to fit his audience's expectations perfectly without moving too far from what seemed comfortable and appropriate to him.

One of the ways to gain ideas about clothing is through mass communication, since the media concurrently reflect and influence fashions. From Faye Duna-way's beret in *Bonnie and Clyde* to the 18th century shoes in *Dangerous Liaisons*, people expand and modify their wardrobes based on what characters wear in films and on television. Clothing styles of television characters are specifically request-ed by customers in stores, as when clerks are told, "I want the Murphy Brown look" (Cook, 1990).

A story from *The New York Times* column "Metropolitan Diary" explains how to apply this approach successfully:

> Marsha Schorr of Scarsdale, N.Y., has always had a difficult time shopping for the perfect gift necktie for her husband. This time, she decided, it was going to be differ-ent. So it was with new-found confidence that she approached the tie counter in Bloomingdale's in White Plains.
> "Do you watch television?" she asked the clerk.
> "Yes."
> "Do you watch 'Thirtysomething'?"
> "Yes."
> "Good," Mrs. Schorr said. "I'd like a tie for my husband."
> "Elliot?" the clerk wanted to know.
> "No," Mrs. Schorr said. "Michael."
> This time her husband loved his gift. (Alexander, 1990, p. Y19)

Deconstructing what had to have happened for this story to make sense, shows the following sequence: (a) Mrs. Schorr thinks her husband is like a particular television character, Michael; (b) therefore, he would like the clothing that Michael likes; and (c) therefore, a sales clerk who is also familiar with the character of Michael and with his clothing choices can predict, from a selection of ties Michael has never actually worn, which tie Michael would like and thus simultaneously which tie Mr. Schorr would like. This example shows how clothing choices are at times assumed to be synonymous with character. In this case, the tie serves as an icon of a very ephemeral sort: It resembles something Michael would have worn but never actually wore.

In a related example, the former clothing of movie stars is avidly sought after. A new store in Hollywood, called *A Star is Worn*, facilitates the transfer of cast-offs out of the closets of the stars into the closets of their fans (Mitchell, 1990). These are indices, formerly physically part of the star's image, gaining value not from any intrinsic worth but solely from their prior physical connection to celebri-ties. Items of clothing worn by the stars in specific films, rather than in their per-sonal lives, are even more valuable; these are not only indices but also icons (now the new owners can dress to match the image seen on the screen).

Would-be popular culture figures sometimes make deliberate choices about clothing in order to carve out an identity of their own. Witness the two 13-year-olds who got together as the musical group Kris Kross wearing their baseball caps, T-shirts, and overalls backwards. In explanation: They just "decided we had to do something different, so we came up with the clothes thing'' (Watrous, 1992, p. H31). They are creatively using existing social conventions to convey their own messages; clearly, clothing worn backwards does not particularly appeal to adults, but it is attractive to teen-agers as a sign of rebellion against adult norms.[14]

In politics, too, clothing matters. The one fact almost everyone remembers about Imelda Marcos was the revelation that she had 3,000 pairs of shoes, for ''nothing has better captured the world's outrage over the excesses of the Marcos regime'' (Ingrassia, 1986, p. D1). Multiples of anything generally indicate wealth, with extreme numbers indicating extreme wealth. A different pair of shoes every day for nearly 10 years no longer connotes wealth; it connotes obscene, conspicuous consumption far beyond what is appropriate or permissible for the wife of the leader of a country. In response to the stories about Imelda Marcos, a source at the Soviet Embassy said that her then Soviet counterpart, Raisa Gorbachev, might have as many as 10 pairs of shoes but no more: ''It couldn't be more because there's no need to have more'' (Ingrassia, 1986, p. D3), embodying a far more correct position to take.

## CLOTHING AS SEMIOTICS

Clothing was one of the first cultural products studied by semiotics. Bogatyrev's early study of national costume influenced the later development of semiotic theory by Barthes by way of Greimas.[15] Bogatyrev was probably the first to explicitly use the metaphor of language: ''In order to grasp the social functions of costumes we must learn to read them as signs in the same way we learn to read and understand languages'' (1937/1971, p. 83). The most elaborate semiotic analysis of any aspect of clothing is provided by Barthes' *The Fashion System* (1967/1983), an analysis of women's fashion as described in French magazines between 1957 and 1963. Theoretically this work focuses primarily on the relationship between the signifier and the signified; Barthes did not study actual items of clothing but rather the verbal descriptions of clothing published in the fashion magazines.

Clothing has often been the example of choice to explain semiotic concepts.[16] It is valuable for its concrete nature and for its familiarity, both of which make difficult theory easier to understand. The model of language has been used more or less literally, depending on the author. Known for her exceedingly literal use of the metaphor, Alison Lurie, in her detailed reading of what a semiotic analysis of clothing should be, searched out ''foreign'' or ''archaic'' ''words'' as she sought direct parallels from speech to clothing (1981, pp. 3–35).[17] An example of a foreign ''word'' is an Arab turban worn with a Western suit; an example of an archaic ''word'' is an Edwardian velvet waistcoat. Because it is unlikely that every single difference truly makes a difference, what, then, does one analyze? In the following passage, Culler used clothing to explain how to tell what is worthy of study in semiotics:

For example, a semiologist . . . who sets out to study clothing in a culture would ignore many features of garments which were of great importance to the wearer but which did not carry social significance. To wear bright garments rather than dark may be a meaningful gesture, but to opt for brown rather than gray might not. Length of skirts might be a matter of purely personal preference, whereas choice of materials would be rigidly codified. In attempting to reconstruct the system of distinctions and rules of combination which members of a culture display in choosing their own garments and in interpreting those of others as indications of a particular life-style, social role, or attitude, the semiotician would be identifying the distinctions by which garments become signs.

Whatever area he is working in, someone adopting the semiotic perspective attempts to make explicit the implicit knowledge which enables people within a given society to understand one another's behavior. (Culler, 1981, p. 32)

Culler's answer to the question of what to study is that we as semioticians include in our analysis whatever conveys meaning to the people we are studying. If they would know how to interpret it, we should also. If it conveys meaning for them and if it makes a difference to them, then it must make a difference to us. The concrete nature of clothing helps make this theoretical point obvious.

## CLOTHING AS COMMUNICATION

It is difficult to avoid conveying information through clothing. In this, clothing is parallel to the nonverbal channels of communication such as kinesic or proxemic behavior traditionally studied by communication researchers. Whatever the position assumed or whatever the distance maintained between people, there is no "neutral" setting. As Kress pointed out, dressing against the code requires no less an understanding of it than following it:

The constraints are set by what I can afford to pay, by the weather, by a decision to conform or to outrage. I can even dress "ungrammatically" by wearing items of clothing that belong to different styles of dress: I could wear a dinner jacket with a pair of tennis shorts, no shirt, and thongs. And yet, both by dressing according to a code and by dressing in contravention of a code I am constrained by the code. The kinds of items of clothing available in any one time in any one culture, even when I combine them in "impermissible" or "creative" ways, still constitute the limits of what I can construct by way of a message. (Kress, 1988a, p. 15)[18]

By its unexpectedness, wearing a dinner jacket without a shirt calls up and gives considerable attention to the absent but expected combination of jacket with shirt; that which is not present, the shirt, becomes more a focus of attention, not less, through its absence. Surprisingly, this is less a hypothetical example than it may appear. In text accompanying photographs of fashions currently worn about New York, the following description is included: "Model Susan Holmes accessorized

her black-tie ensemble with no shirt, a straw bag, a leather cap and boots''
(Donovan, 1992, p. 50). Note that the *lack* of a shirt is termed an accessory.

In clothing, we have ''a veritable map—it does not exaggerate to say—of
the cultural universe'' (Sahlins, 1976c, p. 179), and it would be a pity to under-
utilize a map of such potential value. One research thrust has been to match clothing to personality type (Rosenfeld & Plax, 1977), but a research focus on the individual should not be permitted to override research on social meanings.[19]
Bogatyrev was but the first to point out a substantial social role in clothing choices,
arguing it would be a mistake to assume they are determined entirely by personality (1936/1976a, p. 15). The difference between these two positions is largely one of context: Bogatyrev was writing of traditional folk costumes in Russia
in the 1930s where there was little role for individual choice; Rosenfeld and
Plax were studying the United States in the 1970s, a time and place when it
was assumed individuals had complete choice over their actions. Both positions
are extreme: If Bogatyrev had looked for it, he probably would have found some
individual variation; with greater distance from their topic, Rosenfeld and Plax
might have realized the considerable role played by peer pressure to dress in
particular ways. (At the point when everyone you know wears blue jeans, they
no longer serve as a marker of individuality among peers, though they may still
function as a marker of distinction between generations, as they did in the
1970s).[20]

When people dress, they put on not only clothes but an attitude, a role, sometimes an entire way of life. Thus, it makes sense that some advertisers have
taken advantage of this implication, advertising the attitude as much as the item
of clothing. Recent television ads are noticeable particularly for this; the J. Peterman catalogs stand out as a comparable print example. In their fall 1991 catalog,
titled ''Owner's Manual No. 12,'' the physical characteristics of their Norfolk
wool jacket are barely described, instead they include a story about a beautiful
woman who wore one and a particular relationship for which it came to stand.
A plain white cotton nightshirt is described as ''what Marie-Antoinette wore to
bed''; their goatskin coat with mouton collar is named ''Lindbergh's coat.'' Some
attributions are more obscure: Their plain white silk shirt is positioned under the
name ''Ingrid'' with no last name appearing in the accompanying text, though
there is extensive description. If you don't understand the invocation of Ingrid
Bergman, you shouldn't buy the shirt. If discerning the subject from incomplete
clues makes you feel that you have special knowledge, then perhaps you should
buy that shirt after all. The clothing in their catalog is expensive, sometimes outrageously so, but then they aren't just selling the clothes: you get the attitude,
the history, the story, behind the clothes as well. Presumably those who make
purchases from the catalog consider their money well spent. This example merits
attention particularly because it is normally assumed that people want to create
their own histories for items, not accept someone else's, ready-made.[21]

# CLOTHING: FROM SIGN TO SOCIAL CODE

As single foods rarely convey complete meanings alone but rather in combinations (meals) and in contexts, so do individual items of clothing rarely convey meanings. By appearing in combinations (outfits) and in contexts, the individual items convey meaning through their juxtaposition more than through unique characteristics. As with the study of foods, many authors have emphasized discrete items and their use rather than considering the mid-level analytic category, in this case entire outfits, so obviously some meaning resides even at the lowest level.

Many times a particular item of clothing is separated from its context and discussed in detail as if it were the only item that counted. This happened with bow ties a few years ago when a spate of popular articles appeared debating whether they were the mark of someone who couldn't be trusted or the mark of an independent thinker (Allen, 1986; Conroy, 1986). The better discussions of bow ties placed them into a social context (T. Clarke, 1991; Combes, 1986).[22] In this case, such details as the connections to age (bow ties as a rite of passage) or gender (as a marker of being male), their role as a socializing agent (father taught sons how to tie them), their place in history (they used to be common but now are not), their role in social change (traditionally, only men wore them; more recently, they were adopted by professional women, in a revised silk version, to complement business suits), or the varying allusions they convey to varying audiences (Pee-Wee Herman or Paul Simon) could all be brought up for discussion. Making these sorts of elaboration possible, the value of presenting context is obvious.

Clothing, like food, is a complex system, and many aspects of clothing are available to convey information from fabric (Stacy, 1988; Weiner & Schneider, 1989) to color (Sahlins, 1976a; J. Schneider, 1987), from design (Lurie, 1981) to fit. We can even discuss the act of shopping for clothes, categorizing shoppers as types: the "get-me-the-hell-out-of-here speed gatherer," who thinks clothes-buying is a necessary evil; the "maven," who knows more about clothes than the sales clerk; or "Homer Simpson's cousin," who spends 3 hours agonizing over a tie (Mullen, 1992). The fact that there is so much room for elaboration permits considerable subtlety of meaning whereby conformity in several aspects can be contradicted by creativity in one. As with all social codes, the more knowledgeable the individual, the more meaning he or she can read into its use, and the more minor distinctions are granted social significance.

Clothing clearly serves as a tool in the social construction of self and others. As McCracken (1988) pointed out, clothing works simultaneously in two quite different ways; in both it may be seen as a *concrete manifestation of social reality* (i.e., it makes social reality visible, turning it into a physical reality as well). First, clothing functions as a vehicle to convey *cultural categories* (such as categories of person defined by rank, sex, marital status, occupation, and so forth), *cultural principles* (such as hierarchy vs. egalitarianism), and *cultural processes* (such as rites of passage), all of which are largely collective endeavors where the individual plays a relatively passive role (i.e., as an individual, you participate in your culture's statements and continue them with little chance of stepping outside of the system). Second, clothing functions as a mechanism to convey *individual meanings*, as when clothing is studied for what it conveys about *social distance* (shifts in the tone of a relationship, mood, etc.) as well as what it conveys about *change* (whether confirmation or initiation of such change). Cultural generalizations are particularly difficult to pinpoint. Although obviously significant, social realities lack the concrete grounding that analysts require. In providing a beginning point, a way to study ephemeral social truths through their physical manifestation, clothing serves a valuable function for social analysts. Being capable of carrying social and individual meanings simultaneously, each social actor's construction of self-image through clothing identifies him or her as part of some group while asserting equally some degree of individuality.

As with food, clothing serves as a marker of changes over time. Its role can be quite subtle, serving to not only demonstrate but initiate changes. As an example of the first, Joseph pointed out that the apron, representing the desirable qualities of a housewife, was incorporated into wedding dresses of the 18th century American elite, symbolizing wifely duties and virtues (1986, p. 10). In this case, the changed meaning of the sign indicated something that had already been accepted, a woman's role in the home.[23] Stacy (1988) provided an example of how clothing can more actively initiate change, in her analysis of the current use of tartan by British punk groups to convey new meanings using an old fabric in unconventional ways. She concluded "By mistreating this previously sacred fabric, by wearing it in very unorthodox ways, and by unconventionally combining it with other, unexpected garments, the fabric itself became transformed, and thus its meaning changed" (1988, p. 53). This is an example of how oppositional readings can unhinge what the dominant group had taken for granted were stable meanings.[24] People convey meanings through references to the same items of clothing used in quite different ways by others, or through new combinations of old elements. Thus, meaning conveyed through clothing changes as the meanings people wish to convey change.

The answer to the question of which aspects of clothing are particularly important to study could, presumably, be similar to the answers provided in chapter 4 for food. Issues of identity and social change are certainly basic and essential. The following pages provide a different analysis this time, however, fusing the issues of identity and change into a single discussion.[25] Clothing is the place where individual, private concerns and societal, public ones intersect, the place where we each identify a visible self within the context of the larger community. One reason to expand beyond the discussion of identity and social change in the last chapter is theoretical: since separation of the synchronic and diachronic is ultimately impossible, separating them for analysis may be potentially misleading. Another reason is intrinsic to discussions of identity. Traditionally researchers study identity as if it were stable and simple. In actuality, identity changes over time and across contexts. As Spivak warned, "One needs to be vigilant against simple notions of identity which overlap neatly with language or location" (1990, p. 38). This chapter expands the concept of identity beyond that presented in the last chapter, incorporating issues of social change through a consideration of the ways in which identity serves as the nexus of individual and social group, between private choice and public display.[26]

## CLOTHING AS MEETING POINT OF INDIVIDUAL AND SOCIETY, PRIVATE AND PUBLIC

Clothing works particularly well as the simultaneous demonstration of individuality and of group membership because the choices are individual, yet once made they are visible to all. The food I eat may be eaten alone, conveying no information to a stranger, but the clothes I wear are displayed every time I step into public view, effectively making a statement to any and all who see me. Because people are aware that others gain information from their clothing, they are more likely to engage in deliberate manipulation of the message conveyed through clothing than through other social codes. An example of this is described by Rick Horowitz (1985), considering the effects of pairing bright yellow socks with a proper business suit. The business suit marks the wearer as someone who knows what is expected, yet the yellow socks are recognized as a sign of individuality. The fact that extreme variation occurs only in a minor sign, the socks, rather than consistently, as would be the case if the entire suit were also yellow, indicates the wearer not only knows the rules but also knows just how far they can be bent before the variation is labeled inappropriate.[27]

We use clothing as a vehicle to convey identity; it "establishes *what* and *where* the person is in social terms. . . . when one has identity, he is *situated*—that is, cast in the shape of a social object by the acknowledgement of his participation or membership in social relations" (Stone, 1962, p. 93). In this way clothing mediates between the individual and the group. People become socially significant (interpretable) for one another through the external signs they display. Knowing this will happen, they facilitate that placement through their choice of signs.

As with other social codes, clothing simultaneously marks membership within groups and draws the line between groups. Anyone who wears clothing like that contained in your closet obviously shares some characteristics with you; those who wear clothing considerably different are less obviously similar (Greimas, 1987, p. 193). A variety of group boundaries are marked by clothing distinctions. The following are several fairly obvious ones: religion, gender, age, occupation, social class, sociopolitical boundaries, and relationship status.

## Religion

As is the case with other signs, clothes are polysemic. In fact, one of the values of clothing as a social code is the way in which the individual signs are polysemous, capable of conveying multiple messages depending upon the audience. In the following example, Lawless demonstrated how the same clothing conveys one message to members of a particular group simultaneously with another message to outsiders:

> Pentecostals look different from others in the community because of the dress codes they have adopted. In general, their dress can be characterized as reminiscent of fashionable styles of about thirty years ago. Pentecostal women always wear dresses, and the dresses they wear are usually of somber colors, fall well below the knees, have long sleeves and high necklines. Outside the home, Pentecostal women are most likely to wear shoes with heels and nylon stockings. Especially in the hot summer months, Pentecostal dress is easily recognizable. Pentecostal women wear no jewelry or make-up, and because they are not allowed to cut their hair, their hair either falls down their backs or is piled high on their heads in a 1950-ish "beehive" hairstyle. It is evident that modern fashion does not dictate what Pentecostal women wear or what they look like. Similarly, Pentecostal men will have shorter hair-cuts than other men in the community and will be clean-shaven; it is not uncommon for Pentecostal men to sport a "burr" or "flat-top" hair-cut. Their clothing, too, is recognizable, as they are most likely to "go to town" in black pants, a white shirt, white socks and black shoes. Even Pentecostal young men are not likely to wear blue jeans for fashion, although they may actually work in them.
>
> From the outsider's point of view, the Pentecostal manner of dressing is a mark of the lower-class. Pentecostals are associated with poor people everywhere who wear old clothes out of necessity and who do not sport fashionable hair-styles because of a lack of opportunity or sophistication. But for the adherents of Pentecostalism, dress embodies an entire complex of notions about "holiness" and what a Pentecostal man or woman represents to the rest of the world and to fellow Pentecostals. (Lawless, 1989, pp. 100–101)

Here clothing serves effectively as a marker of group membership in terms of religious affiliation, though it implies differing connotations to those who recognize it than to those unfamiliar with it. Group members simply ignore the public connotations, substituting their own. Thus, individual choices are clearly framed within the norms of the immediate reference group, in this case, a religious organization; norms followed by the larger society are deemed insignificant. The fact that the larger society assumes information about class rather than religion is noteworthy. Many religions advocate simple clothing norms deliberately, eschewing what is fashionable (usually associated with greater expense and thus with a higher social class) for the sake of principle, in order to make a statement about the ultimate irrelevance of class distinctions to religious understandings.

Religious communities choose clothes as identifying markers deliberately, knowing this requires an explicit public statement as to religious affiliation of the individual, something that might otherwise remain a private matter. Sometimes this becomes problematic for the individual who enters a context where such a statement is deemed inappropriate. For example, The Faith United Church of Christ requires that African *kente* cloth be worn by officers in public as in private as an expression of religious faith and ethnic solidarity. District of Columbia Superior Court Judge Robert M. Scott recently denied a lawyer, John T. Harvey III, permission to wear it before a jury on the grounds that *kente* cloth is generally associated with African-American pride, and might cause a predominantly African-American jury to be prejudiced in favor of the African-American client (the lawyer is also African-American; the judge is White). (In this particular example, the lawyer wore a thin strip of *kente* cloth around his suit collar; others may wear *kente* cloth in other forms: ties, stoles, or hats.) Harvey's response was to request assignment of the trial to a different judge (Gaines-Carter, 1992). It is pertinent that Harvey had worn the *kente* cloth in other court appearances, and none of the other judges had objected. *Kente* literally means "whatever happens to it, it will not tear," and *kente* cloth, traditionally worn by West African royalty, is becoming a powerful symbol of African-American pride in the United States (Gaines-Carter, 1992).

In the above examples, members of a particular religious group desire to follow the guidelines, despite the problems this may cause for them when interacting with members of other religions. Alternatively, it is equally possible for individuals to desire to not follow their religion's guidelines despite legal requirements to do so. In modern-day Iran, women are required to be completely covered in compliance with Islamic guidelines for dress. However, some women, wishing to conform to Western fashions, modify the rules slightly, testing the limits of what the system will permit by wearing jean jackets over the traditional *rapoush* or overcoat (a long outer garment which covers a woman from head to toe) adding rhinestone-studded sunglasses, or wearing miniskirts and sheer blouses underneath the *rapoush* (Sciolino, 1992).[28] By so doing, they meet the letter of the law but not the intent.

## Gender

In addition to religion, clothing frequently conveys *gender* information as another way of publicly indicating an individual's role within the larger social realm.[29] People respond to individuals differently because of the way they are dressed; in cultures where gender identity is considered critical information, it is marked clearly through clothing. In such cultures, even babies are not too young for gender marking; "dressing the child in blue invests the child with masculinity; in pink, with femininity" (wrote Stone in 1962, pp. 105–106, describing common practice in the United States 30 years ago as now). Through so simple a matter as color choice, parents change the baby in symbolic terms, making it a member of a particular group. Even so minor a change is significant, for it results in differential treatment: "The pink-clad child is *identified* differently. It is 'darling,' 'beautiful,' 'sweet,' or 'graceful'; the blue-clad child is 'handsome,' 'strong,' or 'agile' " (Stone, 1962, p. 107). Treating gender differences in adults, Helene Roberts (1977) documented the connections between laced corsets and women's roles in the 19th century, when clothing literally defined which activities were possible.[30]

Analyzing gender information conveyed by dress, F. Davis suggested that in the United States today, men have a restricted dress code, whereas women have an elaborated code (1988, p. 32). This fits well with the original conception of elaborated and restricted codes from Bernstein, where the group using an elaborated code could also use a restricted code, but the group using the restricted code had no access to the elaborated one. In parallel terms, women are permitted access to some of the elements of the male dress code (as when professional women wear adapted versions of ties with their adapted business suits), whereas men are unable to utilize most elements of the female dress code with equal facility.

An example of an attempt by men to utilize a traditionally female aspect of dress (not clothing but accessories in this case) is the wearing of one or more earrings, fairly common in the urban United States today. In explaining his own decision to pierce one ear, Douglas Ford suggested that "A feminine detail on a masculine body meant we weren't following the old script" (1986, p. 58). Interestingly, he reported that his explanation of his action varies, depending on audience. Older women accept the fact that it was an exchange—he bought his wife an engagement ring, she bought him a gold earring; older men accept the parallel to tattoos of his father's generation, both being a sign of love and toughness.[31]

As this example demonstrates, rigid gender distinctions in clothing and accessories may be gradually fading. As Barthel pointed out, modern consumer society "invites both men and women to live in a world of appearances and to devote ever more attention to them" (1988, p. 183). My younger male students quite readily report spending as much time shopping as their female counterparts, enjoying it equally; they appear just as knowledgeable about current fashions. At the same time, the current backlash against feminism may lead to a reversal in this trend, reinforcing distinctions once again.

## Age

Equally, clothing serves to publicly mark the relationship of the individual to the group in terms of *age*, demonstrated clearly in Lurie's overview of the ways clothing changes with coming of age (1981, pp. 37–59). Obviously the transition is clearest in cultures where adults and children wear quite specific clothing, visibly different one from the other.[32] Historically, the recognition of childhood as a separate stage of development was associated with the change from children's clothing as identical to adult clothing to distinct styles (Aries, 1962; Ewing, 1977). The large number of mail order catalogs today devoted solely to children's clothing and the popularity of children's clothing specialty stores attest to the increasingly separate role granted children in modern American culture.

Sometimes clothing considered appropriate for adults is adopted by children as a marker of their impending change in social status. Training bras, for example, are sold to young girls who do not yet require them functionally but who want them (or whose parents want them) for the social connotations of maturity and coming of age (McLaughlin, 1989). Other items of clothing serve a comparable role. When I was twelve, all the girls were suddenly enamored of black fishnet stockings, a choice that horrified our parents, who associated them with prostitution. Viewing them as a marker of age and sophistication, we insisted on buying them.

Children are more likely to be given rules to follow for clothing than adults and to try harder to circumvent the rules. The actor Jeremy Irons described how he followed the letter of the rule but not the intent at private school in England: "We had a regulation gray suit and I managed to get mine lined with gold or burgundy material. The school didn't like the lining—they saw it as subversive—but I was wearing their suit, so they couldn't do anything about it" (Lindsay-Hogg, 1991, p. 72). This is a subtle change, playing with the boundary between public (he followed the rules by wearing their suit) and private (he discovered a way to break the rules by adding a lining of his own choice in a place not immediately obvious). As such he made a distinction between their control over his body and their lack of control over his mind, thus maintaining some control over his private self despite their attempts to control his public self.

## Occupation

One of the more obvious ways in which the individual fits within the social group, having a particular social role, is through *occupation*, and clothing often conveys substantial information about one's occupation. Many of the studies conducted in psychology and sociology have focused on this aspect, as did one of the few within communication (Gorden, Tengler, & Infante, 1982).[33] Obviously the considerable popular literature on "dressing for success" assumes a substantial connection between how one dresses and the job one will obtain and keep, as do frequent articles in the popular press (e.g., Dowd, 1991b; Gross, 1986).

The more accurate analysis discovers that there is no one correct way to dress for success. There is, for example, a distinction between what you wear when you want to be considered for a job and what you choose when you actually have it. "As a fast-rising underling, you want to excite. As a CEO, you want to soothe" (Sterba, 1987, p. 7D). In translation: Wear some flamboyant touches while moving up the corporate ladder, so people will notice you but go bland when you reach the top as befits your new standing as a public representative and symbol of the company. Others give the opposite advice: First, demonstrate your ability to fit in as you progress through the ranks; then, once you have been put in charge, do as you like. These contradictory statements indicate the considerable influence of context on behavior, whether clothing or anything else. Ultimately, the only rule is: Discover what the rules are in the contexts of importance to you and how far you can bend the rules without repercussions (or accept the consequences).

## Social Class

Social class is another way to study the place of the individual within the group, and sociologists often look for distinctions in social class made publicly visible through clothing.[34] Generally, the focus of their studies is a single group at a single time period in a single place, a synchronic study.[35] Traditionally, degree of fashionableness has been closely associated with class differences: those who had enough money could buy new clothes frequently, remaining on the cutting edge of fashion, whereas those who lacked the funds had to make do with clothes deemed out of fashion (Polhemus & Proctor, 1978). This has changed to some extent over the past few decades, as a larger percentage of disposable income is spent on clothing and as clothes are more frequently the object of theft, even while worn on the bodies of those who properly own them. Expensive coats, in particular, have changed from displays of wealth to excuses for violence; those who wear them may be displaying the successful theft as a gang initiation (clearly a subversive reading) rather than a high salary (the dominant reading).[36]

As Hebdige pointed out, what distinguishes the clothing (and other) choices of British working class subcultural groups is a willingness to call attention to the conventions of the code rather than taking it for granted. "By repositioning and recontextualizing commodities, by subverting their conventional uses and inventing new ones, the subcultural stylist gives the lie to what Althusser has called the 'false obviousness of everyday practice' " (1979, p. 102). He found Levi-Strauss' concept of *bricolage* valuable for its focus on combining old elements in improvised combinations to generate new meanings (1979, pp. 102–106). Through *bricolage*, old elements are effectively stripped of their original meanings, leaving them available for new meanings. Whether the country's flag is sewn on the back of a parka or converted into a tailored jacket, in either case, it clearly has been rendered incapable of the transparency of meaning usually accorded the flag. New uses require new meanings if and when, by their very existence, they serve to destroy the old.

In punk style, "the most unremarkable and inappropriate items—a pin, a plastic clothes peg, a television component, a razor blade, a tampon—could be brought within the province of punk (un)fashion. . . .The perverse and the abnormal were valued intrinsically" (Hebdige, 1979, p. 107). Through the unexpected combinations of items, punk style makes a statement about the ways in which people make choices or combine old elements in new ways. Dying hair bright red or jet black serves as a comment on the artifice of dying hair in the traditional natural colors. Punk is simply the most obvious of the oppositional subcultures; the underlying critique of social codes as human constructions is certainly valid. Punk style can appropriately be described as "self-conscious semiosis."

## Sociopolitical Identity

Clothing can convey particularly subtle details of sociopolitical identity, useful for potentially complex or contradictory messages. Deshen (1989) provided an example of a rabbi who traditionally wore a traditional white garment to celebrate the High Holy Days (Rosh Hashanah and Yom Kippur) in Tunisia; once in Israel, he changed to the European-styled black suit more commonly worn there. Eventually he had a white suit made for the holidays, as a compromise move, matching the color of one tradition with the design of the other to indicate publicly the dual loyalty he felt privately.

Perhaps the best example of using clothing to publicly express sociopolitical identity is Mohandas Gandhi, who "deliberately used costume not only to express his sociopolitical identity, but to manipulate social occasions to elicit acceptance of, if not agreement with, his position" (Bean, 1989, p. 366). As Bean demonstrated in her excellent case study, Gandhi taught his followers the ability of clothing to transform social and political identities:

> When Gandhi, clothed in loincloth and *chadar* [traditional shawl], was received by the Viceroy Lord Reading in 1921, his followers (and his opponents) also saw that costume can be used to dominate and structure a social event. The most important result of those meetings was that Gandhi, wearing his opposition to English values and representing the people of India, was accepted to negotiate as an equal with the representatives of the British Empire in India. Gandhi forced the Empire to compromise its standards and thus demonstrated the power of the freedom movement he led. (Bean, 1989, p. 373)

By wearing traditional Indian clothing made from traditionally hand-woven cloth, Gandhi communicated his disdain for Western civilization and material possessions as well as his pride in Indian civilization.[37] When Gandhi wore the same clothing to a later meeting (February 1931) with another British representative, it caused an equal stir. No less a figure than Winston Churchill responded to the affront in a speech in England:

> It is . . . alarming and also nauseating to see Mr. Gandhi, a seditious Middle Temple lawyer, now posing as a fakir of a type well-known in the East, striding half-naked up the steps of the Vice-regal palace, while he is still organising and conducting

a defiant campaign of civil disobedience, to parlay on equal terms with the representative of the King-Emperor. (James, 1974, p. 4985)

In the fall of that year, visiting King George at Buckingham Palace, Gandhi reiterated that same point. There was some discussion of whether or not he would even be received at the Palace if he refused to wear appropriate (meaning British) clothing, but in the end he was. Asked later by a reporter if he thought his loincloth correct dress for the Palace, he quipped, "The King was wearing enough for us both" (Shirer, 1979, p. 166).[38] In Bean's terms, Gandhi *wore his opposition to English values*, making that opposition visible to all. By meeting publicly with Gandhi as the representative of India dressed as he chose on these and other occasions, the British, who had previously legislated clothing styles in India, revealed their loss of political power over India.[39]

Gandhi responded in print to the newspaper comments about his clothing choices when he participated in the Round Table Conference in London in the fall of 1931, saying:

> My dress, which is described in the newspapers as a loin-cloth, is criticized, made fun of. I am asked why I wear it. Some seem to resent my wearing it.
>
> When Englishmen visit India, do they forsake their European clothing and adopt our Eastern dress, which is much more suitable to the climate? No. And there is the answer to those who ask why in England I wear the dress to which I am accustomed, the dress of India.
>
> If I came here to live and work as an English citizen, then I should conform to the customs of the country and should wear the dress of an Englishman. But I am here on a great and special mission, and my loin-cloth, if you choose so to describe it, is the dress of my principals, the people of India. Into my keeping a sacred trust has been put. A special duty has been given me to perform. I must, therefore, wear the symbol of my mission. (Gandhi, 1931/1971, pp. 79–80)

But the matter was more subtle and political than he expressly admitted here. Gandhi changed his own clothing as his political needs and understandings changed over the years. To summarize briefly: In 1914, he dressed as an Englishman in a suit. In 1915, he first wore Kathiawari peasant clothing in India, consisting of *dhoti* (loincloth), *angarkha* (robe), upper cloth, and turban, and later wore a loose shirt and pair of trousers. In 1916, he wore a dark-colored prototype of the later "Gandhi cap." In 1919, this had become the white homespun Gandhi cap. As of 1921, he began wearing the *dhoti* alone, primarily because *khadi* (homespun cloth) was scarce and expensive, so it was important to wear as little of it as possible.[40] These choices were all politically motivated and each reflected what was important to him at the time. After 1921, his clothing did not change again, except for the regular addition of a *chadar* (shawl), and the majority of the photographs of him document the combination of *dhoti* and *chadar*.

Gandhi's goal in England in 1931 was to obtain independence for India. By wearing traditional Indian clothing rather than accepting the choices mandated by the British (see Fig. 5.1), Gandhi made his refusal to be part of the British system, governed by the British, visible to all. (This example is actually far more complex than implied here. Briefly, the British forbade the Indians from processing the cotton they grew as a way of supporting British mills. The *dhoti* was a support of village life—as against urbanization—and Indian independence—from Britain—simultaneously.) In conclusion, by accepting the representative of India in the clothing of his choice, the British took the first step toward granting India independence.

## Relationship Status

Gifts of clothing are used frequently to make a statement about the existence or status of a relationship between individuals. They serve this function variously whether given privately or publicly, whether worn privately or publicly. Structurally, relationships fall between individuals and larger groups and, as such, are an excellent topic for investigation when connections between the individual and

FIG. 5.1.    Mohandas Gandhi attending the Round Table Conference in London, September 1931. Courtesy AP/Wide World Photos.

the larger community are at issue. Gifts of clothing are common within close relationships. Understood as a statement about the gift giver's knowledge of the recipient's tastes or needs, they are a statement of level of intimacy. In some parts of the world, the giving of clothing (or special types of cloth) as a gift is highly ritualized.[41] Elsewhere the giving of clothing is more open to individual choice.

Although gifts of clothing generally express closeness, clothing can also be used to introduce distance into a relationship.[42] Imagine the impact of giving a gift of clothing to a close friend or relative, having carefully chosen it to suit your understanding of their tastes, and having it returned. This can be understood as denial of an attempted statement of intimacy. When this happens, distance is introduced into the relationship. There is a related tradition in the modern United States of mothers-in-law giving their daughters-in-law clothing suited not to the recipient's tastes but to the giver's, deliberately chosen to influence the recipient's future choices. This can be understood as an attempt at control by the mother-in-law, visibly demonstrating what she considers correct and appropriate clothing choices. As the implicit critique of the daughter-in-law's usual choices is clearly understood, this technique is far from subtle and usually not altogether successful.

## CONCLUSION

As early as 1847, the *Quarterly Review* argued that clothing was a form of communication: "Dress becomes a sort of symbolic language—a kind of personal glossary—a species of body phrenology, the study of which it would be madness to neglect" (as quoted in H. E. Roberts, 1977). Today most authors take the metaphor of language less literally, yet the comment sounds surprisingly current. Clearly there is still agreement with the sentiment. Clothing is one of the many ways in which people create and exchange meanings in communication; as such, it rewards study.

## NOTES

1. As such, clothing is the likeliest of the three nonverbal codes considered at length in this volume to be included in nonverbal communication texts, if any of them are.
2. Rosencrantz (1972) provided an interesting analysis of her students' clothing awareness and the information they gained from first impressions. See Lennon (1986) for discussion of the role played by clothing in the formation of first impressions generally; also Barthel (1988, p. 62).
3. Even with food, however, there are limits on privacy. There are a certain number of occasions for which it is viewed as appropriate to eat as part of a group, for example, lunch meetings or office parties. The rare person who refuses to *ever* eat in public becomes a source of comments for taking privacy too far.
4. See, for example, Horn (1975), who used the phrase as the title of her book.

5. Some of the current concern with the body as a social phenomenon (Featherstone, Hepworth, & Turner, 1991) incorporates discussion of clothing and fashion (e.g., Emberley, 1987; Wollen, 1987). In such work clothing and/or fashion is considered an extension of the body, a reasonable approach, though different from the one proposed throughout this volume. There is a wide range of publications within anthropology on various aspects of adornment; for examples, see Brain (1979); Mascia-Lees and Sharpe (1992). Finkelstein is a good resource on the commodification of the body; see especially her comments on the various surgical procedures available to change the body that "treat the body as if it were a plastic vehicle to be restyled to suit the individual's wishes and meet the dictates of fashion" (1991, p. 104).

6. Research on fashion has often been closely connected to the study of advertising and marketing, for obvious reasons. Wills and Midgley (1973) provided a good collection of classic writings on fashion; Solomon (1985) is a collection of more current research; E. Wilson (1985) is an excellent historical overview of the role played by fashion in society. Note that Barthes (1967/1983) is a study of fashion rather than clothing more generally. It is interesting that only fashion and not clothing is granted an entry in Sebeok (1986b).

7. Bogatyrev (1937/1971) is a study of traditional folk costumes rather than of clothing in general. Kuper (1973) is another good example of a study of costume in this sense of the word.

8. Polhemus and Procter made the interesting suggestion that fashion "has always been linked with those situations of social mobility where it is possible to be a social climber" (1978, p. 13), thus linking change in fashion quite specifically to the feasibility of change in social status. One of the few communication studies of clothing specifically describes the use of costumes in theater to convey meaning (Seligman, 1974). The classic study of changes in fashion over time is Richardson and Kroeber (1940).

   The following quote by Baudrillard on fashion points to the role played by frequent change:

   > Fashion is one of the more inexplicable phenomena, so far as these matters go: its compulsion to innovate signs, its apparently arbitrary and perpetual production of meaning—a kind of meaning drive—and the logical mystery of its cycle are all in fact of the essence of what is sociological. The logical processes of fashion might be extrapolated to the dimension of "culture" in general—to all social production of signs, values and relations. (Baudrillard, 1981, pp. 78–79)

9. Joseph (1986) provided a thorough study of uniforms, emphasizing particularly the ways in which clothing serves both as metaphor and as metonym. He described how clothing serves as a *total metaphor* when someone borrows symbols for their complete and literal designation (e.g., a CIA undercover agent, not wanting to be unmasked, wears an entire outfit from another role (1986, p. 17)). In describing clothing as *metonymic*, he listed particular items that serve as key symbols: the badge of a police uniform, the cap of nurse, the stethoscope of an intern (1986, p. 21). Metonymy is also at work when minimal symbols are chosen. In these cases, the least symbol necessary to suggest a uniform serves the purpose formerly served by the entire uniform (e.g., nuns today may wear only a ring with a cross on it in lieu of the entire traditional habit (1986, p. 24)).

10. One of the interesting differences between formal and informal uniforms is that it is easier to "lie" with an informal uniform. One merely needs to know where to buy the proper style of business suit and get some advice on appropriate combinations of tie, shirt, and shoes in order to look the part of a well-dressed businessman. (And a lie of this sort is not illegal, as it would be to purchase and wear a formal uniform without authorization.) The more familiar one is with the conventions of a particular informal uniform, the easier it is to discern subtle differences of meaning. For example, the exact type of blouse a woman wears with her formal navy suit can make a big difference in how it is interpreted. Obviously color plays a role here, as does fabric (the difference between silk and cotton, for example, can be very large) and cut (clearly there is a meaning attached to a high versus a low neckline, but there is also meaning to raglan sleeves

versus straight cut). Also, knowledge of the individuals involved can be critical. If I know that you are wearing your standard outfit today, that is interpreted differently from knowing that you are out of uniform. Even slight differences can be understood to convey meaning. Someone who always wears a lot of jewelry is less liable to receive comments on a particular item than someone who rarely does. And the absence of a familiar item (say, a wedding ring) that one has become accustomed to seeing can itself be meaningful.

11. Others stress additional functions. P. Glynn (1982) proposed that the main function of clothing is sexual arousal; Steele (1985) made a similar point. Q. Bell (1976) applied and updated Veblen to a theory of clothing as conspicuous outrage. Gurel (1975) provided a reasonable overview of four functions frequently assumed by a wide range of authors: modesty, immodesty, protection, and adornment.

    Other lists of the ways in which clothing functions abound. R. P. Rubinstein (1985) listed eight functions of clothing (and/or bodily decoration, making no distinction between the two): (a) to separate group members from nonmembers, (b) to place the individual in the social organization, (c) to place the individual in a gender category, (d) to indicate desired social conduct, (e) to indicate high status or rank, (f) to control sexual activity, (g) to enhance role performance, and (h) to give the individual a sense of security (1985, p. 245). An overlapping list is proposed by Roach and Eicher (1979), who treated adornment as aesthetic experience; definition of social role; statement of social worth; indicator of economic status; political symbol; indicator of magico-religious condition; facility in social rituals; reinforcement of belief, custom, and values; recreation; and sexual symbol. A seemingly contradictory function, to hide identity, is also available. For example, the Ku Klux Klan uses clothing to hide identity rather than to reveal it (L. Langer, 1959). In this case, individual identity is thoroughly and deliberately buried in group identity.

    Closely related to the discussion of current function is the discussion of origin. Archaeologists have posited a variety of reasons for the development of clothing: protection from the environment (though this would presume the presence of clothing in extreme environments, and such presence is *not* universal); protection from supernatural forces (still viewed as quite probable); concealing the body out of shame (a theory now thoroughly demolished); efforts to attract attention to the body, particularly to attract sexual interest (not general enough to account for all wearing of clothing); and to indicate status and rank (a major element, though also probably not a general enough rationale to account for all clothing). Schwarz (1979) provided a good summary of the basic argument for each of these positions. As with other attempts to explain origins, a combination of several theories is likely the most reasonable answer.

12. Bogatyrev considered the case of clothing in theater, where clothes are a sign of a sign, not a sign of a material thing (1938/1976c, p. 33). That is, a diamond ring worn by an actor signifies the same thing to the audience regardless of whether it is a real diamond or not, though this would not be true off stage.

13. See also Stone (1962); Kaiser (1985); Lennon and Davis (1989).

14. For discussion of how children learn about clothing not from their parents but from their peers, see Kernan (1973).

15. For discussion of the historical connections, see J. Thomas (1989, pp. 50–51).

16. For example, Barthes (1964/1967, pp. 25–26); Culler (1981, p. 31); Leach (1976, pp. 55–56). See also the satirical piece by MacCannell (1973) on hat tipping, and Manning's (1991) serious analysis of T-shirts, surely a nonserious item of clothing.

17. The fact that a review of Lurie's book in a communication journal recommended it for a place on the cocktail or bedside table rather than the bookshelf is surely significant (Fayer, 1984).

18. After the passage quoted here, Kress remarked that clothing is a simple code in comparison with "the most highly developed and most finely nuanced cultural code, language" (1988b, p. 15), a comment I would dispute. Assuming language to be the most central social code, many researchers have further assumed it is the most complex, but until some of the other social codes have been studied in similar detail, we cannot be sure that it actually is the most complex.

19. Another research possibility has been the study of clothing metaphors as a part of rhetorical style (Adams, 1990), obviously a quite different approach to clothing than that proposed here. This research is closely paralleled to analyses of clothing worn by characters in works of literature (e.g., Baumgarten, 1986; Valverde, 1989; see also Harris & Owens, 1990).

20. Related to research on personality type are discussions of the ways in which people use clothing to convey mood. Some countries have more established conventions for this than others. For example, in Japan, kimonos traditionally served as mechanisms for conveying subtle information about mood and intention (Van Matre, 1992). These were reportedly sufficiently conventional that many people could be relied upon to decode the message as intended.

21. Because clothing conveys geographic information simply by its design or fabric, it is sometimes used to announce that one has traveled, and many tourists choose examples of the clothing worn in the places they visit as souvenirs. Obviously this works only if the clothing is sufficiently different from that worn at home. Often the clothing is substantially different and the additional messages conveyed, such as a lack of understanding of current fashion, are deemed inappropriate, so the foreign clothing remains unworn, conveying its message only to the traveler (Steinberg, 1990).

22. For a contextualization of neckties in general, see Finkelstein (1991, pp. 113-129).

23. Berger presented a comparable analysis of change in a single item of clothing over time. In describing what he termed *denimization*, he proposed that the shift in attitude towards the acceptability of blue jeans indicates a change in attitudes toward work and play (1984a, p. 81). Here the relationship between the clothing and social change is complex; it could reasonably be argued that the rapid acceptance of denim was in part responsible for bringing about change.

24. Collins provided related examples:

> When the punk rocker tears holes in her jeans and closes them with safety pins, or when the fashion designer adds a mink collar to a purposely faded denim jacket, both construct specific signs with quite divergent ideological values—but in each case, the meaning produced is predicated on the violation of the sign's earlier incarnations (e.g., as cowboy work clothes, or cheap, casual dress). (Collins, 1989, pp. 17-18)

25. See Stromberg (1990) for another combination of the study of identity with the study of change: how ideologies work to change identities.

26. Other useful comments on identity come from Feldman (1979), who argued for the idea of "nested" identities. For example, geographically, someone could be a resident of a particular floor in a particular building in a particular neighborhood, suburb, city, state, and country, each identity "nested" within a larger identity. All of these factors together comprise geographical identity; only some are relevant for any particular interaction.

27. Hand-painted fish ties would be another example of permissible deviation from the rules. These are generally worn on only a few occasions by men in otherwise proper business suits.

28. Feldman and McCarthy (1983) provided a fascinating study of the connections between the *burkha*, a garment concealing a woman from head to toe, and mobility of Moslem women in Bangladesh. They argued that the garment increases the ability of women to fully participate in the larger society, thus maintaining rather than diminishing their status.

29. See Hodge and Kress (1988, p. 102) as well as Gottdiener (1977).

30. See also Deborah Warner (1978) on the impact of social reform on women's clothing choices. For further discussion of the connection between clothing and movement, especially the range of behaviors permitted by particular clothes, see Keali'inohomoku (1979). Clothing that followed the lambada dance craze provides another example, for it not only permits specific movements but fits the theme of lambada, described as simultaneously "feminine, sensual, and athletic" (Herman, 1990).

   The inverse is also possible: Clothing particular to specific activities may gain sufficient adherents that the original function is no longer necessary for the clothing to be worn. For example, clothing sold by upscale outdoor catalog companies such as *Patagonia*, is now worn by those who can afford the cost but who do not really need the additional characteristics for which they are paying. If one does not intend to go hiking and rafting, one really does not need supplex nylon (known for its ability to resist tears and dry quickly), but the fabric has a distinctive look and feel, and is now popular, regardless of its intended function. Those who wear these items out of their intended function may be frustrated nature lovers stuck indoors, or may simply be displaying arcane knowledge and conspicuous consumption.

31. For documentation of the way in which piercing a single ear has moved to piercing other body parts and interviews with those who choose to be pierced, see Trish Hall (1991).

32. Lönnqvist (1979, p. 101) described the use of clothing to mark the transition from child to adult among the gypsies of Norway; see also Tamar Horowitz (1982) on the role played by clothing in adolescence.

33. See de Marly (1986) for an extensive discussion of the connections between clothing and occupation.

34. See R. T. Horowitz (1975) for a good introductory bibliography.

35. R. T. Horowitz (1975) provided an example of this approach in analyzing class differences in fashion in Britain in the 1960s.

36. The "coatnapping" that resulted in the murder of the teen-ager wearing the coat someone else desired as described in Tuerina and Edmund (1992) is unfortunately but one recent example of the way in which clothing can become an excuse for violence.

37. The choice of traditional cloth and traditional clothing was not happenstance but critical: The British mandated that India grow cotton but send it to England for weaving and then buy back the finished cloth at great expense. Gandhi wanted to break the cycle by having the cloth woven in India.

38. See Payne (1969, pp. 413–414) for further description of the meeting at Buckingham Palace.

39. For further discussion of Gandhi and the deliberate manipulation of clothing as communication, see Bayly (1986); Merriam (1975).

40. Bean (1989, pp. 366–367) supplied greater detail than that given for each of his costumes here.

41. Gittinger presents one example:

> Among the Batak [of Sumatra] there is a hierarchical structuring that determines the appropriateness of a certain type of gift textile relative to the age and social status of the receiver, and the occasion. The most sacred and prestigious of all textiles is the *ragidup*, a dark cloth with white patterned end panels. This is the most important gift the bride's father bestows upon the groom's mother during the wedding ceremony. It is a statement of the bride-giver's superior status and protective and fructifying role. The *sibolang*, a textile that goes to the father of the groom, has a similar significance. Paralleling these two in relative prestige, but imbued with a slightly different character is the *ragi hotang*, which is the highest-ranked textile to be given to the bride and groom. (Gittinger, 1979, pp. 95, 101)

Note here that tradition prescribes particular types of cloth be given to all of the significant players in the ceremony.

42. This is true of the Tuareg, where men wear veils to create a degree of distance between self and other, a barrier to the intimacy otherwise unavoidable due to the overlapping of social roles in this group (Murphy, 1964).

# Chapter 6

# Objects as Sign and Code

Objects are the most varied and numerous of the social codes, covering the widest range. Anything made by human hands for human purposes can be considered an object, thus the topic is broad, including everything from household items (teapots) to ritual items (candlesticks), from gifts (children's birthday presents) to buildings (houses). Clothing technically fits the description of something made by humans for humans and fits in this category as well, but by convention it is deemed sufficiently important to merit separate consideration. Objects accompany food (the refrigerator it is stored in, the pots it is cooked in, the dishes it is served in, the table it is eaten on), and clothing (the hangers and drawers used for storing the clothes, the objects worn with the clothing called accessories, the suitcases containing the clothes when traveling). And some few straddle the boundary between clothing and object: In which category do masks fit, for example?[1]

Wherever people go and whatever they do, they make objects for their own use. Like food, some objects are physically necessary (shelter to protect from the weather, tools for agriculture, needles for sewing). Objects are a human universal—every group makes some sort of objects for themselves, though the categories vary widely. Some animals are capable of making tools, though none produce the profusion of objects accompanying human settlement. Thus, the term *homo faber*, people as makers and users of objects, is an appropriate appellation.

Unlike food that is consumed and clothing that goes out of fashion or is outgrown only to be discarded, objects are notable for their duration. "The object derives power from its fixity" said Bronner (1986, p. 2). Unless they have been victims of fire or war, most people, no matter how poor, have at least some objects in their possession that have been theirs for years if not decades and value them appropriately. These range from a grandparent's furniture to an uncle's

127

baseball cards, from wedding gifts to a childhood lucky charm. In any case, they serve multiple purposes, at least one of which is to help shape a particular version of the past as people prefer to remember it.

There are many types of objects. An object can be any one of the following: a *tool* (useful for something), a *commodity* (having exchange value), or a *sign* (having social value).[2] Or it can be all of these at once. Obviously objects in their role as signs are of greatest interest in this chapter. Objects are valuable for their connection to the past,[3] for their connection to the supernatural,[4] for what they reveal about the use of technology,[5] or social stratification,[6] but most of all for their ability to make values, ideas, and assumptions concrete. People create objects for their own use, incorporating those meanings of importance to them, yet by their very nature, objects in turn change people, constraining future behavior based on past assumptions.[7] If one buys a table and four chairs, the table and chairs embody an assumption as to how many people one normally expects to feed at one time. Consequently, with growth and change one must replace past, constraining objects with new ones more suited to current choices.

Different, overlapping terms are used in the study of objects. One is *material culture*, the broadest term, that actually refers to any concrete manifestation of culture (food and clothing are included in this broader term), though sometimes used in a way implying a more limited scope. This term already has been used in the Introduction to Part II in accord with its most frequent meaning as a cover term inclusive of all material manifestations of culture and so is not available here for use in the more limited sense of objects alone. A more specific term reserved just for objects, though less common, is *artifacts* (alternately, *artefacts*). Material culture and artifacts have been the terms of choice in folklore, in anthropology, in American civilization studies, and in history.[8] Another term used is *goods*, referring primarily to economic possibilities, viewing objects as commodities to be bought and traded and given away; this usage is preferred by either economists or economic anthropologists.[9] These authors hold that "commodities, like persons, have social lives" (Appadurai, 1986a, p. 3) and take it as their task to study those lives. The more casual term *things* also refers to objects as a category, often as a synonym for whatever more technical term is used first.[10] Conventionally the study of *human habitation* is separated from the study of objects, though it would also fit within the basic definition. Houses, villages, and cities are all important enough to merit their own analysis. Architects, city planners, archaeologists, and occasional folklorists are the primary authors of studies in these areas.[11] My term of choice is *objects*, as the broadest term available.

Like food and clothing, one advantage of studying objects is the range of topics available. This is a complex social code with many parts open to interpretation. From the makers who produce the objects, to the details of the objects themselves including history and cultural variation, to their movement from maker to consumer, to their use in context, there is more than enough material available to study.[12] Kopytoff pointed out that the biography of an object is similar to the biography of a person, thus, the questions one must ask are comparable: What are the possibilities inherent in the period and culture, where does it come from, who made it, what has been its career so far, what is the ideal career for such a thing, how does its use change with age, and what happens when it is no longer useful? (1986, p. 66).

Exemplifying how to follow the biography of an object, Nemy described how a particular bassinet moved in and between a small group of family members and friends over several decades. Such movement is possible because no one really needs a bassinet for more than about 6 months; at that time, the baby has grown and moves on to a crib. So the bassinet becomes available for use with the next baby. In traditional societies with many children in each family, one family might use a bassinet or its equivalent many times; in the modern-day United States it is hardly worth the price of purchase for the one or two children per family. Thus, the bassinet in this story was available for loan to extended family and friends. As this bassinet moved around, it developed a reputation as a good luck charm; more importantly, it served to mark the boundaries of a friendship network. Those included in the network liked the bassinet for that very reason: one of the mothers who borrowed it reported "I liked the idea of something used by friends and friends of friends" (Nemy, 1989, p. Y29).

Other objects serve as a tie between generations rather than across a kin/friendship network. Even so mundane an object as a baseball can serve as a repository of memory. In this case, the issue is not to maintain possession of a particular baseball (for baseballs wear out faster than bassinets and are cheaper and easier to replace) but to remember the act of throwing a baseball between parent and child. As one participant in such a chain reported, "My dad and my boys and I are all linked by this simple act of throwing a round, white ball with raised red seams. We are connected by the arc it travels from parent to child, across generations and time" (Rowen, 1992, p. 24). Clearly here the use of the object, rather than any intrinsic characteristics, makes it memorable.

Sometimes it is neither the object nor its use that is foregrounded but the placement of the object into a collection.[13] A classic example from literature is Laura's collection of glass animals in *The Glass Menagerie* by Tennessee Williams. A surprising number of people have collections, ranging from art objects collected by the wealthy and eventually given to art museums for everyone to appreciate to baseball cards collected by young boys, occasionally sold for profit. Predictably there are age and gender differences in what people collect: "men collect images of power; women collect the diminutive and the domestic" (Salmans, 1989, p. 5F).

In all of these studies, the authors assumed that "things have no meanings apart from those that human transactions, attributions, and motivations endow them with" (Appadurai, 1986a, p. 5). Thus, social scientists study objects not for their abstract aesthetic characteristics but as vehicles capable of conveying human meanings. The social meanings given to objects do not necessarily have any direct connection to their physical attributes, for objects are "only one part—the least ephemeral and most perceptible part—of a dynamic process of human thought and action" (M. O. Jones, 1975, p. 12). It is a mistake to assume that meaning lies in the object itself, for as is the case with the elements of other social codes, objects serve only as the medium through which meaning is conveyed. Objects "are part of the symbolic process that continuously recreates the world by imposing meaning and order on it" (Upton, 1985, p. 87).

## OBJECTS AS SEMIOTICS

Objects have been minimally touched by semiotic theory over the past 30 years and widely ignored before that. Levi-Strauss and Barthes are cited as grandfathers in the field; despite this, their comments are brief, more suggestive than complete. Levi-Strauss considered objects one part of culture, as most anthropologists do now and always have done, mentioning them occasionally but rarely choosing them as the subject of a major discussion. He is generally cited for his concept of *bricolage*, the creation of new meaning through recombinations of preexisting elements, though he emphasized myths more than concrete objects even here (1966b, pp. 16–21).

In his early writings, Barthes used objects as an example of how to apply semiotic theory, much as he used food and clothing; however, they never became a topic in their own right. In a recent publication of a 1964 oral presentation, Barthes gave his most complete comments on objects, pointing out that "there is always a meaning which overflows the object's use" (1988, p. 182). This, of course, is why objects are an appropriate semiotic subject. They serve not merely as physical constructions but as social constructions. There are two other particularly interesting points in this piece by Barthes: (a) He warned specifically against the use of linguistics as a model for the study of objects, suggesting that "the isolated object is already a sentence" (1988, p. 186); and (b) he stressed the polysemous nature of objects, arguing this characteristic is even greater than for other types of signs.

Baudrillard is generally credited with having done the most to analyze objects from the viewpoint of semiotics, developing some of the initial comments by Barthes. He pointed out that objects serve best as a focus for social meanings, not in and of themselves an appropriate focus of study:

> The empirical "object," given in its contingency of form, color, material, function and discourse (or, if it is a cultural object, in its aesthetic finality) is a myth. How often it has been wished away! But the object is *nothing*. It is nothing but the different types of relations and significations that converge, contradict themselves, and twist around it, as such—the hidden logic that not only arranges this bundle of relations, but directs the manifest discourse that overlays and occludes it. (Baudrillard, 1981, p. 62)

Others may not be so willing to describe physical objects as myths, but it is good to be reminded that people react not to the physical object but to its social implications. Because objects so obviously have physical boundaries, it is easy to think of them as discrete units, but their social meanings appear when they are used in connection with other objects, in systems of meanings; thus, it is useful to consider them as myths. Baudrillard's phrase "bundle of relations" appropriately emphasizes the combination of concepts existing in any one concrete object. At one and the same time I may consider the teapot I am using to be functional (it holds the tea), to be aesthetically pleasing (it is beautifully designed), and to be a memory jog (it was a gift from a particular friend). These various meanings do not take away from each other; they join together to multiply the teapot's value for me.

Within semiotics there have been several overviews (Krampen, 1979a, 1979b, 1986; Nöth, 1990, pp. 440–445) and infrequent studies of particular types of objects such as flags (Weitman, 1973) or masks (Ogibenin, 1975), but surprisingly little concerted discussion of what a semiotics of objects would entail and surprisingly few extended case studies.[14] Incidentally, these authors generally do exactly what Barthes warned against, taking the metaphor of language quite literally.

Probably the most suggestive application of semiotic theory to objects is found in the early Russian semiotics of culture, taking objects to be a significant part of the material world, available for study with food and clothing (and numerous other aspects of culture passed over here). Tokarev summarized this approach well, stressing that an object lives through the people who use it: "A material object cannot interest the ethnographer unless he considers its social existence, its relationship to man—to the person who created it and the person who makes use of it" (1985, p. 79). His comments are brief but suggestive; there is apparently an extensive literature yet to be translated into English. In a long list of what has been studied within the Soviet tradition to date, Tokarev included all of the obvious topics: connections between material culture and the natural world, link to economic pursuits, ethnic traditions, geography, gender, age, social structure, class, religion, aesthetics, and social change. He concluded with a reminder to emphasize material objects not as intrinsically interesting creations but in their "social aspect," the ways in which human relations are realized through material objects, particularly the ways in which they serve as a means both of uniting and of segregating people.

## OBJECTS AS COMMUNICATION

The earliest nonverbal communication text, Ruesch and Kees (1956), included an entire chapter on objects. Using photographs to demonstrate their statements, they emphasized primarily the ways in which people arrange objects to display order and disorder, pointing out that people shape their surroundings to introduce order. One characteristic of order is arranging parts into a whole, and their photographs capture different presentations of parts into various wholes. They used the metaphor of language fairly literally, defending it by the argument that the "exchange of messages codified in material terms fulfills all the criteria of language" (1956, p. 89).

Recent collections of readings in nonverbal communication very occasionally include one or two articles on objects. Katz and Katz (1983a), for example, included a brief selection from a book by Michael Korda, discussing the use of objects as status markers in the business world. More recently, objects have been studied within communication as products, looking at the extent to which advertisements successfully imply judgment about people's character traits based on brands (Baran, Mok, Land, & Kang, 1989). Advertisements, of course, are deliberately designed to magically attach social and personal meanings with particular objects and do successfully so function (Raymond Williams, 1980a, p. 185).[15] In addition, there have been a few recent studies of objects as a form of communication within organizations, but these have been as slight in their theoretical conclusions as in their impact on the field.[16] On the whole, objects have been surprisingly little studied within communication, leaving the topic wide open for future research.

## OBJECTS: FROM SIGN TO SOCIAL CODE

The classic study of an object considers a single item, placing it in appropriate context as explanation of its meanings.[17] Even archaeologists, who have only objects available to study but never their users and who therefore traditionally have emphasized physical characteristics over patterns of use, are surprisingly explicit today about their goal being "to explore systematically the linkage between the constitution of social reality and material-culture production and use" (Tilley, 1990a, p. vii). The same is true of historians and art historians.[18] Stott (1987), using Northwest Coast bentwood boxes as her focus, provided an extensive list of which additional information would be necessary to ensure a complete study. Bentwood boxes are noted particularly for sophisticated and difficult woodworking technique; the wood is bent to make the corner rather than joined (see Fig. 6.1). Stott's list of what to study is quite comprehensive, including such ideas as: the relationship between ceremonial functions and social structure, modifications and substitutions over time, and sociocultural change related to boxes as to other aspects of Northwest Coast Indian material culture.[19]

It is intriguing that objects have so much more quickly been placed into a more complete context when searching for their meaning than clothing and food. Perhaps because objects are more physically separated from people, who neither eat them nor wear them, researchers have been able to distinguish themselves from objects, recognizing the significance of not only one object but also a cluster, a group, or a related set.

Even the most mundane objects convey meanings. Describing New York in the 1930s, Irving Howe pointed out, "To read the *News* meant that you belonged, it was a paper for plebeians on the run; to read the *Times* signaled alien yearnings, perhaps some vision of getting away. No one made such things explicit, no one needed to" (cited in Braunstein & Joselit, 1991, p. 15). In a similar vein, Rapoport pointed out, "If I am a 'good' person in the US I have a nice front lawn, in Peru an elaborate front door, in Puerto Rico an appropriate metal grille" (1982, pp. 28–29).[20] If newspapers and front doors convey meaning, how much more might be conveyed by the objects people privilege as important?

The basic question in studying objects, as with other forms of material culture, can be phrased as, "Which information does a culture choose to communicate and to whom?" One reasonable answer proposed is "a community's historic perception of its impelling problems in the context of its value system and its image of the world" and "how, according to the group's experience in the course of time, those problems may be resolved" (Thompson, 1969, p. 332). Thompson suggested that the answers are hidden in the codes of a culture's various symbolic systems; it is the job of the student of culture and communication to translate these codes.

FIG. 6.1   Kwakiutl bentwood box.
In the collection of the Milwaukee
Public Museum, catalog number
17772/4615. Photo by Don Lintner,
University of Wisconsin-Parkside.

Behavior does not always seem to make sense unless attended to in the context of a social code. Glaser presented an example of spending money in order to look like one is not:

> A very funny story is that we were doing this market and the client decided that it was essential to have a concrete floor. Why? Because one of the signals that it is not a fancy place is that you have a concrete floor. They took over an old failed market. It had a perfectly good tile floor. And at a cost of $50,000 they tore up that perfectly good tile floor so that they could reveal the rather crummy-looking concrete underneath! (Glaser, 1985, p. 470)

In this particular instance, the convention of having a concrete floor to connote "cheap market" took priority over the actual (and considerable) expense associated with a tile versus concrete floor. The audience would not have known that the tile floor was already in place and would have assumed that money had been spent to lay it, therefore, the expenditure of money was understood to be necessary in order to signify its opposite: the lack of expenditure of money.

Numerous questions about the use of objects may be addressed; several of these are now briefly considered.

## How Do People Learn to Interpret Objects?

As is the case for the rest of culture, the answer is from many sources: from parents, from mass media, from friends, from schools, and from businesses. This is only a problem when there is a conflict in values and that conflict is made obvious in distinctions between preferred objects (as when a feminist has a daughter who specifically prefers frilly dresses to more functional pants, or when a child of nonviolent parents wants toys associated with violence). "It soon became clear that my child did not want what I wanted him to want. Instead, he wanted what his culture wanted him to want. Other kids would show up at the sandbox with Robocops and Barnyard Commandos. I began to suppose that values are communicated the same way as the common cold" (Ellsberg, 1991, p. 14). At the very least, just as colds are more frequently acquired by children in day care settings than those kept at home because they are exposed to more different cold viruses, so children who are placed together with other children learn new expectations and values from them, including the use of particular objects such as toys.

It is possible to creatively manipulate differing assumptions among various subcultural groups. Van der Veer Hamilton (1991) described how the purchase of a red sports car shortly before her 70th birthday, shortly after her 50th college reunion and her 45th wedding anniversary, served as a statement about psychological youth as opposed to physical aging. That it functioned as such a statement is attributable to the assumption that most people at her point in life drive pale-blue, 4-door Buicks and Oldsmobiles. She was able to communicate psychological youth through an object, in this case through a particular type and color of car, only because of previously existing widespread associations between particular types of people and particular cars.[21] She did not create the context within which her choice makes sense, but if she understands that context she can utilize it successfully to convey information.

## How Are Objects Acquired?

We obtain objects through trade or purchase (exchanging goods, labor, or money in order to acquire new goods, through theft (taking them for ourselves, though they legally belong to someone else), or through gift (others giving them to us). Geary noted that for a long time gift and theft were more significant methods of property circulation than trade because commerce suggests a degree of neutrality that was uncommon before the end of 12th century in Europe; trade "if carried on with one's friends, was base, and if with one's enemies, cowardly" (1986, p. 173). Today, in most of the Western world at least, it is more common for people to purchase what they require than to trade for it or to steal it. Obviously all of marketing, advertising, and public relations is connected to the purchase of objects, and there is a huge literature on all of these topics within communication. However, it is more revealing to discuss gifting behavior, so that is my focus here.

Gifting behavior is particularly of interest in a study of how people communicate through objects, as a mechanism for exchanging meanings. We give objects to each other, exchanging part of our reality for part of someone else's, imposing our assumptions on their expectations. According to Baudrillard:

> In symbolic exchange, of which the gift is our most proximate illustration, the object is not an object: it is inseparable from the concrete relation in which it is exchanged, the transferential pact that it seals between two persons: it is thus not independent as such. It has, properly speaking, neither use value nor (economic) exchange value. The object given has symbolic exchange value. This is the paradox of the gift: it is on the one hand (relatively) arbitrary: it matters little what object is involved. Provided it is given, it can fully signify the relation. On the other hand, once it has been given—and *because* of this—it is *this* object and not another. The gift is unique, specified by the people exchanging and the unique moment of the exchange. It is arbitrary, and yet absolutely singular. (Baudrillard, 1981, p. 64)

The importance of gifts and gifting behavior is such that most people can generally attach a source to all of the objects in their homes that were gifts years and even decades after they have been acquired. The fact of giving is sufficiently a factor in their possession of an object that people will often keep objects for which they have no need or even that they dislike simply in memory of their giving.

People preserve their memories of occasions marked by gifting in photographs, thus maintaining a record for the future. Sometimes they establish a formal tradition of recording who gave what as gifts are opened so the information is properly preserved and appropriate givers are formally thanked later. (As in a wedding shower, where someone generally is designated the task of writing down who gave what in a record book especially sold for that singular purpose.)

People specifically train children in the giving and receiving of gifts through birthday parties, where the ritual of opening gifts in front of the assembled group is a major act within the larger event. Children are explicitly taught that it is the intent to give that counts and not the gift chosen. At the same time, they are often implicitly taught that this is a lie and that the gift itself actually matters a great deal. They can generally be relied on to learn both messages.

In the United States today, the most important gift-giving ritual crosses the boundary between the sacred and the secular worlds. It is, of course, the giving of Christmas presents. In this ritualized behavior, gifts are given primarily within kin networks, functioning as "a method of dealing with relationships that are important but insecure" (Caplow, 1982, p. 391). Thus, Christmas gifts are given to spouses and their family members and to children. In both cases, gifts are "addressed to persons whose goodwill is wanted and cannot be taken for granted" (Caplow, 1982, p. 391). In Goffman's terms, gifts are understood as *tie-signs*, valuable primarily for the evidence they contain about relationships (Goffman, 1971, p. 194).[22]

The classic example of gift behavior widely cited for its apparent contradiction of the modern global economic system is the giving away of wealth among several Northwest Coast Indian groups including the Kwakiutl and the Bella Coola. Lee provided some details of one such ceremony:

> A precisely formulated case of creating value is found in the so-called coppers of the Bella Coola. These are thin pieces of copper of a special shape and size, which are displayed at public occasions, and eventually are destroyed to "make bone" for a returned dead relative. A copper, whose recognized value is known as three hundred dollars is broken in two, or thrown into the fire; its value flows out of it and into the dead. Now the copper, which a minute ago was full of value, is completely empty of value.
>
> Presently the owner of the copper picks it up and gives it to a poor man, who cleans and straightens and repairs it and sells it to a chief for perhaps twenty dollars which can be spent only for acquiring food to be given away publicly. That is, the twenty dollars are given away as a gift to infuse value into the copper, which now contains value to the degree of twenty dollars. The chief now proceeds to increase the value of the copper. Perhaps he gives it a name with the appropriate public display; and gives away fifty dollars to validate the display. He next invites guests, displays the copper, has it passed from hand to hand—has it fully participate in the event—and gives away gifts to the amount of eighty dollars. He does this gradually, for all growth is a matter of time. He cannot merely assign a value to it; nor can

he infuse value into it all at once. Eventually, when enough value has been imbued, so that the copper can function at a dance of the returned dead, the owner flings it in the fire, and again it is emptied of its value.

The white traders quickly spotted the importance of the coppers, and before long had flooded the market with them. They thought of them naturally as having value, or as representing value; perhaps as analogous to our paper money. But the coppers neither had nor lacked value in themselves. They were symbols only in the sense in which the symbol had been presented here; they acquired and conveyed only the value inherent in the situation in which they participated. No one wanted to buy a copper unless he was ready to go through the long and expensive procedure of infusing it with value. So the flood of coppers brought no inflation; the value of coppers neither could rise nor fall, through such manipulation. Being true symbols, they could acquire valid existence and value only through participation in meaningful situations. (Lee, 1964, pp. 84–85)

The conflict described here between a system in which all coppers are understood to have particular value based on their design (the way money obtains its value) and a system in which a copper can only obtain value when particular behaviors and ceremonial requirements have been met reflects substantial differences in cultural assumptions—giving away what has value in order to gain status versus acquiring what has value to gain status (see Fig. 6.2). The Northwest Coast tradition of giving away wealth through the destruction of objects symbolizing wealth is uncommon but not unparalleled. For example, the Sioux give star quilts to honor people and to others on behalf of the honored. When given away, "star quilts bestow respect on both the giver and the receiver" (Albers & Medicine, 1983, p. 131).

There has been less emphasis on theft behavior than on gifting as a form of communication, yet it is also an important resource for social information. Most often, gifting and theft should be understood as social opposites for just as gift behavior encourages social connections, theft generally destroys them. And yet, petty theft may be a rite of initiation among teen-agers in formal and informal groupings, thus demonstrating solidarity within group boundaries while simultaneously demonstrating a lack of identification with other groups (particularly the world of adults).

Sometimes information is gained from what is stolen that could not be easily gained any other way. Hamilton (1990) suggested that far more is learned by discovering which books are stolen from the New York Public Library than by reading best-seller lists. The latter only reveals which books people were willing to pay money for not whether they read them afterwards. The former reveals which books were important enough that someone had to have them; had to have them badly enough to risk fines or even arrest. (On the incomplete list he compiled were the Bible, how-to-books, books on sex, the occult, and antiestablishment books.)

## Which Objects Are Appropriate Choices for Study?

Traditionally, as was the case for food and clothing, the objects most frequently studied to date have been those identified in some way as central, as key symbols rather than peripheral ones. Yet even the most mundane object can be used as a way in to a system of meaning.[23] Any item incorporates in its form some information about maker and user, production techniques, and expected uses. If enough context and background information is known (and this is, of course, critical), any item can be used as the beginning point in understanding an entire way of life. Thus, as with food and clothing, a wide variety of objects used as part of communication in everyday life is appropriate for and available for study.

FIG. 6.2.   Kwakiutl copper. In the collection of the Milwaukee Public Museum, catalog number 16646/4361. Photo by Don Lintner, University of Wisconsin-Parkside.

Of all objects humans create, objects used in changing a house (the physical entity) into a home (the social entity) have attracted the most attention. This is because the home is the location of the largest collection of objects important to people. "The home contains the most special objects: those that were selected by the person to attend to regularly or to have close at hand, that create permanence in the intimate life of a person, and therefore that are most involved in making up his or her identity" (Csikszentmihalyi & Rochberg-Halton, 1981, p. 17). In fact, this is one definition of a home: the place where people are able to surround themselves with symbolic meanings of what is important in their lives. They have more control over what goes into their homes than other objects used in other places, thus, such objects convey more information.[24]

Within the home, the traditional center was the hearth, the fireplace in the middle of a small house serving as physical and social center (Glassie, 1968).[25] In order to be warm in cool climates, people gathered near to the fire, thus, everyone was grouped together in one place in older homes as opposed to the current practice of spreading out in different rooms. It is still quite common for living rooms in Europe and the United States to have fireplaces, though these are now more for display than warmth. Today, the social center of most homes in the United States is the kitchen. Close friends are defined as those who have permission to use the back door, entering directly into the kitchen as family members often do, rather than through the front door into the living room, the place for receiving strangers and other public company.[26]

Objects in the living room have been studied more than those in any other room, because living rooms are the most publicly available of all the rooms in a home, the one most clearly designed for purposes of display and for others to see rather than for family use.[27] Through the placement of furniture and selection of surrounding objects, people display themselves as they wish others to see them (if not, what they display is that they do not care). This includes even choosing appropriate knickknacks.[28] The smallest object in a living room conveys information to visitors about class, values, interests, and family background.

To those familiar with a person and with his or her home, however, even more information is conveyed. Musello (1992) pointed out that in the small community in Pennsylvania he studied, "when someone looks at your home, they are likely to know what shape the building was in when you bought it, they will have followed what you've done, they know how far you have progressed, and they will have an idea about the course it will likely follow in the future" (p. 42). These others may bring more information to their interpretation of your behavior than you yourself have available! You are unlikely to know how the previous owners conducted themselves with regard to the home; you are equally unlikely to know the pattern of normal usage in a community when you first move in and so cannot comport yourself accordingly, whether you wish to or not. In this way, homes become "a social entity constructed in social activity rather than . . . a strictly material one" (Musello, 1992, p. 43).

## Which Meanings Do Objects Convey?

In theory, objects can convey any meaning. They can indicate information about any component of social identity (gender, age, ethnicity, geographic identity, social class, relationship status, etc.). In fact, despite their broad potential, they are most often used and have most often been documented as markers of social status.

McCracken (1988) provided a fascinating dimension in the study of how objects convey social class and status information through his discussion of *patina*, defined as "the small signs of age that accumulate on the surface of objects" (especially on furniture, silverware, and jewelry). He suggested patina functions "not to claim status but to authenticate it. Patina serves as a kind of visual proof of status" (p. 32). In the modern world where anyone with money can buy anything he or she likes, patina serves as the final barrier between the *nouveau riche* and those who have inherited money. Patina physically reproduces the duration of the family's claim to status; it visibly demonstrates that not only this generation but the several generations preceding it were members of the wealthy class.

As McCracken implied, true wealth has often declined to be showy, preferring subtlety. Thus, Paul Mellon, heir to a family fortune matched by few, is described as follows:

> His clothes never call attention to themselves (nor do they ever look quite new). His taste in neckties is in the area of the "winter regimental." No man was ever a greater stranger to designer hand luggage, and it was remarked not long ago that when he has to carry speeches and papers around they come not in zippered containers made of Italian leather but in a brown paper accordion folder with an elastic tie. (Russell, 1991, p. H1)

Those who have grown up with money are taught not to display it unduly, a technique impossible to copy for those who have recently acquired it, for no one will know to attribute wealth to them unless some indication of wealth is provided. Thus is the nondisplay of wealth by the wealthiest the ultimate marker of status, one like patina that gains its significance by the fact that it cannot be copied. If one neither displays wealth nor has a family reputation for wealth, it is impossible to gain a reputation for having wealth.

At the same time, if status claims were made explicitly, they would be deemed offensive in many cultures (such as the modern United States) where major distinctions in status are not supposed to be relevant. Objects are useful socially precisely because "goods communicate their meaning *sotto voce*. This makes them an especially effective and stealthy means for the communication of certain potentially controversial political messages. Communicated through goods, these messages are largely hidden from the conscious awareness of the recipient" (McCracken, 1988, p. 133). This subtlety is more socially acceptable than an explicit (verbal) claim to status through the recent acquisition of wealth would be.

Which particular object(s) conveys social standing most directly changes periodically. Prior to 1950 in New York, it was the piano: "for upwardly mobile and middle-class people everywhere, the 'sweet tones' of the piano had much to do with creating a proper, suitably domesticated, home environment" (Joselit, 1991, p. 36). In the 1980s, one choice among others was an outrageously expensive fountain pen; in the 1990s, it may be the Hermes Kelly bag, a purse selling for between $2000 and $8000.[29] Equally, the same object conveys different meanings over time. Hebdige (1988b) analyzed the changes in meanings conveyed by the Italian scooter cycle from the 1920s to the 1970s, emphasizing the 1950s in Britain.

Objects lend themselves to exploration of many theoretical issues. Of these, only two are described in any detail here: the way in which objects serve to mediate the dialectic between tradition and creativity and the way in which people use *bricolage* to convey new meanings, making new wholes out of old objects.

## OBJECTS MEDIATE TRADITION AND CREATIVITY

Objects often have been assumed to embody the clash between tradition and creativity. On the one hand, objects are part of how traditions are maintained; on the other, they are means through which changes can be introduced. In a wonderful essay describing the different objects in her office and their connections to her own traditions and to those she has studied, Rayna Green pointed to a pair of beaded Adidas as exemplary. "The Beaded Adidas tell me about the recapturing of identity, an active Indian attempt—in the sneaker's case, a Sioux or Dakota attempt—at owning identity. They say 'I am Indian, but on my own terms' " (1989, p. 66; see Fig. 6.3).

Comparably, Spooner investigated Oriental carpets, remarking that no object successfully indicates social status across cultural boundaries, for it is only within cultures that status-granting objects convey meaning. He explained how, con-

FIG. 6.3.　Beaded sneakers by Victoria Firethunder (Lakota Sioux), circa 1988. Courtesy collection of Rayna Green, Washington, DC.

tradicting the American assumption that Oriental carpets serve as a marker of social status, "the Afghan teenager in the new urban middle class seeks authentic American jeans and alligator (Izod) polo shirts." Thus, "while we seek authenticity in their past (as well as in our own), they seek it in our present" (1986, pp. 229–230).

One part of the study of how objects are implicated in the concepts of tradition and change is the adoption of new objects into an old meaning system. Kopytoff rightly pointed out, "what is significant about the adoption of alien objects—as of alien ideas—is not the fact that they are adopted, but the way they are culturally redefined and put to use" (1986, p. 67). Gell provided the example of fishermen in Sri Lanka who accumulate wealth through the purchase of televisions when they have no electricity and garages when they have no cars. Clearly it is not the *use* of these objects that indicates status, as one might assume, but possession alone. This Gell named *adventurous consumerism* (1986, p. 115).

At times the object represents a change only partially accepted by the culture, and subtle means must be found to integrate this new idea into established expectations and conventions. Thus, Diane Douglas investigated the reasons why sewing machines, objects originally placed on a piece of furniture, grew until they became pieces of furniture themselves:

> The sewing machine threatened Victorian domesticity in two ways. Socially it begged the question of the woman's traditional place at home. Ideologically it challenged the notion of home as a refuge from the outer world of technology. In short, it represented problems in both its functional and symbolic impact. How were those problems alleviated in the physical form "sewing machine" equals "furniture"? First, by hiding the sewing machine from obvious view, its function was effectively sublimated. Then, by encasing the sewing machine in furniture, its form was made specifically appropriate to a domestic setting. (D. Douglas, 1982, p. 26)

Through this resolution, sewing machines simultaneously served to make social changes visible as they occurred and to hide these changes from view (out of sight, out of mind) for those who had not yet adjusted to the difference nor considered the implications.

Changes come about due to a shift in roles, as described here for sewing machines, representing a shift in women's roles within the family and the society, but they also come about in other ways. One other source is the interaction between creators and consumers of objects, especially when these do not belong to the same community and do not have identical expectations. Joyce described the minor changes in Amish quilts requested by customers that when added together resulted in the destruction of key aspects of tradition:

> Eager customers have so cajoled them [Amish quilters] over the past twenty-five years, requesting a small change here and another there, that they have slowly but

surely undermined and finally replaced this rich tradition. Gone are those glorious soft wools, the breathtaking geometric patterns, the handsome dark colors for which the Amish quilts of the nineteenth and early twentieth centuries have become so justly famous. Gradually the customer's preference for popular patterns and figured materials and bright colors have become prominent. . . . This evolution, even revolution, in a venerable artistic tradition has been the *direct* result of customer demands. It was not based on any one buyer's desire to erase a long, rich tradition of a people's ethnic and religious aesthetic. There was no malice of forethought, no deliberate subverting of a people's history. To most buyers, a quilt is a quilt. Their stereotype of brightly colored, stylized, polyester figures as the stuff of all good quilts was not meant to rob the Amish women of their artistic heritage. Nor was it designed to relegate them to paper doll figures interchangeable with all the other quilters of the world. But stereotypes do that. The cost of such change is high, yet it is exacted by a buying public quite unaware of the long-term effects of their seemingly small requests for change. (Joyce, 1983, p. 229)

Presumably no one intends to destroy the tradition they are attempting to purchase, for that would devalue it considerably. However, traditions are complex and subject to many tensions; too many minor changes can destroy the whole fabric, as described here.

In contrast to this sort of outside-influenced change, there are also cases of inside-influenced change: those who create new combinations with abandon, refusing to acknowledge the apparent clashes of cultures. As part of a description of a Yup'ik Eskimo woman tanning muskrat skins, a photographer documenting the tradition reported:

Alice tosses the half-tanned skin on top of the television set, where it makes a small picture of the Rivers's world—the importance of the family, of the traditional lifestyle, and of outside influences. The glass plaques that Mattie has given to Billy and Alice show her feelings about them. The muskrat skin is evidence of continued living off the land, as Eskimos have done right here for thousands of years. Mattie's trophy shows that basketball is now a Yup'ik game. And television, like the radio, the school, and the daily planes, brings the outside world in, and encourages Scammon Bay people to travel out. (Jenness & Rivers, 1989, p. 72)

Thus, the dichotomy between tradition and innovation is at times imposed externally by researchers; here Alice and Billy happily combine television with tanned skins, integrating what is new into their existing system, seeing no apparent contradiction to cause problems.

These examples imply the question of how much change a system can endure before it collapses. The answer partially depends on whether the changes are forced (externally) or accepted gradually (internally), thus determining whether the system has a chance to gradually integrate small amounts of the new into the old successfully or not.

## OBJECTS AS BRICOLAGE

The study of how meanings change over time, how people reuse old objects in new ways, is another approach to the analysis of meanings conveyed by objects. Just because their grandmothers considered particular functions appropriate to specific objects, does not mean people cannot introduce changes. According to Joselit:

> As they made the transition from tenement to apartment, functional objects became ornaments. Cherished copper pots formerly used for making gefilte fish now served as planters, while brass candlesticks, no longer in active service as ritual implements, adorned bookshelves. "There is no need for mother's pot in my kitchen," explained one writer; "it has become an emblem of the past, an ornament in my living room."
> (Joselit, 1991, p. 49)

It is no less respectful, and it conveys no less meaning (though it certainly does convey a different meaning) to move a pot from the kitchen to the living room. In similar fashion, traditional toys that once served a primary function as objects of play may later serve instead as a visible display of ethnic identity (Leeds-Hurwitz, 1989, pp. 53–55). The star quilts mentioned at the beginning of this chapter are an example of how traditional items can be used in new ways: parents of basketball players now give them to members and coaches of other teams, as interschool competitions replace intertribal competitions.[30]

It is not solely the attachment of a new meaning to an old object that is of interest here; there is also the creation of a new *set* of objects that when combined, convey new meanings not previously conveyed by any of the objects separately. Two examples are described in some detail here, quilts and scrapbooks, for each metaphorically as well as literally exemplifies the process. In both cases, the physical piecing together of distinct elements into a new coherent whole serves as metaphor for many types of drawing together old elements into a new whole.

Quilts have traditionally been studied as art objects, for their aesthetic qualities, but they are even more interesting for what is learned from studying the details of their creation and their use. Quilts were traditionally pieced together by a group, thus reinforcing community; made of materials taken from clothing previously worn by family members, thus reinforcing family connections; and passed through several generations, thus serving as a visible reminder of the past in the present. In sum, they served as a physical embodiment of family and community, of connection over time.[31] They also incorporated important cultural assumptions, including such basics as understandings of life and death: coffin quilts, for example, incorporated coffins with the names of relatives sewn in the borders, to be moved to a graveyard in the middle of the quilt as people died (Dewhurst, MacDowell, & MacDowell, 1979, p. 100), thus revealing greater ability to think about and visibly document mortality in 19th century America than in the 20th century.

In 1990 the University of Wisconsin System (UW System) commissioned a quilt as the perfect symbol for itself: the individual blocks brought together to form a whole serve as an appropriate metaphor for the way separate campuses are brought together into a single system. Thus is an old form adapted to a new use. It is a tribute to the flexibility of the quilt as metaphor that the old form serves this new function as well as it ever served the old. A university system is successfully compared to a family with the various parts visibly brought together into a single physical entity serving as sign. Putting this quilt on public display (it now hangs in Brittingham House, official residence of the UW System president) confirms the connection between the parts, reaffirming the validity of the new whole that has been created (see Fig. 6.4).

When a photograph of this quilt was used as a holiday card in 1991 by the president of the UW System, the text on the back of the card mentioned several meanings in addition to the obvious (creation of unity out of diversity): the history of the state (all the flowers chosen are wildflowers native to the original prairie, carefully chosen to represent the area of Wisconsin each UW institution serves), the contribution of women to the state (the quilters were all women, part of the Mad-City Quilters), and the connection between the university and the state (the flower chosen for the border is the wood violet, the state flower). Thus, this quilt has an abundance of meanings simultaneously, only some of which are relevant for each portion of the potential audience: its creators, the president of the UW System, those who see it when they visit the president's residence, residents of each community that has a UW campus. Including an image of the quilt in various forms of promotion carries its meanings to an even larger group: those who received the 1991 holiday card, faculty and staff of each UW campus who read an article about the quilt that represents them in a UW System publication (Durham, 1992), and those who saw it included in a photo of the current UW System President, Katharine Lyall, accompanying a newspaper article about her (Vanden Brook, 1993). It is important to note that the quilt as sign moved easily from one president (Kenneth Shaw) to another (Lyall), for it accompanies whoever fills that role rather than any particular individual.

A completely different set of characteristics of quilts was utilized by the Milwaukee County Zoological Society's Intergenerational Quilt Project ("The Fabric," 1992). This project brought together elementary students (who drew animals of the rain forest in their classes) with residents of nursing homes (who turned the drawings into quilt squares). The resulting quilts served many purposes. They were a useful activity for the students and for the nursing home residents independently (the one group learned biology and art, the other built camaraderie and independence), and they served as a bridge between the generations. Finally, because the resulting quilts were auctioned off to benefit the Zoological Society, they served yet another purpose and audience: The zoo gained funds, while a few people purchased a concrete sign of their role as benefactor, presumably for display in their homes.

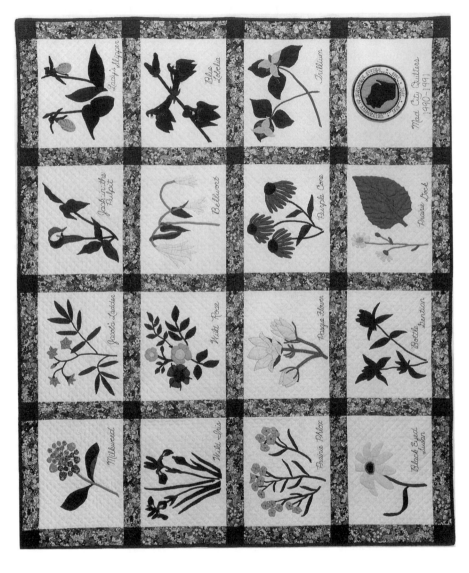

FIG. 6.4.  The University of Wisconsin System quilt. Photo by Jay Salvo, University of Wiscon-

Just as a quilt exemplifies the technique of *bricolage*, so, too, does a scrapbook. Scrapbooks are "a metonymic assemblage of one's social self" (Katriel & Farrell, 1991, p. 5). That is, they provide a place for the detritus of everyday life to be brought together, arranged, and formed into a coherent whole. No matter how confusing and random one's actual life may be, a scrapbook imposes order on the events experienced, so that they may be remembered and retold to oneself and others in a coherent, reasonable manner. As was the case with quilts, scrapbooks create something new and valuable out of what would otherwise be recognized only as trash, having no value or significance, thus strikingly demonstrating that the meaning of objects lies in the wholes created, rather than in the separate parts used in that creation. No one but the creator knows the full story, for that resides in the person rather than in the object.

Both scrapbooks and quilts function in the same way serving as a shorthand for memory, preserving parts of events and lives so that they may be retold later as a performance, imparting meanings to past events and encouraging memories of those past events in future generations. Because of this, neither functions appropriately without a person serving as narrator who understands its history and context. Both can be appreciated, but that is not the same as being understood. If separated from a competent narrator, the scrapbook may or may not be appreciated by later generations for the incidental bits of history preserved; the quilt may or may not be appreciated for its aesthetic qualities. Both impose a new sense of pattern upon seemingly random bits and pieces; however, because the ultimate meaning of that pattern does not reside in the object, human memory and narrative are integral components of the stories told.

There are also differences between these two forms. A scrapbook provides a more flexible conveyance of meanings than a quilt. Scrapbooks are designed to incorporate different media: whereas a quilt can only handle fabric remnants, a scrapbook may include photographs, newspaper clippings, awards, ticket stubs, and birthday cards. And whereas a quilt requires that separate pieces of fabric be sewn together, literally connected, a scrapbook merely requires that they be brought together for joint presentation inside the covers of a single book.

In both cases, the creation of scrapbooks and quilts requires time and energy, and not everyone will take the time to make either. Valuing either is learned through family and friendship networks; those who quilt or maintain scrapbooks influence their relatives and friends to do the same. In both cases, women are traditionally more likely to be the creators, thus saying something about the role played by women as institutional memories and conveyors of tradition, even in modern society.[32]

## CONCLUSION

Objects signify culture by making concepts and assumptions visible. "Objects are references people use to tangibly outline the worlds they know, the ones they try to cope with, and those they aspire to or imagine" (Bronner, 1985b, p. 14).

Objects do not stand alone with their meanings made visible for anyone to see; they are granted meanings by people. These meanings are not revealed unless we as researchers include the people and their use of objects in our investigations. We study objects as one way of investigating the construction of the social world; we learn to interpret objects via the people who give them meaning. Anyone who wishes to study people and the worlds they create can appropriately turn to objects as one beginning point.

## NOTES

1. See Ulrich (1989) for a quite brief but excellent summary of what masks are and how they function. "Masks encourage us to transform ourselves, and empower us to do so. They permit us to replace one reality with another" (1989, p. 9). Napier (1986) provided a longer treatment.

2. See Baudrillard (1981, p. 66) for general discussion of these categories. See Grahame Clark (1986) on the role of particular precious materials (such as ivory, amber, jade, and gold) as status indicators.

3. A detailed listing of possible types of objects by their relationship to the past has been provided by Kirshenblatt-Gimblett: material companions (things that one has for a long time); souvenirs and mementos (things intended to remind of an experience or person); memory objects (things that materialize internal images); collectibles (things collected for themselves, activity future-oriented, not past); ensembles (loosely assembled collection); projects (major effort to do life review); and miniatures (economy of scale with plenum of detail; 1986, p. 329). In a study of which objects serve as cherished personal possessions for the elderly, Sherman and Newman (1977–1978) discovered photographs, religious items (such as Bibles), and symbolic jewelry (such as wedding rings) top the list.

4. Objects are an integral part of religious systems. When we create objects we inadvertently create a physical manifestation of our belief system (Lathrop, 1984). We create meanings for ourselves and for others, often through the same objects at the same time through the power of polysemy. Hole (1977) focused on objects used to protect homes from evil and misfortune, both material and spiritual, looking briefly at a wide variety of examples: horseshoe, lucky hand, and salt among others.

5. Fiddle (1979); Marvin (1988); Rakow (1992).

6. "Thus objects, their syntax, and their rhetoric refer to social objectives and to a social logic. They speak to us not so much of the user and of technical practices, as of social pretension and resignation, of social mobility and inertia, of acculturation and enculturation, of stratification and of social classification" (Baudrillard, 1981, p. 38). Bourdieu (1984) is the classic study of the connections between social class and taste; see also Bronner (1983); P. Cohen (1980).

7. "It is quite obvious that interaction with objects alters the pattern of life; for instance, that refrigerators have revolutionized shopping and eating habits, that automobiles created suburbs and increased geographical mobility, or that television is changing how family members relate to one another" (Csikszentmihalyi & Rochberg-Halton, 1981, p. 14).

8. Among folklorists, see Bronner (1985c). Among anthropologists, see Clifford (1985); Reynolds and Stott (1987); Thompson (1969). Among archaeologists, see Hodder (1982, 1989); Tilley (1990b). Among historians, see Ames (1978); Carson and Carson (1983); Schlereth (1990). Among American civilization studies, see L. Cohen (1980); D. Douglas (1982); Gordon and McArthur (1985).

9. See Appadurai (1986b); Douglas and Isherwood (1979).

10. Csikszentmihalyi and Rochberg-Halton (1981) titled their book *The Meaning of Things*; the word also appears in other titles such as Ferguson's *Historical Archaeology and the Importance of Material Things* (1977) and Appadurai's *The Social Life of Things: Commodities in Cultural Perspective* (1986b).

11. Leone (1977) is an example of how an archaeologist studies a single building for the meanings it conveys. He pointed out that "Every utopian group . . . set out to modify behavior by modifying the physical environment the believers lived in" (p. 56), thus it clearly is useful for analysts of behavior to also study buildings. Gottdiener and Lagopoulos (1986) provided an introduction specifically to urban semiotics; Eco (1973a) provided discussion of semiotics of architecture in more general terms. "Domestic architecture in particular illuminates norms concerning family life, sex roles, community relations, and social equality" (Wright, 1980, p. 1), and so homes are given greatest consideration here. Among folklorists, see M. A. Williams (1991) for her emphasis on the connections between narratives and homes. See also Glassie for the insight that like other objects, buildings are capable of being viewed from the outside but "only architecture can be entered and sensed from within" (1987, p. 236). Among historians, see Hayden (1981), the now classic study of gender and housing.

12. M. O. Jones (1989, p. 251) provided a detailed listing of the major potential categories of study when approaching material culture, divided into technology, producer, consumer, and product-producer interface. There are studies of the makers of objects, for example, Diamonstein (1983) or Spotswood (1975); M. O. Jones (1975) is the classic. Noyes (1989) provided an excellent demonstration of shifting focus from the object to its maker and is particularly good in her use of extensive quotes from those who created the objects she gathered together into a museum exhibit.

13. Danet and Katriel (1989) provided an excellent introduction to the various ways in which collections can be analyzed.

14. There apparently has been more interest in Germany than in the United States devoted to the topic to date. Krampen (1979a) provided extensive citations, stressing in particular the work of Moles, Bense, and von Uexkull, but I have not yet seen this research translated into English.

15. Describing his own efforts as an advertising copywriter, Cadley described the shift in emphasis required, changing a shoe from "a mere lump of leather" into "a footwear statement" (1992, p. 24).

16. Miles and Leathers (1984) and Olson (1985) are typical of this research. Katriel and Farrell (1991) is an exception; it is discussed in some detail here. Katriel's current research (1992) also centers around objects, though her concern is less with particular objects than with their role in museums. Musello (1992) is another exception, in that it is quite strong theoretically, but it is published within a folklore journal by someone now teaching within an anthropology department, so it hardly demonstrates the centrality of the topic to communication. An interesting analysis of the use of building as context in a single television show extends mass communication to the built environment as communication (Goodstein, 1992). Interesting work is being done by the British school of Cultural Studies (Hebdige, 1988a) and may impact the strand of communication study in the United States most heavily influenced by Cultural Studies.

17. For example, Rudofsky (1955) included a fascinating meditation on the history of how people have made use of chairs.

18. As a historian, Wright is typical in her current expansion of what can be learned through the study of buildings:

> There are several ways in which architecture reveals the designer's cultural biases and often those of the larger society as well. When something is built, the process documents underlying structures of work, technology, and economics. It also serves as metaphor, suggesting and justifying social categories, values, and relations. Domestic architecture in particular illuminates norms concerning family life, sex roles, community relations, and social equality. (Wright, 1980, p. 1)

She basically viewed the single family home as the "primary symbol of American cultural values" (1980, p. 294).

19. The complete list follows:

  1. The morphology of bentwood boxes.
  2. The major industry to which the boxes are related.
  3. The relationship of this industry to other major industries.
  4. The relationship of these industries to the economy of the Northwest Coast Indians and to the ecology of the area.

   5. The production of the bentwood box, including materials, tools, techniques and labor.
   6. The relationship between form, production and function.
   7. The relationship between form, production, function and "decoration."
   8. The relationship between the decoration of bentwood boxes and two-dimensional North-
      west Coast Indian art.
   9. The relationship of the two-dimensional art to other kinds of Northwest Coast Indian art.
  10. Characteristics and interpretations of Northwest Coast Indian art.
  11. The relationship between art, society and cosmology.
  12. The distinction between domestic and ceremonial functions of bentwood boxes.
  13. The relationship between bentwood boxes and other containers.
  14. The concept of "container" in Northwest Coast Indian culture.
  15. "Real" and symbolic ceremonial functions of boxes.
  16. The relationship between ceremonial functions and social structure.
  17. Modifications and substitutions over time.
  18. Socio-cultural change related to boxes and other aspects of Northwest Coast Indian
      material culture. (Stott, 1987, pp. 25–27)

I include her list here in its entirety because with a little thought, it might be adapted to provide
a reasonable blueprint for the study of any object.
20. The cross-cultural emphasis on transition or entry points is not insignificant, as Rapoport con-
    tinued (1982, p. 29) by pointing out the frequent use around the world of some sort of physical
    marker of a place where a transition is made (e.g., *Tori* gateways in Japan).
21. Several years ago a student of mine who was a car salesman prepared a guide documenting his
    assumptions about which types of customers were likely to buy which types of cars. For the pur-
    poses of his class assignment, it was a demonstration of how objects serve to indicate social identi-
    ty. For his peers at the car dealership who requested copies, it served as a practical manual for
    newcomers to the job who had not yet consciously figured out all of the connections between visi-
    ble social characteristics and car preferences.
22. The traditional resource on gift behavior is Mauss (1954/1990); see especially the foreword by
    Mary Douglas in this republication (M. Douglas, 1990). For a description of current Canadian
    gifting behavior, see Cheal (1988); for a nice analysis of children's exchanges, see Katriel (1991,
    pp. 167–181).
23. Kress (1988a, p. 7) explained at length the assumptions incorporated into the design and use of
    a garden spade, for example, surely a mundane object.
24. This image of the home as "a personal artistic statement—a symbolic representation of what the
    owner and his wife stood for and valued" was in place by the 1890s in the United States (Clifford
    Clark, 1987, p. 157).
25. For a reminder of the ways in which the entire household revolved around the hearth, see Tay-
    lor's (1991) memoir of childhood in rural Ireland in the 1950s.
26. Discussing New York tenements from 1880 to 1950, Joselit pointed out, "Generally the largest
    space, the kitchen also served as the central point from which the remaining rooms opened. Then,
    again, its centrality was symbolic as well, reflecting the view that the kitchen was indeed the 'hub
    of the home' " (1991, p. 29). See Welsch (1981) for comments on the use of various doors as
    entrance to the home.
27. Living rooms have been studied by sociologists as visible depictions of class distinctions (J. A.
    Davis, 1990; Laumann & House, 1970); by psychologists as a display of composite identity (Csik-
    szentmihalyi & Rochberg-Halton, 1981); by anthropologists as values made visible (Douglas &
    Isherwood, 1979, pp. 5–10); by folklorists as demonstration of ethnic identity and acculturation
    (Teske, 1979).
28. "Knickknacks . . . are highly heterogeneous in stylistic and quality connotations—a Woolworth
    hobnail milk glass or ten-cent-store figurine (low status traditional) is very different from a Steuben
    Glass owl or dolphin (high status modern) or from Royal Doulton and Hummel figures (high
    status traditional)" (Laumann & House, 1970, p. 199).

29. It is interesting to study the imitations of expensive objects and the implications they have for making statements about status. Kazanjian (1991) commented on this issue.
30. The *Wotonia Wonapi*, newspaper for the Fort Peck Reservation in Poplar, Montana, printed a photograph of this exchange, with no accompanying article or author ("Parents of Poplar Indian," 1992, p. 9). My thanks to Sue Glanz for bringing the photo to my attention.
31. Polacco (1988) made this point in a children's book more insightfully than any academic article I have read. She showed how outgrown and worn-out clothing from an immigrant generation was turned into a quilt in order to preserve memories and prompt family stories, following the quilt through various uses over several generations, using it as witness to innovations as well as reminder of traditions.
32. Letty Pogrebin provided one explanation of why this has been so in her discussion of a related role, that of keeper of the family secrets: "Secrets were female currency. While men controlled commerce and the history of nations, women used family history as their negotiable instruments. Knowledge is power, but clandestine knowledge is power squared; secrets could be withheld, exchanged and leveraged as tools of intimacy and woman-to-woman advice" (1992, p. 22).

# From Communication
# Behavior to Semiotic Theory

Part I presented semiotic theory; Part II moved away from theory to the description of actual communication behavior. It is the task of Part III to return from behavior back to theory and to reevaluate as necessary. With this in mind, Part III presents the beginnings of a new discussion emphasizing the *interrelations between codes*, using food, clothing, and objects as examples.

Expanding the study of signs to include the larger groupings known as codes (as proposed in Part I) is more adequate than limiting the investigation to signs alone, but in the end, even this much context for the interpretation of a sign is often insufficient. Certainly social actors do not perceive the world one code at a time; they take other codes into account as well in their efforts to interpret any sign. Only analysts divide the world into individual codes, treating them as separable entities, studying one while simultaneously ignoring others.

Context beyond the code has not previously been recognized as necessary within semiotic theory, so there is no common term available to name a group or set of codes. One term proposed for the set of codes used by a single group is a *culture* (Uspensky et al., 1973, p. 26). Despite the fact that this term has been used by others for other things, such usage conforms to the discussion presented in chapter 1, and it is the term adopted here. Culture is not limited to the definition ''set of codes,'' but most definitions include this meaning among others.

A more obscure term, *semiosphere*, defined by Lotman as describing the semiotic space within which languages [read codes] exist and function (1990, p. 123), has also been proposed and is certainly more unique with the advantage of not being used to describe anything else. However, it means something slightly different from what I intend here: Lotman referred to the *realm* of the semiotic, to the place within which semiotic codes have meaning but not really to the combined whole of semiotic codes, so it is not quite the correct term. Thus I am forced to stay with the over-used term culture.[1]

Part III consists of a single chapter exploring the various ways in which individual codes connect with other codes. It provides the next higher level in the hierarchy of levels presumed throughout this volume: first signs, then codes, then cultures. Each of these is embedded in the others. A sign makes its appearance within a code; a code is but one of many in a culture. At the same time, each word is written in the plural, for no one sign, no one code, no one culture can be studied bereft of its company.

Thus, finally, there is an adequate explanation of the title of this volume. It provides an introduction of semiotic theory to a communication audience, drawing upon the structural resources semiotics provides: from signs (particularly symbols), to codes (particularly social codes) to cultures (beginning with the modern United States for the simple reason that it is closest to hand). Each term is irreducibly plural, for the social world includes not single entities but pluralities and the study of any one sign, one code, one culture, is inadequate for many purposes. Taken together the terms form a hierarchy, a series of analytic concepts increasing in magnitude: signs are a part of codes, codes are a part of cultures. In all cases both cultural variability (I don't eat grubs, but others may) and the common denominators of human behavior (we all must eat to survive) are of specific interest.

If in the end, semiotic theory serves as a useful tool for investigations of how humans create and exchange meanings, then it is valuable to the study of communication. If on the other hand, we as researchers descend to debating the fine points of terminology *ad infinitum*, then it grants us nothing essential. If we use it to study only synchrony, ignoring diachrony, we have not utilized its full potential. If we pretend it is a predictive tool that describes rigid categories leaving nothing to individual creativity, we misinterpret reality. If we assume that we as analysts can either stand outside of the system we study or project our meanings onto others, we mislead ourselves. As with other tools, it is ours to use (or misuse) as we will.

**NOTE**

1. Still other terms have been used by other authors for related meanings. For example, Fleming (1990) referred to the set of artistic genres he considered as a *concert*, a term acceptable for his needs but inappropriate to nonartistic genres.

# Chapter 7

# Cultures

Just as the proper context for understanding a single sign is a code (a set of signs and rules for their use), so the proper context for understanding a single code is a culture (a set of codes and rules for their use). No culture is made up of only a single isolated code, no matter how complex it may be. Different cultures share the basic types of codes they incorporate; language, food, clothing, and objects are only the beginning, but they are all basic codes included in every culture. Initially signs were treated as discrete units for purposes of introduction, but ultimately they must be understood as integrally related. Similarly, codes were presented as separable units for purposes of introduction. Although useful analytically, this is not how they actually exist: *In social life codes are woven together as a coherent whole in intricate and mutually-influencing ways.* Together they make up what is sometimes termed the *social fabric*, a metaphor valuable particularly for its emphasis on the extent to which the various parts of life form a single coherent whole.[1]

"Individual sign systems, although they presuppose immanently organized structures, function only in unity, supported by one another" (Uspensky et al., 1973, p. 1). Just as a sign requires knowledge of the appropriate code for interpretation, so a code requires familiarity with the appropriate culture. For example, the act of drinking tea, when considered alone, conveys but little; understanding the implications of choosing tea over coffee, or water, or beer for members of a particular group conveys a little more. However, eventually tea must be understood in relation to particular objects (the cup, or mug, or glass in which it is presented, the table on which it stands, the implement with which it is stirred, etc.). The person drinking the tea wears particular clothing while holding the cup, or mug, or glass, and so either the objects or the clothes can become a major contributing factor in the event.

**155**

As Glassie (1991) pointed out, "The collection is our key expressive mode. Others make up the parts, but we make the wholes" (p. 264). He spoke here of collections formed within the boundaries of a single code; his statement takes on even greater significance when applied to that most human of activities, bringing elements of different codes into coherent arrangement as a new whole that speaks to us and for us to others. Just as it is a creative act to make a new actuality out of old possibilities within codes, so it is equally (if not more) creative to make a new whole combining and contrasting elements drawn from separate codes. In both cases people participate in an act of creativity through synthesis. We make separable parts that are individually meaningful into new wholes, creating new meanings as we go.

Understanding that codes join together to make up larger wholes (cultures) implies, for purposes of analysis, movement beyond considering any one code alone to a consideration of interrelations between two or more. Ideally as researchers we would always consider *everything* of potential relevance, in this case every social code simultaneously, but that would be mistaking the map for the territory. Enlarging the scope of our analysis to such an extent would obviate analysis, for it would become an impossibility. All we can hope to do is to bear in mind the interactive nature of codes, expanding our consideration accordingly and moving in different directions for each analysis, as seems appropriate depending upon unique circumstances.

For example, in his discussion of American foodways, Camp moved beyond the food itself to include discussion of the ways in which requesting recipes serves as an evaluation of the food:

> The custom of asking the cook who prepared a dish to furnish a copy of the recipe leads to a compiled cookbook that is a more useful record of the acquaintances of the recipient of the recipes than his or her tastes or cooking preferences. Asking for a recipe is a gesture demanded in situations where praise is generally directed toward the cook, and chiming in may not reflect the true judgment or tastes or each recipient of a copy. But, like Christmas cards from distant and seldom-seen relatives, recipe cards once received are difficult to throw away. Various recipes, whether clipped from newspapers or gathered from acquaintances, often find their way to a drawer or filecard box, where they may come to constitute a barely organized social register of a cook and homemaker. (Camp, 1989, p. 98)

Understanding the role of requests for recipes and knowing what happens to recipe cards once they have been given is potentially valuable information in an effort to understand how people give social meanings to food. Researchers learn something new by considering the recipe box as social register, something we would not have known if we had limited our scope to details of food preparation or presentation.

Similarly, cookbooks are an integral part of what people do with food. Cookbooks are demonstrably important: More cookbooks are sold than any other publication except the Bible (Fordyce, 1987, p. 85). In addition, special cookbooks are prepared as fundraisers for organizations, as a record of particular occasions, even in memory of particular individuals. Alan Davidson (1990) commented on the idea of a cookbook in memory of a person:

> There is a custom which I have met only in Thailand, whereby a person composes a small cookbook before her or his death, so that it can be distributed as a keepsake to the mourners attending the funeral. . . .
>
> The idea is attractive. With what better keepsake could one depart from a funeral? What other would equally well keep one's memory green among friends? If one is to issue some sort of posthumous message, avoiding anything egotistical or hortatory, is not a simple message about enjoyable food the best that could be devised? It is true that one could equally compose a list of "books I have enjoyed," but that might seem didactic, even patronising; whereas a little bouquet of recipes arrives on a more relaxed note: "take them or leave them, it's up to you, I just wanted you to have them." (A. Davidson, 1990, p. 27)

Just as researchers learn something new by viewing recipe cards as a social register, we can potentially learn something new by expanding the boundaries of our interest in food to include cookbooks.[2] In the use described by Davidson, cookbooks serve as a *memento mori*, a reminder of the inevitability of death; elsewhere they have other functions. But in all cases they enlighten us more than would consideration of food alone.[3]

The appropriate conclusion to the analysis suggested in previous chapters is the introduction of vocabulary permitting the analysis of the complex interrelations of different codes within a single culture or across cultural boundaries. My goal in this chapter is to provide a series of new vocabulary words for the analysis of progressively larger slices of reality and to appropriately set the topics of investigation into an adequate context. This is a step into unknown territory and must be made tentatively, for this moves beyond what semiotic theory can directly recommend to what it implies but has not previously explored. The semiotic concepts presented earlier do not directly encourage an analysis of connections between codes, giving little guidance to efforts at analysis, nor a statement of generalizations about these sorts of phenomena. By taking this step, it is my intent to achieve a new understanding of what communication involves. For me, this is what communication research can return to semiotics: an extension of the theory in a new direction.

The majority of semiotic theory fails to make this final analytic step, to move beyond the single code to the culture as a whole and beyond to the mutual influences existing among cultures.[4] As was pointed out earlier, semiotic writing tends to the abstract, more often discussing details of terminology than analyzing concrete behavior. Such discussions have not generally required a larger analytic set than the code. In what semiotic literature moves away from abstract theorizing, there is a clear preference for analysis of single signs first and single codes after. There is no theoretical argument against the value of moving beyond codes; neither have there been substantial calls for it. What would then have to be termed ''insubstantial'' calls for such a step are the vague comments or even vaguer implications that the world consists of a set of codes, such as commonly made by Eco and Barthes. These authors implied much of what I state explicitly here, but they never pursue the thought to its logical conclusion. In part due to their fuzzy nature, such calls have been followed up neither by their authors nor by others. The more significant problem, I suspect, is a practical constraint, rather than theoretical: It is far more difficult to study the ways in which multiple codes interact and have mutual influence than to study a single code. As was the case with the study of individual signs, it is probably always easier to study one analytic unit at a time but probably more adequate to study the connections between several.

Communication also has turned away from adequately confronting the problem of mutual influence of codes. Nonverbal communication is the obvious place one might expect to find such research, but it has become accepted practice to study single codes separately, as if they had no mutual influence. Introductory texts reflect this with the standard outline enumerating the major channels (codes) to be covered in a particular book but attempting no final synthesis. Only the studies linking gaze or gesture to speech within interaction provide an exception to the norm, and these rarely show a willingness to increase their scope beyond the two or very occasionally three codes emphasized by the authors.[5] The early research within nonverbal communication certainly took this wider approach for granted, but it did not follow through with an adequate solution to the problem of how to successfully study the multicode nature of communication in all its complexity.[6]

The Russian semiotics of culture approach states most bluntly the mandate to study relations among social codes as they function within particular cultures:

> The view according to which cultural functioning does not occur within any semiotic system (let alone within a level of a system) implies that in order to describe the life of a text in a system of culture or the inner working of the structures which compose it, it does not suffice to describe the immanent organization of separate levels. We are faced with the task of studying the relations between structures of different levels. (Uspensky et al., 1973, p. 25)

Their term system is comparable to my use of the term code; thus, the mandate is to move beyond explanation of how discrete social codes operate separately to a description of the types of connections possible among these.[7] Yet even here there is little explicit discussion of the new vocabulary required to pursue their notions.

Researchers need terms that describe connections among codes and characteristics of multiple codes as mutually influencing. In order to hold this discussion, however, more than the connections among codes needs to be addressed,

for the same concepts function in similar ways across several domains. At least
the following three basic contexts are related and as such can be appropriately
described using the same vocabulary: (a) the connections among codes, (b) the
changes in single codes over time, and (c) the connections among codes of different cultures. Describing the connections among codes is my primary theoretical
concern here, yet if the concepts valuable in that discussion are equally of value
to two other issues as well, they should be incorporated. These three topics are
tightly interwoven due to the similarity in the basic processes to be described.
Much as I hate to increase the semiotic vocabulary list, if new words aid in understanding communication, then they are of value. Thus I reluctantly present
a small set of new concepts to be added to the basic terminology presented previously in this volume.[8]

In the following pages, the basic concepts of *continuity, layering, reinterpretation,
transformation, revival, assimilation, appropriation*, and *syncretism* are described. These
terms are potentially useful in describing connections among codes, changes within codes over time, and connections across cultures. In addition, three forms of
*balance* among codes are proposed: replication, compensation, and selective elaboration. These apply primarily to the study of codes within a single culture.


## CONTINUITY

The concept of *continuity* is the simplest and therefore an appropriate starting point.
Continuity refers to maintenance of the status quo over time: A particular sign
is associated with a particular meaning or meanings within a single culture or
subculture; such meaning remains constant over time.[9] Continuity is the base-
line; if nothing causes a change, then there is continuity. Unless there is deliberate effort to change them, signs will mean the same thing tomorrow that they
meant today. (The question of how this is possible also needs to be addressed;
the brief answer is through teaching the meanings for signs to children and thus
to future generations.)

For example, when a child carries a backpack, or bookbag, or satchel, or brief-
case of some sort to school, it means today what it meant last year. This is a practical solution to the problem of carrying books and lunch from home to school
and back again. As such, it becomes a sign for ''student''; a student has books
and other materials, therefore, through metonymy, the backpack alone indicates
the status of student and/or the activity of going to school. The exact characteristics of the object change over time; the materials, design, and colors are different
over the years, but there is a consistent image of a child carrying school-related
items in some sort of hand-held, fabric/leather/paper/plastic carryall. The image
gains meaning for observers through a mental matching with previous examples;
the child passing my living room window today reminds me of other children, other
days, other years, other cities. I am reassured about the similarities between the

present and the past and encouraged to make assumptions about the likely future. This is the value of continuity: It provides reassurance, insisting that even if some of the details change, the basics will remain dependable.

For the Cuna Indians of Panama, the *mola* (colorful handsewn appliqué) worn by the majority of the women is "a symbol, perhaps the most salient symbol, of Cuna culture, of *Cunaité*" (Sherzer & Sherzer, 1979, p. 1077). All women wear *molas*, regardless of age. Thus, *molas* serve to demonstrate the similarities between young girls and their grandmothers and to function as a sign of connection with the past and continuity into the future (see Fig. 7.1).

When Gandhi emphasized the continuity between past and present traditions in India through his choice of clothing by wearing the *dhoti* (loincloth), this led ultimately to the adoption of the *charkha* (spinning wheel) for weaving the cloth for the *dhoti* as a symbol of independence (Merriam, 1975). Calling for continuity in one social code implied, no, required, continuity in the other. Particular types of clothing require particular types of cloth be available, and spinning was the best way to obtain it. Thus, a decision to wear the *dhoti* had implications not only for the clothing code (not wearing British clothing, for example) but also for the object code (someone had to spin the cloth to make the *dhoti*). Thus, a choice of continuity in one code led to implications of continuity in another.

Yet it would be quite wrong to assume that cultures and codes would remain constant with absolute continuity from one generation to the next if left to themselves. Lotman and Uspensky suggested "the dynamism of the semiotic components of culture is evidently connected with the dynamism of the social life of human society" (1978, p. 223). That is, dynamism (or change) is inseparable from culture; people begin by using what they know as a base and then move ahead by changing it into something new. Thus, there is a need for a series of

FIG. 7.1.   Cuna *mola*. In the collection of the Milwaukee Public Museum, catalog number 58365/19138. Photo by Don Lintner, University of Wisconsin-Parkside.

other theoretical concepts to describe the ways in which signs and codes change over time.[10]

## LAYERING

Buried within the concept of continuity is the assumption that the meaning(s) associated with a particular sign is (are) shared by participants and observers. And yet, signs are polysemous, capable of conveying multiple meanings simultaneously. The concept of *layering* is a logical consequence of polysemy. When an old sign acquires a new meaning yet retains the original meaning as well, that is layering.[11] Layering results primarily either from extended use of a sign over time (so there is opportunity for elaboration) or from multiple audiences using the same sign, attributing different meaning to various characteristics.

When the type (brand, design, color, etc.) of backpacks brought to school is granted particular meaning by the children carrying them, they have added a layer of meaning to the sign. Now it does not only mean an object for carrying other objects conveniently that connects to the related need for such an object in the past and stands in for school and scholar but also conveys information about whether a child is up to date on current styles and colors. *Any* characteristic that is distinguishable to *any* population of users can be used to convey meanings. Thus what to a parent appears to be a display of nearly identical backpacks in a department store is, to a child, a potential minefield. It is no wonder a child spends time thinking about the choice, time the adult may not understand. To a parent, a backpack that seems sturdy is a good value, but the additional meanings conveyed by minor differences in color, material, or design matter to the child who must display the backpack before peers.

When the Cuna *mola* is put on the walls of tourist offices and in the airport, "It signifies that the Cuna are in Panama, part of Panama. . . . No words could say this as well as a *mola*" (Sherzer & Sherzer, 1979, p. 1077). This is another example of layering, of adding meaning to meaning. The *mola* no longer means "the person wearing this item is Cuna" but now, by extension, it means "the place where this *mola* appears is a place where the Cuna live."

Just as an object can be changed from an item of clothing intended to be worn on the body to an art object intended to be put on the wall, an object from the sacred realm can be brought into the secular world; this also results in layered meanings. For example, organs were originally found only in churches, but later moved to parlors, where they retained some of the original connection to the sacred realm but also acquired a new meaning: encouraging social bonding between family and community members who came together to sing (Ames, 1980). These organs were enjoyed in homes in part due to their previous connections to churches; yet the attachment to the sacred was not so great that they could not survive being transposed to a new context, where new meanings would be given primacy.

Any important symbol attracts multiple meanings. The more important it becomes, the more likely it is to attract still further meanings, thus gaining in import;
the process is cyclical. Barthes (1973) considered how this has occurred with the
Eiffel Tower, noting how layer upon layer of diverse implication has been put onto
the same sign over time. His description includes the following meanings of the
Tower: symbol of Paris, modernity, communication, science, metallurgy, trans-
portation, democracy, tourism, subversion, ascension, lightness, plant, animal,
female, and male. He concluded "the Tower is everything that man puts into it,
and that is infinite" (p. 182). The Eiffel Tower is an extreme example, being a key
symbol, but to a lesser extent some layering of meanings occurs for many signs.

Like layering within a single code, layering across codes implies the accumulation of meanings over time. In this case, meanings make sense when matched
to prior meanings not within a code but across codes, thus requiring considerably more cultural knowledge for interpretation. The eventual inclusion of the
*charkha* (spinning wheel) as symbol on the Indian flag is an example of layering
across codes, for it relies upon knowledge of the connections between a particular
item of clothing (the *dhoti*) and a particular object (the *charkha*) if the viewer is
to correctly understand the implication. The spinning wheel signified independence, and thus was appropriately included on the Indian flag, for it referred viewers to a previous statement about independence made by the wearing of the *dhoti*
and its requirement that the *charkha* be available to spin the cloth to make the
*dhoti* (Merriam, 1975) (see Fig. 7.2).

Intertextuality can be described as one form of layering. When applied to multiple social codes, intertextuality implies a metaphoric relationship between a sign
in one social code and a sign in a second. An example is an advertisement for
a car, the Lexus SC400, making use of the tag line "Only your milk should be

FIG. 7.2.  Flag of India.

homogenized.'' Interpreting this ad requires certain knowledge about the processing of milk (homogenization makes all milk the same), implying that a similar process is at work in cars (all cars today have been made to look the same), finally offering this particular car as a solution to the problem of sameness. Implicitly the ad plays upon two additional assumptions: (a) only children drink a lot of milk, whereas adults generally move on to something else; therefore, if you are not a child, you should have outgrown cars that are like milk; and (b) milk is bland, and the adventurous will seek something more exciting; thus a new and different type of car is appropriate (see Fig. 7.3).

## REINTERPRETATION

Over time, a sign having multiple meanings may lose one or more of them. The concept of *reinterpretation* refers to the fact that when multiple meanings operate simultaneously, some of the old meanings may drop out of the system, relinquishing their place to the new. For example, as a child grows older, he or she may be taken camping and may discover a new role for a backpack, that of carrying supplies while hiking. Thus, the previous meanings attached to design may be superseded. Those characteristics considered stylish by peers may be particularly unhelpful when the backpack is actually needed to carry substantial weight, and so the child may change meanings granted the same sign over time. A backpack designed in a teardrop shape, putting the majority of the weight at the waist rather

FIG. 7.3.   Toyota Lexus ad by Team One Advertising. Photograph by Rick Rusing.

than shoulders, may become more valued than one designed as an oval, despite previous preference.

Similarly, *molas* can also be reinterpreted, and can change their primary meanings over time and across space. "Outside Panama, in New York, Paris, or Tokyo, for example, the *mola* no longer symbolizes the Cuna *per se*, but rather 'primitive' craftsmanship, the idea, somehow constantly enlightening in the 'civilized' world, that technologically primitive, non-literate peoples also have art, an art which can be colorful, complicated, and generally attractive" (Sherzer & Sherzer, 1979, pp. 1077–1078). This is reinterpretation rather than a layering of meanings, for the original meaning of "this item indicates Cuna identity" has been lost. No Cuna person need accompany the *mola* to Tokyo; thus, there may be no person nearby to be identified as Cuna when the *mola* is put on display. There is a significant difference between putting a *mola* on display in Panama, where there are Cunas and where a general statement to that effect is understood as having been made, and putting a *mola* on display in Tokyo, where there may be no Cunas around, and no statement about identity can be true.

Similarly, reinterpretation has occurred when the Cuna adapt their traditional appliqué designs to suit the tourist trade. The Milwaukee Public Museum collection includes a jaguar mask made by modifying the traditional technique to an entirely different design. Stretching the traditional boundaries of the category *mola* considerably, this mask, as a non-traditional form, does not make the expected statement about the Cuna identity of the owner, for the Cuna have need of no such masks and do not make them for their own use. A quiet statement about

FIG. 7.4.   Cuna jaguar. In the collection of the Milwaukee Public Museum, catalog number 65951/28220. Photo by Don Lintner, University of Wisconsin-Parkside.

the Cuna identity of the maker is still evident, however, through the maintenance of traditional techniques in the creation of this new object (see Fig. 7.4).[12]

Diderot's story "Regrets on Parting with my Old Dressing Gown" demonstrates how elements of different codes can be related through reinterpretation. After buying a new dressing gown, Diderot discovered that this new item of clothing appeared too elegant for the objects in his study that were older and less fashionable, thus the new purchase implied the consequent replacement of the remainder of his possessions. Finally, after replacing the majority of furnishings in his study, the sole remaining piece, an old braided carpet, took on a new meaning. "It will remind me of what I used to be, and Pride will have to come to a standstill at the threshold of my heart" (1772/1964, p. 313). Thus did changing an item of clothing (the dressing gown) lead to a new significance of an object (the braided carpet) for its owner.

## TRANSFORMATION

On some occasions, an entire sign, not just individual meanings, may drop out of use. If it was no longer needed, this is considered as normal growth and change and there is no need for a particular name for the process. However, if the sign dropped out of the system due to external pressures rather than internal ones, it may still be needed. In this case, a new sign can be granted the old meanings. This is termed *transformation*: the substitution of a new sign for an old. Transformations often occur as a result of emigration from one place to another, accompanied by involuntarily leaving the materials necessary for the production of a sign behind.

Peterson explained how one particular example of transformation occurred within the Hmong communities in the United States:

> Far from the Laotian forests of greening bamboo, a Hmong assembly line worker gathers plastic strapping from a factory floor; later he will weave the strips into baskets for collecting garden vegetables, packing clothing, and storing needlework. The brightly colored baskets circulate within the Hmong community, fulfilling traditional requirements for portability and storage capacity. The Hmong basketmaker has effected a material translation, substituting petroleum-based fiber for the natural resource of bamboo. (Peterson, 1988, p. 107)

Here, the baskets are still needed, but the original material of which they were made, bamboo, is no longer conveniently available due to the resettlement of the Hmong. The new material matches the old for convenience, low cost, pliability, and approximate size (see Fig. 7.5).

Transformation can be required by a variety of changes in context. In this case, the major change was a move from Laos to the United States; in others, it might be destruction of materials or a decision that a particular material is an inappropriate choice. Few Alaskan artists now carve ivory, despite historical precedent, but use synthetic materials or other natural materials in its stead (the use of fossilized ivory being one solution).

A different cause for transformation is the voluntary integration of a new sign into an old system, not because a particular old sign is no longer available, but just because the new one becomes available. Edwards (1982) examined how a single new food (the Western-style wedding cake) has been successfully incorporated into an entirely divergent food system (the Japanese wedding reception), concluding that it was made possible by the transfer of still operable traditional meanings to the new item (the cake represents children and fertility, both meanings previously associated with Japanese weddings). Similarly, Kuper described the use of individual pieces of Western clothing as ornament to traditional dress in Swaziland; the new items were given old meanings, accepted as a new variation on the old theme of decoration. Western skirts were similar to their traditional leather skirts and could be worn by married as well as unmarried women without significantly changing the implied meanings, thus they were adopted fairly quickly into the existing system (1973, p. 356). In whatever system, new items will be added periodically, and a mechanism permitting this must be available.

Transformation as it occurs across the boundaries existing among codes is somewhat different from that occurring within single codes. In this case, the term is

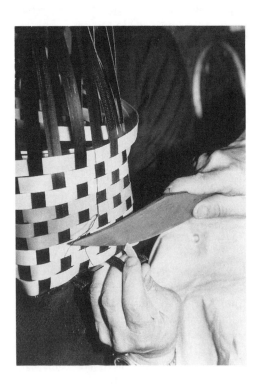

FIG. 7.5.   Chia Ker Lor making a Hmong basket. Photo by Sally Peterson, courtesy of The Balch Institute for Ethnic Studies.

intended to invoke images of a delicate balance between related elements in diverse codes, such that changing a sign in one code implies the need to change a different sign in another code.

The movie *The Breakfast Club* is valuable for its narrow focus on five character types in modern American high schools and for the creative way in which various social codes are used to convey the exact nature of each character. Claire, known as the "princess," has been given diamond earrings by her father. A match for this in terms of food has been found in the sushi her mother prepares for her lunch. In both cases, an implication of money and time spent by parents along with attention to what currently carries weight as a status symbol is successfully conveyed. John, exemplifying the "criminal," is given no objects by his parents; neither is he given food for lunch. Brian, the "brain," has a peanut butter and jelly sandwich, milk, and a thermos of soup for his lunch, successfully indicating the ordinary, the bland, the everyday, the normal, especially in comparison with the other students. Changing any one of these signs would require concatenating changes (transformations) in all of the others, across codes as well as within them.

## REVIVAL

Sometimes a sign is permitted to lapse by one generation, only to be recovered before it has been fully lost by the next. The concept of *revival* refers to the process whereby a sign previously used within a particular group to convey a particular meaning has dropped out of currency, only to be granted new life by a later generation (Isaacs, 1988). Within the United States, revivals are particularly evident between the first and third generations of immigrants. The first generation is so busy becoming acculturated that some traditions are not passed to the second generation; by the third generation the lack is noticed, and attempts are made to recover the tradition before it can be permanently lost. Graves presented an example:

> Pennsylvania German craftspeople and their Pennsylvania German customers consciously reach back to their historical tradition to draw on those artistic and cultural forms which they see as having relevance in today's world. They are rejuvenating forms which were getting "tired," such as hex signs [small hand-painted designs, most often abstract] and *fraktur* [illuminated manuscripts], and they are reviving, bringing back to life, "dead" forms such as decorated chests [furniture with painted designs on the front]. (Graves, 1988, p. 121)

It is more meaningful to bring back a sign that once was valued by one's own ancestors than to make up a new one for modern use, for it has "resonance." Conveying not only the meaning that was lacking, it also reminds modern users of the history invoked, giving them a sense of their own place in the social world.

Susan Stewart described a related concept, what she termed *distressed genres*. Her choice of the word distressed is intended to bring to mind the creation of so-called "new antiques," objects resembling old things but readily recognizable as new. These are similar in function to revivals but are clearly recognizable as imitations of the original forms. Her examples emphasize literary imitations of traditional forms of verbal art such as when authors write their own proverbs, fables, or fairy tales for inclusion in a longer text (1991, pp. 66–101).[13]

## ASSIMILATION, APPROPRIATION, SYNCRETISM

The terms presented thus far (continuity, layering, transformation, and revival) primarily address the use of signs within a single culture. But cultures have permeable boundaries, permitting the movement of signs between and among cultures. The concepts of assimilation, appropriation, and syncretism are all particularly valuable in describing the acquisition and use of signs across cultural boundaries. *Assimilation* refers to the relatively straightforward acquisition of a sign by one culture from another. In this case, the original meaning is generally adopted as well as the sign, more or less completely incorporating a small piece of a foreign culture into the host culture.[14]

For example, pizza has been adopted and thoroughly assimilated from Italy into modern U.S. culture. Over time, it has been gradually changed, both in form and meaning. In Italy today, pizza looks nothing like the U.S. variety, and it holds none of the implications of cheap, fast food, eaten in specialty restaurants rather than in homes, particularly loved by children and teen-agers. Given enough time, the possible variations of an assimilated sign multiply, and it acquires its own traditions. It would be difficult today to remove pizza from the American diet, because it has been so thoroughly integrated into the expectations of the possible.

Sometimes when a sign is acquired, the meanings are changed substantially. *Appropriation* refers to the taking of a sign in use by one culture for a new use in another culture, giving it a new meaning in the process.[15] Unlike assimilation's often positive connotations (one group has a good idea, and another group copies it; imitation being the sincerest form of flattery, the first group does not mind), appropriation often carries negative connotations (a group takes the empty form of another group's signs, ignoring the substance and using the signs in a new way that the originators consider bizarre and inappropriate).

For example, a sacred object may be turned into an aesthetic object through appropriation, as is the case with many museum acquisitions (S. Jones, 1983). This is why many Native American groups today are requesting the return of their sacred objects. It is distressing to see one's own sacred objects treated as aesthetic objects by others, even if no harm or insult is intended. In a complex case of real-life appropriation of religious symbols, the city of Jerusalem is deemed holy by three religious groups (Jews, Christians, and Moslems), though for differing reasons. Each feels the others have appropriated their signs, changing the "real" meaning in the process.

*Syncretism* moves a step beyond appropriation in its integration of signs to address the joint creation of a new set of meanings. This involves the blending of two traditions, so that a new whole is formed, one valued equally by members of both "parent" groups. Given enough time, assimilation and appropriation can lead to syncretism, especially in cultures sharing a physical boundary, thus increasing the likelihood of continued mutual influence. When Native Americans put bead designs on mass-produced sneakers instead of on hand-made moccasins, that is syncretism, the combining of two traditions in new and unique ways. As described by Rayna Green and quoted in chapter 6, this example was positively valued and served as an enticing physical example of how to simultaneously display two identities. However, when similarly beaded sneakers are produced in larger numbers and sold through catalogs, that is appropriation. They no longer indicate an individual's double cultural identity but have been turned into merely aesthetic objects. At the same time, their appeal is largely due to the originally traditional nature of the beadwork, as demonstrated by the following catalog description:

> Always new, forever old. This seeming contradiction best describes the hand-beaded fashions created by Melody Lightfeather, a talented artist who draws her inspiration from her Pima Indian heritage. Melody says her goal is "to preserve an old way in a contemporary time." To do this, she transforms stylish fashions into timeless works of art. It's no wonder she has garnered hundreds of awards for her artistic talents as well as a growing demand for her hand-beaded collection. To meet this welcome demand, Melody now employs many Native American artisans from New Mexico to help with the hand-beading. (*Second Nature*, 1992, p. 32).

Such decorated shoes may still function as an example of syncretism for their designer, Melody Lightfeather, and they may function as an example of syncretism for the various Native American artisans responsible for the hand-beading. But they cannot function as syncretism for those who purchase them if they are a false statement of double identity; they can only function as appropriation (putting someone else's signs to new use). In this case, the appropriation may be intended as positive (a statement of ideological and financial support for Native American crafts, perhaps, especially as these shoes are quite expensive); in other cases, the appropriation may have more obviously negative connotations (see Fig. 7.6).

Moving a step further away from the original meaning of hand-beading commercially produced sneakers, there is at least one additional variant.[16] Imitation hand-beaded sneakers are now available that are *not* made by Native American artisans in the United States but made in China and that are *not* hand-beaded (they are made by machine with long strands of beads sewn to the fabric) and that do *not* follow traditional patterns. In this case, not only is the wearer unable to say "I am Indian" but the maker is unable to say it; not only are the sneakers mass produced but now the beading is as well[17] (see Fig. 7.7).

## BALANCE AMONG CODES AND WITHIN CULTURES

In addition to the previous descriptions, it is possible to describe the various social codes of a culture as being in *balance* in a variety of ways, such that decisions in one directly influence decisions in another. There are at least three forms of balance among codes: (a) they can be in a relationship of *replication* (when one becomes more elaborate, so do the others), (b) of *compensation* (when one becomes more elaborate, others become more simplified), or (c) *selective elaboration* (when one or more codes are emphasized while others are ignored).[18] Each of these is described and illustrated in the following pages.

Replication between or among codes is the most obvious relationship and the one most often expected. It implies that the separate codes move together, in the same direction. If one code is elaborated, so are the others; if one is formal, so are the others. In mainstream American weddings, this leads to the suggestion that the same degree of formality is appropriate in all areas, such that the choice of a traditional long white gown with satin buttons down the back implies particular choices in other codes. Ponce described how the choice of wedding

FIG. 7.6.   Beaded sneakers by Melody Lightfeather. Photo courtesy of *Second Nature* Catalog, a subsidiary of the National Wildlife Federation.

dress impinges upon the wedding cushions (to hold the wedding rings) in a Mexican-American wedding:

> Wedding cushions were not generally sold in stores, nor always in bridal shops. The small pillow-like cushions were made to order to match the material and style of the bride's dress. They were always white and usually made of the identical satin or chiffon worn by the bride. The cushions were trimmed with an abundance of lace, ribbons and soft-pink rosettes. Oftentimes, the bridal couple's initials were embroidered on the cushions with tiny seed pearls. After the wedding, the cushions were stored as a memento. (Ponce, 1989, pp. 64–65)

Note the assumption here that the object (cushions) must match the clothing (bride's dress) exactly, even to the use of the identical fabric.

As another example of replication, D. H. Rubinstein reported that in Micronesia "the geometric principles and problems inherent in measuring canoe length, laying floor supports for large cage-like fish traps, or constructing the sides and roofs of houses, are the same as those embodied by the woven patterns in women's skirts" (1987, p. 68).[19] This is a fairly literal example with the same geometric pattern simply being duplicated from object (canoe) to clothing (skirt). This case demonstrates that once particular designs have been chosen or adopted by a culture, they are often used and reused across codes.

In the modern United States, direct matching of this nature is often assumed to be a mark of additional expense, as when a designer makes draperies out of the same fabric as the sheets, picking up the pattern in the wallpaper as well.

FIG. 7.7. Imitation Indian style beaded sneakers made in China. Courtesy collection of Nancy Osterreich Lurie. Photo by Don Lintner, University of Wisconsin-Parkside.

Knowing that sheets and drapes and wallpaper are traditionally made by different manufacturers, using different fabrics and designs, leads to a connotation of added expense when these match. Although such matching was originally available only to those able to afford customized materials, today it is possible to purchase such elaborately matched materials commercially, through wallpaper stores, for an expensive look without additional actual expense.

A quite different form of balance between social codes is compensation, where increasing elaboration (or formality, etc.) in one code implies decreasing elaboration (or formality, etc.) in another (or, potentially, in several others). This is similar to what G. Bateson has termed *complementary differentiation* (1972, p. 68). Here, two codes remain closely connected, as they were in the case of replication, but one is the inverse of the other; *more* of one results in not more but *less* of the other.

In some family celebrations, food serves as an indication of formality and marker of special event, but clothing is irrelevant. Many of my students have reported upon the elaborate menus prepared by their families at Thanksgiving, yet they insist that no special clothing is expected or even tolerated. Anyone who dresses up in an attempt to match levels of formality between clothing and food would indicate a noticeable lack of appropriate knowledge of family traditions. (New girl/boyfriends brought to the family are frequent sources of such inadvertent mismatches.) Other students reported equally strong family traditions of dressing up for the Thanksgiving meal, noting that anyone who refused to dress up would be guilty of inappropriate behavior (and again, new boy/girlfriends are mentioned as not yet fully competent participants). The first described is an example of compensation; the second an example of replication. Each group of students is quite adamant about the appropriateness of their own assumptions and quite surprised by the differences displayed within even so small a community (most of them live within a few miles of each other).

Due to the complexity of culture, it is possible for both replication and compensation to occur simultaneously. This seems complicated but actually is not. An example makes the point clear. In a description of University of Pennsylvania English professor Paul Korshin, the similarity between his use of food, clothing, and objects was commented upon at length in an article describing his ideas, his classes, and his personality. Hughes provided the following anecdote set in a faculty committee meeting during lunch hour with each member responsible for bringing their own lunch:

> Korshin, resplendent as usual in his custom-tailored London suit, arrived with a wicker hamper, which he placed on the table before him. He opened it up and pulled out a linen napkin, then a half-bottle of claret, then a long-stemmed wine glass, then a fork and knife, and finally a serving dish filled with duck à *l'orange*, which he began serving to himself, ever-so-carefully, onto a china plate. (Hughes, 1991, p. 41)

In this story, what is particularly noteworthy is the simultaneous fit between codes utilized by Korshin as one individual, carefully replicated, and the lack of fit between his usage of these codes and those of the other professors who had lunches consisting of "a paper bag with a cheese sandwich in it, and maybe a piece of fruit" (Hughes, 1991, p. 41). Thus do replication and compensation go hand in hand. The meaning of an individual who has carefully matched his own public display of food, clothing, and objects is reframed when placed in a context of a group where such detailed forethought and such careful matching are considered inappropriate. It is precisely the (knowing and deliberate) lack of fit with peers that makes this episode memorable. If Korshin had simply done what everyone else considered appropriate, there would have been nothing to comment upon.

In some cases, one or two codes are chosen for *selective elaboration*, ignoring the ability of other codes to convey social information equally well. For example, the various sorts of tea ceremonies held around the world clearly emphasize drink and occasional other aspects of food choices; but some also emphasize either clothing or objects as well. Fujioka described the prominence of the objects used in the Japanese tea ceremony, most significant of which is the tea bowl: "Because of the tea bowl's importance, assembling a collection of fine pieces has always been one of the primary pursuits of tea masters" (1973, p. 15). Other items utilized include the water jar, whisk, tea scoop, caddy, ladle, waste-water jar, and lid rest. The actual ceremony is strictly choreographed: the host cleans the bowl, whisk, caddy, and scoop; tea is placed in the bowl, whipped to a froth with the whisk; the tea is slowly consumed by one guest at a time; the guests examine the utensils and discuss their makers; they may examine the few decorations in the tea hut (a flower or scroll); then they leave.

In contrast to the emphasis placed on the objects used in serving tea in Japan, Steele (1988) described the clothing women wore in late 19th century Paris for a particular event labeled "le five o'clock tea."[20] Certainly special china and silver were expected, but the clothing became the focus of attention. A wide range of possibilities was permissible, so long as there was greater elaboration than usual and a large number of frills, often accompanied by gloves and hat (see Fig. 7.8). In both cases, the act of drinking tea takes on particularly subtle shades of meaning when placed into appropriate context. In Japan, the tea ceremony developed as a ritualized celebration of the everyday performed by men, where actions were more important than words and conversation was rigidly limited to discussions of immediate context. In Paris, the 5 o'clock tea was an occasion for a group of women to get together and talk generally, with few limits on topic. Wearing a silk teagown with frills appropriate to a Parisian tea would no more be considered appropriate in Japan than using a tea bowl and whisk appropriate to a Japanese tea ceremony would be deemed appropriate in Paris. More subtly, elaborating upon clothing in place of objects in Japan or objects in place of clothing in Paris would be perceived by those with local knowledge as equally inappropriate.

## CONCLUSION

Jane Young (1991) suggested that the most powerful cultural images are polysemous or multivalent, for they are ambiguous and open to manipulation. (Thus,
layering increases flexibility, whether within or across codes.) I would agree, but
would expand her comment. When several of the concepts outlined here operate
concurrently within a single context, meanings are multiplied, and the event grows
in implication. That is why we may react strongly to the sale of Chinese imitation
Native American beaded sneakers or a jaguar mask made using traditional techniques but sold only to tourists. These are complex signs, conveying information
on several different levels simultaneously. And that is why the story about Korshin is memorable for multiple competencies are displayed simultaneously. Ambiguity permits participants to find certain connections more significant
(meaning-filled) than others, revising the decision as context changes.

The ideas presented here can be applied to various subcultures within the United
States as to various cultures around the globe. They can be applied to any social
codes, not only the three described in some detail in these pages. They should
help make sense of any event, whether large or small, public or private, formal

FIG. 7.8.  "The Cup of Tea" by
Alfred Stevens, circa 1874. Courte-
sy of the Musée royal de Mariemont
(Morlanwelz, Belgium).

or informal, planned or spontaneous, sacred or secular. Yet what has been presented so far is only a beginning, not an end. The theoretical concepts presented in
this chapter have never been brought together previously and require further consideration before it is certain which are most useful and which must be reconsidered.

## NOTES

1. This conception of culture as composed of a series of interrelated codes is not substantially different from the assumptions of structural anthropology, as put by Levi-Strauss (1963, see particularly pp. 95–96).
2. A. Davidson considered the implications of creating a funeral cookbook outside the Thai cultural
   framework, even writing down his "gloomy imaginings" of how such cookbooks would likely
   be received by his friends after his death (1990, p. 28).
3. Another example of extending beyond food to a particular aspect of context is Staub (1989), where
   the restaurant within which the food is sold and the people interacting in the restaurant become
   the focus of attention.
4. Anthropology makes this move theoretically with ethnographies presenting a culture as a set of
   related systems; however, in practice, each system (code) by tradition is described in a separate
   chapter with limited discussion of the influence any one has on the others. In order to find calls
   for study of the connections among codes within cultures one needs to return to early anthropology and the emphasis placed by such authors as Margaret Mead and Ruth Benedict on the discovery of cultural patterns. However, much of that early work was either more superficial in its
   understanding or less well-integrated than one might wish. Anthropologists then as now often
   shy away from consideration of how the various codes within a single culture are related, opting
   instead to emphasize one to the exclusion of the others. This is a reasonable temporary solution
   to the problem of cultural complexity, but it means that the ultimate goals of first, understanding
   a culture in its totality and second, understanding connections among cultures have been set aside,
   to be met in the indefinite future.
5. Goodwin (1981), Heath (1986), and Kendon (1990) are all good examples of the combination
   of several nonverbal channels into a single analysis.
6. See Leeds-Hurwitz (1987) for further discussion. Intercultural communication may yet grapple
   theoretically with the interface of multiple codes. One promising route is Edward Hall's suggestion that there are high-context cultures and low-context cultures (1984, pp. 59–77), a concept
   that if followed to its logical conclusion, brings one to a comparison of codes not only within but
   across cultures.
7. Elsewhere in the same article these authors also hint at the need to study the connections among
   cultures, though they provide no details of what this would entail (Uspensky et al., 1973, p. 5).
8. Whenever possible, I have adapted terms from those already available for related purposes and
   identified my source.
9. I have specifically borrowed the term from Thompson and Cornet (1987, p. 93), though it is in
   common usage with much the same implication.
10. For further discussion, see Leeds-Hurwitz and Sigman with Sullivan (in press).
11. I have taken the term from Glassie (1991, p. 264).
12. Conquergood (1992) included a stunning example of reinterpretation, though it was not described
    as such. One of his photographs was of a Barbie doll dressed in *pa ndau* [flower cloth], the tradi-
    tional Hmong appliqué technique. Just as with the Cuna jaguar discussed here, a statement about
    the cultural identity of the maker is implied but has been detached from any comparable state-
    ment about the identity of the user.

13. Hobsbawn and Ranger (1983) addressed a similar concern when they described the creation of a false past, though they are more interested in the ways this functions to promote group cohesion than in detailed analysis of what has been created.

14. I take this term from the colloquial usage.

15. I have taken the word most directly from Nicholas Thomas (1991), though it is in wide colloquial use as well.

16. My thanks to Nancy Oestreich Lurie for calling this example to my attention; such shoes were actually given to her by a Native American friend who knew of her interest in traditionally beaded sneakers and are included in this volume as illustration.

17. See Wieder and Pratt (1990) for further discussion on demonstrating one is an Indian among Indians.

18. The word replication is used by D. Rubinstein (1987) in much the same sense I intend it here. This is similar in some ways to what G. Bateson means by symmetrical differentiation (1972, p. 68). Martindale (1990, 237 ff.) referred to cross-genre influences within the arts as "synchrony."

19. Another example is the match between naming behavior and use of buildings: when naming behavior became more informal in the rural United States, guests began entering these same homes by the back door rather than the front door directly into the kitchen and the food instead of the parlor (Welsch, 1981).

20. This is the French version of the British custom of taking high tea at 5:00 p.m. For some reason the time has been kept as an integral part of the event's name, leading to potential confusion when "le five o'clock tea" is scheduled for a different hour.

# References

Abrahams, R. (1985). Equal opportunity eating: A structural excursus on things of the mouth. In L. K. Brown & K. Mussell (Eds.), *Ethnic and regional foodways in the United States: The performance of group identity* (pp. 19-36). Knoxville: University of Tennessee Press.

Ackerman, D. (1990). *A natural history of the senses.* New York: Random House.

Adams, J. C. (1990). Linguistic values and religious experience: An analysis of the clothing metaphors in Alexander Richardson's Ramist-Puritan lectures on speech "Speech is a Garment to Cloathe Our Reason." *Quarterly Journal of Speech, 76,* 58-68.

Adler, T. (1981). Making pancakes on Sunday: The male cook in family tradition. *Western Folklore, 40,* 45-54.

Albers, P., & Medicine, B. (1983). *The hidden half: Studies of Plains Indian women.* Lanham, MD: University Press of America.

Aldrich, S. P. (1985, March 17). Breakfast gravy: Northerners just don't know what they're missing. *The Milwaukee Journal,* Wisconsin Magazine, p. 27.

Alexander, R. (1990, April 29). Metropolitan diary. *The New York Times,* p. Y19.

Allen, H. (1986, February 5). Ok, Smarty: What's the story behind your bow tie? *The Milwaukee Journal,* p. B2.

Ames, K. (1978). Meaning in artifacts: Hall furnishings in Victorian America. *Journal of Interdisciplinary History, 9,* 19-46.

Ames, K. (1980). Material culture as non-verbal communication: A historical case study. *Journal of American Culture, 3,* 619-641.

Anderson, E. N. (1988). *The food of China.* New Haven: Yale University Press.

Anderson, J. A. (1971). Scholarship on contemporary American folk foodways. *Ethnologia Europeae, 5,* 56-63.

Anderson, J. A. (1990). Preface. *Communication Yearbook, 13,* 11-15.

Appadurai, A. (1986a). Commodities and the politics of value. In A. Appadurai (Ed.), *The social life of things: Commodities in cultural perspective* (pp. 3-63). Cambridge: Cambridge University Press.

Appadurai, A. (Ed.). (1986b). *The social life of things: Commodities in cultural perspective.* Cambridge: Cambridge University Press.

Appleby, J. (1990). In search of Benjamin Franklin. *The Pennsylvania Gazette, 89,* 35.

Aries, P. (1962). *Centuries of childhood.* New York: Random House.

Arnott, M. L. (Ed.). (1975). *Gastronomy: The anthropology of food and food habits*. The Hague: Mouton.

Arnott, M. L. (1983). Philadelphia bread re-assessed. In A. Fenton & E. Kisban (Eds.), *Food in change: Eating habits from the Middle Ages to the present day* (pp. 34-40). Glasgow, Scotland: John Donald Publishers in association with the National Museums of Scotland.

Aune, J. A. (1983). Beyond deconstruction: The symbol and social reality. *Southern Speech Communication Journal, 48*, 255-268.

Bailey, R. W., Matejka, L., & Steiner, P. (1978). Preface. In R. W. Bailey, L. Matejka, & P. Steiner (Eds.), *The sign: Semiotics around the world* (pp. vii-viii). Ann Arbor: Michigan Slavic Publications.

Bakhtin, M. (1971). Discourse typology in prose. In L. Matejka & K. Pomorska (Eds.), *Readings in Russian poetics: Formalist and structuralist views* (pp. 176-196). Cambridge, MA: MIT Press. (Original work published 1929)

Bakhtin, M. (1981). *The dialogic imagination*. (C. Emerson & M. Holquist, Trans.). Austin: University of Texas Press.

Balducci, G. (1976). Umberto Eco in New York: An interview. *Communication Quarterly, 24*, 35-38.

Baran, S. J., Mok, J. J., Land, M., & Kang, T. Y. (1989). You are what you buy: Mass-mediated judgments of people's worth. *Journal of Communication, 39*, 46-54.

Barrows, S., & Room, R. (Eds.). (1991). *Drinking: Behavior and belief in modern history*. Berkeley: University of California Press.

Barthel, D. (1988). *Putting on appearances: Gender and advertising*. Philadelphia: Temple University Press.

Barthes, R. (1967). *Elements of semiology*. (A. Lavers & C. Smith, Trans.). New York: Hill and Wang. (Original work published 1964)

Barthes, R. (1972). Steak and chips. In R. Barthes, *Mythologies* (pp. 62-64). New York: Hill & Wang.

Barthes, R. (1973). The Tour Eiffel. In J. Bryan & R. Sauer (Eds.), *Structures implicit and explicit* (pp. 163-184). Philadelphia: University of Pennsylvania Press.

Barthes, R. (1979). Toward a psychosociology of contemporary food consumption. In R. Forster & O. Ranum (Eds.), *Food and drink in history: Selections from the Annales: Economies, societes, civilisations* (Vol. 5, pp. 166-173). Baltimore, MD: Johns Hopkins University Press. (Original work published 1961)

Barthes, R. (1982a). *A Barthes reader*. S. Sontag (Ed.). New York: Hill & Wang.

Barthes, R. (1982b). Food decentered. In *Empire of signs* (pp. 19-22). New York: Hill & Wang.

Barthes, R. (1983). *The fashion system*. (M. Ward & R. Howard, Trans.). New York: Hill & Wang. (Original work published 1967)

Barthes, R. (1988). *The semiotic challenge*. (R. Howard, Trans.). New York: Hill & Wang.

Basso, K. H., & Selby, H. A. (1976). *Meaning in anthropology*. Albuquerque: University of New Mexico Press.

Bateson, G. (1972). *Steps to an ecology of mind*. New York: Chandler.

Bateson, G. (1979). *Mind and nature: A necessary unity*. Toronto: Bantam.

Bateson, G., & Mead, M. (1942). *Balinese character: A photographic analysis*. New York: New York Academy of Sciences.

Bateson, M. C. (1984). *With a daughter's eye: A memoir of Margaret Mead and Gregory Bateson*. New York: Morrow.

Bateson, M. C. (1989). Language, languages, and song: The experience of systems (1968). In R. W. Rieber (Ed.), *The individual, communication, and society: Essays in memory of Gregory Bateson* (pp. 129-146). Cambridge/Paris: Cambridge University Press/Éditions de la Maison des Science de l'Homme.

Bateson, M. C. (1990). *Composing a life*. New York: Penguin.

Baudrillard, J. (1981). *For a critique of the political economy of the sign*. St. Louis: Telos.

Bauman, R., & Sherzer, J. (Eds.). (1974). *Explorations in the ethnography of speaking*. New York: Cambridge University Press.

Baumgarten, M. (1986). Clothing and character. In D. N. Miller (Ed.), *Recovering the canon: Essays on Isaac Bashevis Singer*. Leiden, Netherlands: Brill.

Bayly, C. A. (1986). The origins of *swadeshi* (home industry): Cloth and Indian society, 1700-1930. In A. Appadurai (Ed.), *The social life of things: Commodities in cultural perspective* (pp. 285-321). Cambridge: Cambridge University Press.

Bean, S. S. (1989). Gandhi and *khadi*, the fabric of Indian independence. In A. B. Weiner & J. Schneider (Eds.), *Cloth and human experience* (pp. 355-376). Washington, DC: Smithsonian Institution Press.

Bell, A. R. (1990). Separate people: Speaking of Creek men and women. *American Anthropologist, 92*, 332-345.

Bell, M. (1983). *The world from Brown's Lounge: An ethnography of Black middle-class play.* Champaign: University of Illinois Press.

Bell, Q. (1976). *On human finery.* London: Hogarth.

Ben-Amos, D. (1977). The context of folklore: Implications and prospects. In W. R. Bascom (Ed.), *Frontiers of folklore* (pp. 36-53). Boulder: Westview.

Berger, A. A. (1984a). Denimization. In *Signs in contemporary culture: An introduction to semiotics* (pp. 80-82). New York: Longman.

Berger, A. A. (1984b). Foods as signs. In *Signs in contemporary culture: An introduction to semiotics* (pp. 170-172). New York: Longman.

Berger, A. A. (1984c). Signs and identity. In *Signs in contemporary culture: An introduction to semiotics* (pp. 95-103). New York: Longman.

Bernstein, B. (1966). Elaborated and restricted codes: An outline. In S. Lieberson (Ed.), *Explorations in sociolinguistics* (pp. 126-133). Bloomington: Indiana University Press.

Bernstein, B. (1975). *Class, codes and control.* London: Routledge & Kegan Paul.

Birdwhistell, R. L. (1970a). *Kinesics and context: Essays on body motion communication.* Philadelphia: University of Pennsylvania Press.

Birdwhistell, R. L. (1970b). Social contexts of communication. In *Kinesics and context: Essays on body motion communication* (pp. 95-98). Philadelphia: University of Pennsylvania Press.

Birdwhistell, R. L. (1972). A kinesic-linguistic exercise: The cigarette scene. In J. J. Gumperz & D. Hymes (Eds.), *Directions in sociolinguistics: The ethnography of communication* (pp. 381-404). New York: Holt, Rinehart & Winston.

Blaxter, M., & Paterson, E. (1983). The goodness is out of it: The meaning of food to two generations. In A. Murcott (Ed.), *The sociology of food and eating* (pp. 95-105). Hants, England: Gower.

Blumer, H. (1969). *Symbolic interactionism: Perspective and method.* Englewood Cliffs: Prentice-Hall.

Bogatyrev, P. (1971). *The function of folk costume in Moravian Slovakia.* (R. G. Crum, Trans.). The Hague: Mouton. (Original work published 1937)

Bogatyrev, P. (1976a). Costume as sign. In L. Matejka & I. Titunik (Eds.), *Semiotics of art: Prague School contributions* (pp. 13-19). Cambridge, MA: MIT Press. (Original work published 1936)

Bogatyrev, P. (1976b). Folk song from a functional point of view. In L. Matejka & I. Titunik (Eds.), *Semiotics of art: Prague School contributions* (pp. 20-32). Cambridge, MA: MIT Press. (Original work published 1936)

Bogatyrev, P. (1976c). Semiotics in the folk theater. In L. Matejka & I. Titunik (Eds.), *Semiotics of art: Prague School contributions* (pp. 33-50). Cambridge, MA: MIT Press. (Original work published 1938)

Botscharow, L. J. (1990). Paleolithic semiotics: Behavioral analogs to speech in Acheulean sites. In M. L. Foster & L. J. Botscharow (Eds.), *The life of symbols* (pp. 63-79). Boulder: Westview.

Bourdieu, P. (1980). The aristocracy of taste. *Media, Culture, and Society, 2*, 225-254.

Bourdieu, P. (1984). *Distinction: A social critique of the judgment of taste.* (R. Nice, Trans.). Cambridge, MA: Harvard University Press.

Brady, I. (Ed.). (1991). *Anthropological poetics.* Savage, MD: Rowman & Littlefield.

Brain, R. (1979). *The decorated body.* London: Hutchinson.

Braunstein, S. L., & Joselit, J. W. (Eds.). (1991). *Getting comfortable in New York: The American Jewish home, 1880-1950.* Bloomington: Indiana University Press.

Brennan, T. (1991). Social drinking in Old Regime Paris. In S. Barrows & R. Room (Eds.), *Drinking: Behavior and belief in modern history* (pp. 61-86). Berkeley: University of California Press.

Bringeus, N. (1981). The thrive-bit: A study of cultural adaptation. In A. Fenton & T. M. Owen (Eds.), *Food in perspective: Proceedings of the third international conference on ethnological food research, Cardiff, Wales, 1977* (pp. 31–55). Edinburgh, Scotland: John Donald.

Bronner, S. J. (1983). The house on Penn Street: Creativity and conflict in folk art. In J. M. Vlach & S. Bronner (Eds.), *Folk art and art worlds* (pp. 123–149). Ann Arbor: UMI Research Press.

Bronner, S. J. (Ed.). (1985a). *American material culture and folklife: A prologue and dialogue.* Ann Arbor: UMI Research Press.

Bronner, S. J. (1985b). The idea of the folk artifact. In S. J. Bronner (Ed.), *American material culture and folklife: A prologue and dialogue* (pp. 3–39). Ann Arbor: UMI Research Press.

Bronner, S. J. (1985c). Visible proofs: Material culture study in American folkloristics. In T. J. Schlereth (Ed.), *Material culture: A research guide* (pp. 127–153). Lawrence: University Press of Kansas.

Bronner, S. J. (1986). *Grasping things: Folk material culture and mass society in America.* Lexington: University of Kentucky Press.

Brown, L. K., & Mussell, K. (1985). Introduction. In L. K. Brown & K. Mussell (Eds.), *Ethnic and regional foodways in the United States: The performance of group identity* (pp. 3–15). Knoxville: University of Tennessee Press.

Brown, W. R. (1978). Ideology as communication process. *Quarterly Journal of Speech, 64*, 123–140.

Brummett, B. (1979). Gary Gilmore, power, and the rhetoric of symbolic forms. *Western Journal of Speech Communication, 43*, 3–13.

Brummett, B. (1980). Symbolic form, Burkean scapegoating, and rhetorical exigency in Alioto's response to the "Zebra" murders. *Western Journal of Speech Communication, 44*, 64–73.

Brummett, B. (1981). Gastronomic reference, synecdoche, and political images. *Quarterly Journal of Speech, 67*, 138–145.

Bryant, J., & Anderson, D. R. (Eds.). (1983). *Children's understanding of television: Research on attention and comprehension.* New York: Academic.

Bryson, L., Finkelstein, L., MacIver, R. M., & McKeon, R. (Eds.). (1964). *Symbols and values: An initial study. Thirteenth Symposium on the Conference on Science, Philosophy and Religion, 1952.* New York: Cooper Square.

Burke, K. (1968). Definition of man. In *Language as symbolic action* (pp. 3–24). Berkeley: University of California Press.

Burke, K. (1989). *On symbols and society.* (J. R. Gusfield, Ed.). Chicago: University of Chicago Press.

Bynum, C. W. (1987). *Holy feast and holy fast: The religious significance of food to Medieval women.* Berkeley: University of California Press.

Cadley, J. (1992, September 13). About men: Shoe garnish. *The New York Times Magazine*, p. 24.

Camp, C. (1989). *American foodways: What, when, why and how we eat in America.* Little Rock: August House.

Caplow, T. (1982). Christmas gifts and kin networks. *American Sociological Review, 47*, 383–392.

Carbaugh, D. (1985). Cultural communication and organizing. In W. B. Gudykunst, L. P. Stewart, & S. Ting-Toomey (Eds.), *Communication, culture, and organizational processes* (pp. 30–47). Newbury Park, CA: Sage.

Carbaugh, D. (1988). *Talking American: Cultural discourses on Donahue.* Norwood, NJ: Ablex.

Carbaugh, D. (1990). *Cultural communication and intercultural contact.* Hillsdale, NJ: Lawrence Erlbaum Associates.

Carey, J. W. (1975). A cultural approach to communications. *Communication, 2*, 1–22.

Carey, J. W. (1989). Culture as communication: Essays on media and society. Boston: Unwin Hyman.

Carlisle, S. G. (1982). French homes and French character. *Landscape, 26*(3), 13–23.

Carroll, L. (1871). *Through the looking glass and what Alice found there.* New York: Grosset & Dunlap.

Carson, B., & Carson, C. (1983). Things unspoken: Learning social history from artifacts. In J. Gardner & G. Adams (Eds.), *Ordinary people and everyday life* (pp. 181–203). Nashville: American Association for State and Local History.

Cassirer, E. (1944). *An essay on man.* New Haven: Yale University Press.

Cavan, S. (1966). *Liquor license: An ethnography of bar behavior*. Chicago: Aldine.

Cheal, D. (1988). *The gift economy*. London: Routledge.

Chen, V. (1990/1991). *Mien tze* at the Chinese dinner table: A study of the interactional accomplishment of face. *Research on Language and Social Interaction, 24*, 109–140.

Cherry, C. (1980). The communication explosion. In M. L. Foster & S. H. Brandes (Eds.), *Symbol as sense: New approaches to the analysis of meaning* (pp. 249–267). New York: Academic.

Cherwitz, R. A. (1981). Charles Morris' conception of semiotic: Implications for rhetorical criticism. *Communication Quarterly, 29*, 218–227.

Clark, C. E., Jr. (1987). The vision of the dining room: Plan book dreams and middle-class realities. In K. Grover (Ed.), *Dining in America, 1850–1900* (pp. 142–172). Amherst/Rochester: University of Massachusetts Press/Margaret Woodbury Strong Museum.

Clark, G. (1986). *Symbols of excellence: Precious materials as expressions of status*. Cambridge: Cambridge University Press.

Clarke, D. S., Jr. (1990). *Sources of semiotic: Readings with commentary from antiquity to the present*. Carbondale: Southern Illinois University Press.

Clarke, T. (1991, March 17). Lasting impressions. *The New York Times Magazine, Part 2*, p. 32.

Clifford, J. (1985). Objects and selves: An afterword. In *Objects and others: Essays on museums and material culture*. Madison: University of Wisconsin Press.

Clines, F. X. (1990, July 22). Tea at dusk in Tashkent is a ritual for men alone. *The New York Times*, p. Y6.

Cohen, L. A. (1980). Embellishing a life of labor: An interpretation of the material culture of American working-class homes, 1885–1915. *Journal of American Culture, 3*, 752–775.

Cohen, P. (1980). Subcultural conflict and working-class community. In Centre for Contemporary Cultural Studies (Ed.), *Culture, media, and language: Working papers in cultural studies, 1972–79* (pp. 78–87). London: Hutchinson.

Cohen, Y. A. (1961). Food and its vicissitudes: A cross-cultural study of sharing and nonsharing. In Y. A. Cohen (Ed.), *Social structure and personality: A casebook* (pp. 312–350). New York: Holt, Rinehart & Winston.

Collins, J. (1989). *Uncommon cultures: Popular culture and post-modernism*. New York: Routledge.

Combes, A. (1986, February 2). The bow's art. *The New York Times Magazine*, pp. 56–58.

Conquergood, D. (1992). Fabricating culture: The textile art of Hmong refugee women. In E. C. Fine & J. H. Speer (Eds.), *Performance, culture, and identity* (pp. 206–248). Westport, CT: Praeger.

Conroy, S. B. (1986, February 5). A sneak attack: Fans of bow ties talk back to an outspoken critic. *The Milwaukee Journal*, pp. B1, B2.

Cook, C. (1990, March 25). Talk of the tube: TV fashions do well in the ratings, too. *The Milwaukee Journal*, p. G4.

Cooley, R. E. (1983). Codes and contexts: An argument for their description. In W. B. Gudykunst (Ed.), *Intercultural communication theory: Current perspectives* (pp. 241–251). Beverly Hills: Sage.

Corcoran, F. (1981). Towards a semiotic of screen media: Problems in the use of linguistic models. *Western Journal of Speech Communication, 45*, 182–193.

Coutu, W. (1962). An operational definition of meaning. *Quarterly Journal of Speech, 27*, 59–64.

Cromley, E. C. (1990). *Alone together: A history of New York's early apartments*. Ithaca, NY: Cornell University Press.

Cronen, V. E., Pearce, W. B., & Harris, L. M. (1982). The coordinated management of meaning: A theory of communication. In F. E. X. Dance (Ed.), *Human communication theory* (pp. 61–89). New York: Harper & Row.

Cronkhite, G. (1986). On the focus, scope, and coherence of the study of human symbolic activity. *Quarterly Journal of Speech, 72*, 231–246.

Culler, J. (1977). *Ferdinand de Saussure*. Harmondsworth: Penguin.

Culler, J. (1981). *The pursuit of signs: Semiotics, literature, deconstruction*. Ithaca, NY: Cornell University Press.

Culler, J. (1988). *Framing the sign: Criticism and its institutions*. Oxford: Basil Blackwell.

Cussler, M., & De Give, M. L. (1952). *'Twixt the cup and the lip: Psychological and socio-cultural factors affecting food habits.* New York: Twayne.

Csikszentmihalyi, M., & Rochberg-Halton, E. (1981). *The meaning of things: Domestic symbols and the self.* Cambridge: Cambridge University Press.

Danet, B., & Katriel, T. (1989). No two alike: Play and aesthetics in collecting. *Play & Culture, 2,* 253–277.

Davidson, A. (1990). Funeral cookbook. In A. Davidson (Ed.), *A kipper with my tea: Selected food and essays* (pp. 27–28). San Francisco: North Point.

Davidson, H. R. E. (Ed.). (1977). *Symbols of power.* Cambridge: D. S. Brewer and Rowman & Littlefield for the Folklore Society.

Davis, F. (1988). Clothing, fashion and the dialectic of identity. In D. R. Maines & C. J. Couch (Eds.), *Communication and social structure* (pp. 23–38). Springfield, IL: Charles C. Thomas.

Davis, J. A. (1990). *Living rooms as symbols of status: A study in social judgment.* New York: Garland.

De Lauretis, T. (1984). *Alice doesn't: Feminism, semiotics, cinema.* Bloomington: Indiana University Press.

De Marly, D. (1986). *Working dress: A history of occupational clothing.* London: Batsford.

Deely, J. (1990). *Basics of semiotics.* Bloomington: Indiana University Press.

Deely, J., Williams, B., & Kruse, F. E. (1986). Preface. In J. Deely, B. Williams & F. E. Kruse (Eds.), *Frontiers in semiotics* (pp. viii–xvii). Bloomington: Indiana University Press.

Deshen, S. A. (1989). Ethnicity and citizenship in the ritual of an Israeli synagogue. In E. Oring (Ed.), *Folk groups and folklore genres: A reader* (pp. 114–123). Logan: Utah State University Press.

Deutsch, K. (1966). On theories, taxonomies, and models as communication codes for organizing information. *Behavioral Science, 10,* 1–17.

Dewhurst, C. K., MacDowell, B., & MacDowell, M. (1979). *Artists in aprons: Folk art by American women.* New York: E. P. Dutton in association with the Museum of American Folk Art.

Diamonstein, B. (1983). *Handmade in America: Conversations with fourteen craftmasters.* New York: Harry N. Abrams.

Diderot, D. (1964). Regrets on parting with my old dressing gown. In *Rameau's nephew and other works* (pp. 309–317). (J. Barzun & R. H. Bowen, Trans.). Indianapolis: Bobbs-Merrill. (Original work published 1772)

Dolgin, J. L., Kemnitzer, D. S., & Schneider, D. M. (1977a). Introduction: "As people express their lives, so they are ..." In J. L. Dolgin, D. S. Kemnitzer, & D. M. Schneider (Eds.), *Symbolic anthropology: A reader in the study of symbols and meanings* (pp. 3–44). New York: Columbia University Press.

Dolgin, J. L., Kemnitzer, D. S., & Schneider, D. M. (Eds.). (1977b). *Symbolic anthropology: A reader in the study of symbols and meanings.* New York: Columbia University Press.

Donnellon, A. (1986). Language and communication in organizations: Bridging cognition and behavior. In H. P. Sims, Jr., D. A. Gioia, & Associates (Eds.), *The thinking organization: Dynamics of organizational social cognition* (pp. 136–164). San Francisco: Jossey-Bass.

Donovan, C. (1992, May 31). What they're wearing: BLACK . . . What they'll be wearing: RED. *The New York Times Magazine,* pp. 50–51.

Dorgan, R. (1986, April 6). No Ovaltine? *The Milwaukee Journal,* Wisconsin Magazine, p. 21.

Douglas, D. (1982). The machine in the parlor: A dialectical analysis of the sewing machine. *Journal of American Culture, 5,* 20–29.

Douglas, M. (1966). *Purity and danger.* London: Routledge & Kegan Paul.

Douglas, M. (1970). *Natural symbols.* New York: Random House.

Douglas, M. (1971). Deciphering a meal. In C. Geertz (Ed.), *Myth, symbol, and culture* (pp. 61–81). New York: W. W. Norton.

Douglas, M. (1979). Accounting for taste. *The Bridge, 10,* 15–16.

Douglas, M. (1982a). Food as an art form. In M. Douglas, *In the active voice* (pp. 105–113). London: Routledge & Kegan Paul.

Douglas, M. (1982b). Food studied as a system of communication. In M. Douglas, *In the active voice* (pp. 82–104). London: Routledge & Kegan Paul.

Douglas, M. (1984). Standard social uses of food: Introduction. In M. Douglas (Ed.), *Food in the social order: Studies of food and festivities in three American communities* (pp. 1–39). New York: Russell Sage Foundation.

Douglas, M. (1987). *Constructive drinking: Perspectives on drink from anthropology.* New York: Cambridge University Press.

Douglas, M. (1990). Foreword: No free gifts. In M. Mauss, *The gift* (pp. vii–xviii). London: Routledge.

Douglas, M., & Isherwood, B. (1979). *The world of goods.* New York: Basic.

Dowd, M. (1991a, January 20). Starched in Connecticut: Review of *The way of the WASP* by Richard Brookhiser. *The New York Times Book Review,* pp. 1, 34.

Dowd, M. (1991b, May 26). Yes, but can she make them swoon? *The New York Times,* p. E3.

Duncan, H. D. (1962). *Communication and social order.* New York: Bedminster.

Du Plessix Gray, F. (1981). The escape from fashion. *The Dial, 2,* 43–47.

Durham, G. (1992). Quilt symbolizes UW System ties to its Wisconsin heritage. *Wisconsin Ideas, 8,* 10–11.

Dwyer, J. P. (Ed.). (1975). *Studies in anthropology and material culture.* Providence: Brown University Press.

Dyen, D. J. (1988). *Pysanky*: Craftsmanship, ritual meaning, and ethnic identity. In S. D. Staub (Ed.), *Craft and community: Traditional arts in contemporary society* (pp. 99–106). Philadelphia: Balch Institute for Ethnic Studies and the Pennsylvania Heritage Affairs Commission.

Eco, U. (1973a). Function and sign: Semiotics of architecture. In J. Bryan & R. Sauer (Eds.), *Structures implicit and explicit* (pp. 131–153). Philadelphia: University of Pennsylvania Press.

Eco, U. (1973b). Social life as a sign system. In D. Robey (Ed.), *Structuralism: An introduction* (pp. 57–72). Oxford: Clarendon.

Eco, U. (1976). *A theory of semiotics.* Bloomington: Indiana University Press.

Eco, U. (1980). Towards a semiotic enquiry into the television message. In J. Corner & J. Hawthorne (Eds.), *Communication studies: An introductory reader* (pp. 131–150). London: Edward Arnold.

Eco, U. (1986). On symbols. In J. Deely, B. Williams, & F. E. Kruse (Eds.), *Frontiers in semiotics* (pp. 153–180). Bloomington: Indiana University Press.

Eco, U. (1990). Introduction. In Y. M. Lotman, *The universe of the mind: A semiotic theory of culture* (pp. vii–xiii). London: I. B. Tauris.

Edwards, W. (1982). Something borrowed: Wedding cakes as symbols in modern Japan. *American Ethnologist, 9,* 699–711.

Ellis, D. G., & Hamilton, M. (1985). Syntactic and pragmatic code usage in interpersonal communication. *Communication Monographs, 52,* 264–279.

Ellis, R. (1983). The way to a man's heart: Food in the violent home. In A. Murcott (Ed.), *The sociology of food and eating* (pp. 164–171). Hants, England: Gower.

Ellsberg, P. R. (1991, January 13). Our toys are us. *The New York Times Magazine,* pp. 12, 14.

Emberley, J. (1987). The fashion apparatus and the deconstruction of postmodern subjectivity. *Canadian Journal of Political and Social Theory, 11,* 39–50.

Enninger, W. (1984). On the role of artifactual signification and communication in the organization of speaking. *Papers in Linguistics, 17,* 53–88.

Erlich, V. (1969). *Russian formalism.* The Hague: Mouton.

Ewing, E. (1977). *History of children's costume.* New York: Charles Scribner's Sons.

The fabric of friendship. (1992, Spring). *Alive, 12,* p. 11.

Farb, P., & Armelagos, G. (1980). *Consuming passions: The anthropology of eating.* Boston: Houghton Mifflin.

Fayer, J. M. (1984). Review of Alison Lurie, *The language of cloth* [sic]. *Southern Speech Communication Journal, 49,* 217.

Featherstone, M., Hepworth, M., & Turner, B. S. (Eds.). (1991). *The body: Social process and cultural theory.* London: Sage.

Feldman, S. D. (1979). Nested identities. *Studies in Symbolic Interaction, 2,* 399–418.

Feldman, S., & McCarthy, F. E. (1983). Purdah and changing patterns of social control among rural women in Bangladesh. *Journal of Marriage and the Family, 45,* 949–959.

Fenton, A., & Kisban, E. (Eds.). (1983). *Food in change: Eating habits from the Middle Ages to the present day*. Glasgow, Scotland: John Donald Publishers in association with the National Museums of Scotland.

Fenton, W. N. (1974). The advancement of material culture studies in modern anthropological research. In M. Richardson (Ed.), *The human mirror: Material and spatial images of man* (pp. 15–36). Baton Rouge: Louisiana State University Press.

Ferguson, L. (Ed.). (1977). *Historical archaeology and the importance of material things*. New York: Society for Historical Archaeology.

Fernandez, J. W. (1982). The dark at the bottom of the stairs: The inchoate in symbolic inquiry and some strategies for coping with it. In J. Maquet (Ed.), *On symbols in anthropology: Essays in honor of Harry Hoijer, 1980* (pp. 13–43). Malibu: Undena.

Fiddle, S. (1979). The telephone as physical object. *Journal of Communication, 29*, 69–74.

Finkelstein, J. (1989). *Dining out: A sociology of modern manners*. Cambridge, England: Polity.

Finkelstein, J. (1991). *The fashioned self*. Cambridge, England: Polity.

Fiol, C. M. (1989). A semiotic analysis of corporate language: Organizational boundaries and joint venturing. *Administrative Science Quarterly, 34*, 277–303.

Firth, R. (1973a). Food symbolism in a pre-industrial society. In R. Firth, *Symbols: Public and private* (pp. 243–261). Ithaca, NY: Cornell University Press.

Firth, R. (1973b). *Symbols: Public and private*. Ithaca, NY: Cornell University Press.

Fish, S. (1979). Normal circumstances, literal language, direct speech acts, the ordinary, the every-day, the obvious, what goes without saying, and other special cases. In P. Rabinow & W. M. Sullivan (Eds.), *Interpretive social science: A reader* (pp. 243–265). Berkeley: University of California Press.

Fiske, J. (1982). *An introduction to communication studies*. London: Methuen.

Fiske, J. (1983). General editor's preface. In T. O'Sullivan, J. Hartley, D. Saunders, & J. Fiske (Eds.), *Key concepts in communication* (pp. ix–x). London: Methuen.

Fiske, J. (1985). The semiotics of television. *Critical Studies in Mass Communication, 2*, 176–183.

Fiske, J. (1987). *Television culture*. London: Methuen.

Fiske, J. (1988). Critical response: Meaningful moments. *Critical Studies in Mass Communication, 5*, 246–251.

Fiske, J. (1989). Moments of television: Neither the text nor the audience. In E. Seiter, H. Borchers, G. Kreutzner, & E. Warth (Eds.), *Remote control: Television, audience and cultural power* (pp. 56–78). London: Routledge.

Fleming, W. (1990). *Concerts of the arts: Their interplay and modes of relationship*. Pensacola: University of West Florida Press.

Ford, D. (1986, March 2). About men: An earring. *The New York Times Magazine*, p. 58.

Fordyce, E. T. (1987). Cookbooks of the 1800s. In K. Grover (Ed.), *Dining in America, 1850–1900* (pp. 85–113). Amherst/Rochester: University of Massachusetts Press/Margaret Woodbury Strong Museum.

Foster, M. L. (1980). The growth of symbolism in culture. In M. L. Foster & S. H. Brandes (Eds.), *Symbol as sense: New approaches to the analysis of meaning* (pp. 371–397). New York: Academic.

Foster, M. L. (1990a). Analogy, language, and the symbolic process. In M. L. Foster & L. J. Botscharow (Eds.), *The life of symbols* (pp. 81–94). Boulder: Westview.

Foster, M. L. (1990b). Introduction. In M. L. Foster & L. J. Botscharow (Eds.), *The life of symbols* (pp. 1–8). Boulder: Westview.

Foster, M. L., & Brandes, S. H. (Eds.). (1980). *Symbol as sense: New approaches to the analysis of meaning*. New York: Academic.

Foster, S. W. (1988). *The past is another country: Representation, historical consciousness, and resistance in the Blue Ridge*. Berkeley: University of California Press.

Francoeur, L. (1985). The dialogical semiosis of culture. *American Journal of Semiotics, 3*, 121–130.

Frank, L. L. (1966). The world as a communication network. In G. Kepes (Ed.), *Sign image symbol* (pp. 1–14). New York: George Braziller.

Franks, D. (1985). The self in evolutionary perspective. In H. A. Faberman & R. S. Perinbanaya-gam (Eds.), *Studies in symbolic interaction, Supplement 1: Foundations of interpretive sociology: Original essays in symbolic interaction* (pp. 29–61). Greenwich: JAI Press.

Freeman, S. A., Littlejohn, S. W., & Pearce, W. B. (1992). Communication and moral conflict. *Western Journal of Communication, 56,* 311–329.

Friedrich, G. W., & Boileau, D. M. (1990). The communication discipline. In J. A. Daly, G. W. Friedrich, & A. L. Vangelisti (Eds.), *Teaching communication: Theory, research, and methods* (pp. 3–18). Hillsdale, NJ: Lawrence Erlbaum Associates.

Fry, D. L., & Fry, V. H. (1986). Semiotic model for the study of mass communication. *Communication Yearbook, 9,* 443–462.

Fujioka, R. (1973). *Tea ceremony utensils.* New York/Tokyo: Weatherhill/Shibundo.

Gailey, A. (1989). The nature of tradition. *Folklore, 100,* 143–161.

Gaines-Carter, P. (1992, May 23). D.C. lawyer told to remove African *kente* cloth for jury trial. *The Washington Post,* pp. F1, F3.

Gandhi, M. (1971). Myself, My Spinning-Wheel and Women. In Publications Division, Ministry of Information & Broadcasting, Government of India (Ed.), *The Collected Works of Mahatma Gandhi* (Vol. 48, pp. 79–81). Ahmedabad, India: Navajivan. (Original work published 1931)

Gasparov, B. (1985). Introduction. In A. D. Nakhimovsky & A. S. Nakhimovsky (Eds.), *The semiotics of Russian cultural history* (pp. 13–29). Ithaca, NY: Cornell University Press.

Geary, P. (1986). Sacred commodities: The circulation of medieval relics. In A. Appadurai (Ed.), *The social life of things: Commodities in cultural perspective* (pp. 169–191). Cambridge: Cambridge University Press.

Geertz, C. (1966). *Person, time and conduct in Bali: An essay in cultural analysis.* New Haven: Yale University, Southeast Asia Studies.

Geertz, C. (1973). *The interpretation of cultures.* New York: Basic Books.

Gell, A. (1986). Newcomers to the world of goods: Consumption among the Muria Gonds. In A. Appadurai (Ed.), *The social life of things: Commodities in cultural perspective* (pp. 110–138). Cambridge: Cambridge University Press.

Gerbner, G., Gross, L., Eleey, M., Jackson-Beeck, M., Jeffries-Fox, S., & Signorelli, N. (1977). *Violence profile no. 8: Trends in network television drama and viewer conceptions of social reality 1967–1976.* Philadelphia: The Annenberg School of Communications, the University of Pennsylvania.

Giddens, A. (1984). *The constitution of society: Outline of the theory of structuration.* Berkeley: University of California Press.

Gillen, J. (1944). Custom and range of human response. *Character and Personality, 13,* 121–131.

Gittinger, M. (1979). *Splendid symbols: Textiles and tradition in Indonesia.* Washington, DC: Textile Museum.

Glaser, M. (1985). I listen to the market. In M. Blonsky (Ed.), *On signs* (pp. 467–474). Baltimore: Johns Hopkins University Press.

Glassie, H. (1968). *Pattern in the material folk culture of the eastern United States.* Philadelphia: University of Pennsylvania Press.

Glassie, H. (1973). Structure and function, folklore and the artifact. *Semiotica, 7,* 313–351.

Glassie, H. (1987). Vernacular architecture and society. In D. W. Ingersoll, Jr. & G. Bronitsky (Eds.), *Mirror and metaphor: Material and social constructions of reality* (pp. 229–245). Lanham, MD: University Press of America.

Glassie, H. (1991). Studying material culture today. In G. L. Pocius (Ed.) *Living in a material world: Canadian and American approaches to material culture* (pp. 253–266). St. John's, Newfoundland, Canada: Institute of Social and Economic Research.

Glynn, P. (1982). *Skin to skin: Eroticism in dress.* New York: Oxford University Press.

Glynn, S. (1986). Beyond the symbol: Deconstructing social reality. *Southern Speech Communication Journal, 54,* 125–141.

Goffman, E. (1959). *The presentation of self in everyday life.* Garden City, NY: Doubleday Anchor.

Goffman, E. (1961). *Asylums.* Garden City, NY: Doubleday Anchor.

Goffman, E. (1963). *Behavior in public places*. New York: The Free Press.

Goffman, E. (1971). *Relations in public*. New York: Harper & Row.

Goffman, E. (1983). The interaction order. *American Sociological Review, 48*, 1–17.

Goldschmidt, W. (1990). *The human career: The self in the symbolic world*. Cambridge, MA: Basil Blackwell.

Goodall, H. L., Jr. (1990). A theater of motives and the "Meaningful orders of persons and things." *Communication Yearbook, 13*, 69–94.

Goode, J. G. (1989). Food. *International Encyclopedia of Communication, 2*, 187–193.

Goode, J. G., Curtis, K., & Theophano, J. (1984). Meal formats, meal cycles, and menu negotiation in the maintenance of an Italian-American community. In M. Douglas (Ed.), *Food in the social order: Studies of food and festivities in three American communities* (pp. 143–218). New York: Russell Sage Foundation.

Goode, J. G., Theophano, J., & Curtis, K. (1985). A framework for the analysis of continuity and change in shared sociocultural rules for food use: The Italian-American pattern. In L. K. Brown & K. Mussell (Eds.), *Ethnic and regional foodways in the United States: The performance of identity* (pp. 66–88). Knoxville: University of Tennessee Press.

Goodstein, E. S. (1992). Southern belles and southern buildings: The built environment as text and context in *Designing Women*. *Critical Studies in Mass Communication, 9*, 170–185.

Goodwin, C. (1981). *Conversational organization: Interaction between speakers and hearers*. New York: Academic.

Goody, J. (1982). *Cooking, cuisine and class: A study in comparative sociology*. Cambridge: Cambridge University Press.

Gordon, J., & McArthur, J. (1985). American women and domestic consumption, 1800–1920: Four interpretive themes. *Journal of American Culture, 8*, 35–46.

Gorden, W. I., Tengler, C. D., & Infante, D. A. (1982). Women's clothing predispositions as predictors of dress at work, job satisfaction, and career advancement. *Southern Speech Communication Journal, 47*, 422–434.

Gottdiener, M. (1977). Unisex fashion and gender role change. *Semiotic Scene, 1*, 13–37.

Gottdiener, M. (1985). Hegemony and mass culture: A semiotic approach. *American Journal of Sociology, 90*, 979–1001.

Gottdiener, M., & Lagopoulos, A. P. (Eds.). (1986). *The city and the sign: An introduction to urban semiotics*. New York: Columbia University Press.

Graves, T. E. (1988). The selling of Pennsylvania German folk art. In S. D. Staub (Ed.), *Craft and community: Traditional arts in contemporary society* (pp. 119–126). Philadelphia: Balch Institute for Ethnic Studies and the Pennsylvania Heritage Affairs Commission.

Green, R. (1989). Beaded Adidas. In C. Camp (Ed.), *Time and temperature: A centennial publication of the American Folklore Society*. Washington, DC: American Folklore Society.

Greimas, A. J. (1983). *Structural semantics: An attempt at a method*. (D. McDowell, R. Schleifer, & A. Velie, Trans.). Lincoln: University of Nebraska Press.

Greimas, A. J. (1987). *On meaning: Selected writings in semiotic theory*. (P. J. Perron & F. H. Collins, Trans.). Minneapolis: University of Minnesota Press.

Gronbeck, B. E. (1983). Narrative, enactment, and television programming. *Southern Speech Communication Journal, 48*, 229–243.

Gronbeck, B. E. (1988). Symbolic interactionism and communication studies: Prolegomena to future research. In D. R. Maines & C. J. Couch (Eds.), *Communication and social structure* (pp. 323–339). Springfield, IL: Charles C. Thomas.

Gross, M. (1986, January 29). It may be unwritten, but a dress code is a fact of life. *The Milwaukee Journal*, pp. B1, B3.

Grossberg, L. (1982). Experience, signification, and reality: The boundaries of cultural semiotics. *Semiotica, 41*, 73–106.

Grossberg, L. (1989). It's a sin: Politics, post-modernity and the popular. In L. Grossberg, T. Fry, A. Curthoys, & P. Patton (Eds.), *It's a sin: Essays on postmodernism, politics, and culture* (pp. 6–71). Sydney: Power.

Grossman, R. (1991, November 24). Tray chic. *The Chicago Tribune*, section 5, pp. 1, 4.

Grover, K. (Ed.). (1987). *Dining in America, 1850–1900*. Amherst/Rochester: University of Massachusetts Press/Margaret Woodbury Strong Museum.

Gudykunst, W. B., & Ting-Toomey, S., with Chua, E. (1988). *Culture and interpersonal communication*. Beverly Hills: Sage.

Guiraud, P. (1975). *Semiology*. London: Routledge & Kegan Paul.

Gumperz, J. J., & Hymes, D. (Eds.). (1972). *Directions in sociolinguistics: The ethnography of communication*. New York: Holt, Rinehart & Winston.

Gurel, L. M. (1975). The function of dress. In L. M. Gurel & M. S. Beeson (Eds.), *Dimensions of dress and adornment: A book of readings* (pp. 3–6). Dubuque: Kendall/Hunt.

Gusfield, J. R. (1963). *Symbolic crusade: Status politics and the American Temperance Movement*. Urbana: University of Illinois Press.

Gusfield, J. R. (1987). Passage to play: Rituals of drinking time in American society. In M. Douglas (Ed.), *Constructive drinking: Perspectives on drink from anthropology* (pp. 73–90). New York: Cambridge University Press.

Gusfield, J. R. (1989). Introduction. In K. Burke (Ed.), *On symbols and society* (pp. 1–49). Chicago: University of Chicago Press.

Guss, D. M. (1989). *To weave and sing: Art, symbol and narrative in the South American rain forest*. Berkeley: University of California Press.

Gutierrez, C. P. (1985). The social and symbolic uses of ethnic/regional foodways: Cajuns and crawfish in South Louisiana. In L. K. Brown & K. Mussell (Eds.), *Ethnic and regional foodways in the United States: The performance of identity* (pp. 169–182). Knoxville: University of Tennessee Press.

Haiman, F. S. (1982). Nonverbal communication and the First Amendment: The rhetoric of the streets revisited. *Quarterly Journal of Speech, 68*, 371–383.

Hall, E. T. (1984). *The dance of life: The other dimension of time*. Garden City, NY: Doubleday.

Hall, L. (1991). *Organizational communication: The process*. Boston: American Press.

Hall, S. (1980). Encoding/decoding. In S. Hall, D. Hobson, A. Lowe, & P. Willis (Eds.), *Culture, media, language* (pp. 128–138). London: Hutchinson.

Hall, S., Hobson, D., Lowe, A., & Willis, P. (Eds.). (1980). *Culture, media, language*. London: Hutchinson.

Hall, T. (1991, May 19). Piercing fad is turning convention on its ear. *The New York Times*, p. Y17.

Halliday, M. A. K. (1976). Anti-languages. *American Anthropologist, 78*, 540–548.

Halliday, M. A. K. (1978). *Language as social semiotic: The social interpretation of language and meaning*. Baltimore: University Park Press.

Hamilton, J. M. (1990, November 18). Is there a klepto in the stacks? *The New York Times Book Review*, pp. 13, 48–49.

Hankiss, A. (1980). Games con men play: The semiosis of deceptive interaction. *Journal of Communication, 30*, 104–112.

Harris, A. C., & Owens, N. J. (1990). Doth apparel the symbol make? A semiotic investigation of symbolic references to dress in selected plays of William Shakespeare. *The American Journal of Semiotics, 7*, 109–130.

Harris, M. (1985). *Good to eat: Riddles of food and culture*. New York: Simon & Schuster.

Harrison, R. (1976). Nonverbal communication. In I. de Sola Pool & W. Schramm (Eds.), *Handbook of communication* (pp. 93–113). Boston: Houghton Mifflin.

Hassan, I. (1987). *The postmodern turn: Essays in postmodern theory and culture*. Columbus: Ohio State University Press.

Hattenhauer, D. (1984). The rhetoric of architecture: A semiotic approach. *Communication Quarterly, 32*, 71–77.

Hattox, R. S. (1985). *Coffee and coffeehouses: The origins of a social beverage in the Medieval Near East*. Seattle: University of Washington Press.

Hawkes, T. (1977). A science of signs. In *Structuralism and semiotics* (pp. 123–150). Berkeley: University of California Press.

Hayden, D. (1981). *The grand domestic revolution: A history of feminist designs for American homes, neighborhoods, and cities.* Cambridge, MA: MIT Press.

Heath, C. C. (1986). *Body movement and speech in medical interaction.* Cambridge: Cambridge University Press.

Hebdige, D. (1979). *Subculture: The meaning of style.* London: Methuen.

Hebdige, D. (1988a). *Hiding in the Light.* London: Routledge.

Hebdige, D. (1988b). Object as image: The Italian scooter cycle. In *Hiding in the Light* (pp. 77–115). London: Routledge.

Heller, M. A. (1982). Semiology: A context for television criticism. *Journal of Broadcasting and Electronic Media, 26,* 847–854.

Henderson, M. C. (1970). Food as communication in American culture. *Today's Speech, 18,* 3–8.

Herd, D. (1991). The paradox of Temperance: Blacks and the alcohol question in nineteenth-century America. In S. Barrows & R. Room (Eds.), *Drinking: Behavior and belief in modern history* (pp. 354–375). Berkeley: University of California Press.

Herman, V. (1990, February 28). Lambada dance craze inspires new designs. *The Milwaukee Journal,* p. 3D.

Hervey, S. (1982). *Semiotic perspectives.* London: Allen & Unwin.

Hirsch, P. M. (1991). Processing fads and fashions: An organization-set analysis of cultural industry systems. In C. Mukerji & M. Schudson (Eds.), *Rethinking popular culture: Contemporary perspectives in cultural studies* (pp. 313–334). Berkeley: University of California Press.

Hirsley, M. (1985, April 28). To Southerners, new Coke just isn't it. *The Chicago Tribune,* Section 1, p. 5.

Hobsbawn, E., & Ranger, T. (Eds.). (1983). *The invention of tradition.* New York: Cambridge University Press.

Hockett, C. F. (1960). The origin of speech. *Scientific American, 203,* 89–96.

Hodder, I. (1982). *Symbols in action: Ethnoarchaeological studies of material culture.* Cambridge: Cambridge University Press.

Hodder, I. (Ed.). (1989). *The meanings of things: Material culture and symbolic expression.* Boston: Unwin Hyman.

Hodge, R., & Kress, G. (1988). *Social semiotics.* Ithaca, NY: Cornell University Press.

Hole, C. (1977). Protective symbols in the home. In H. R. E. Davidson (Ed.), *Symbols of power* (pp. 121–130). Cambridge, England: D. S. Brewer and Rowman & Littlefield for the Folklore Society.

Horn, M. J. (1975). *The second skin: An interdisciplinary study of clothing.* Boston: Houghton Mifflin.

Horowitz, R. T. (1975). From elite fashion to mass fashion. *Archives Européennes de Sociologie, 16,* 283–295.

Horowitz, R. (1985, November 24). Socks it to 'em: A little color can raise a lot of eyebrows in some circles. *The Milwaukee Journal,* p. B8.

Horowitz, T. (1982). Excitement vs. economy: Fashion and youth culture in Britain. *Adolescence, 17,* 627–636.

Hufford, M., Hunt, M., & Zeitlin, S. (1989). *The grand generation: Memory, mastery, legacy.* Seattle: University of Washington Press.

Hughes, S. M. (1991, October). The unforgettable Dr. Korshin. *The Pennsylvania Gazette,* pp. 31–37, 41.

Humphrey, L. T. (1988). "Soup night": Community creation through foodways. In T. C. Humphrey & L. T. Humphrey (Eds.), *"We gather together": Food and festival in American life* (pp. 53–68). Ann Arbor: UMI Research Press.

Humphrey, T. C., & Humphrey, L. T. (Eds.). (1988). *"We gather together": Food and festival in American life.* Ann Arbor: UMI Research Press.

Hymes, D. (1974). *Foundations in sociolinguistics.* Philadelphia: University of Pennsylvania Press.

Ingersoll, D. W., Jr., & Bronitsky, G. (1987). Foreword. In D. W. Ingersoll, Jr. & G. Bronitsky (Eds.), *Mirror and metaphor: Material and social constructions of reality* (p. xi). Lanham, MD: University Press of America.

Ingrassia, M. (1986, April 9). Shoes to burn: Her excess was measured by the pair. *The Milwaukee Journal*, pp. D1, D3.

Innis, R. E. (Ed.). (1985). *Semiotics: An introductory anthology*. Bloomington: Indiana University Press.

Isaacs, S. L. F. (1988). Redware revival and re-presentation: A Pennsylvania pottery tradition. In S. D. Staub (Ed.), *Craft and community: Traditional arts in contemporary society* (pp. 127–130). Philadelphia: Balch Institute for Ethnic Studies and the Pennsylvania Heritage Affairs Commission.

Jakobson, R. (1971a). The dominant. In L. Matejka & K. Pomorska (Eds.), *Readings in Russian poetics: Formalist and structuralist views* (pp. 82–87). Cambridge, MA: MIT Press. (Original work published 1935)

Jakobson, R. (1971b). Results of a joint conference of anthropologists. In *Selected writings* (Vol. 2, pp. 554–568). The Hague: Mouton.

Jakobson, R. (1971c). *Selected writings* (Vols. 1–3). The Hague: Mouton.

James, R. R. (Ed.). (1974). *Winston S. Churchill: His complete speeches, 1897–1963* (Vol. 5). New York: Chelsea House.

Jameson, F. (1987). Foreword. In A. J. Greimas, *On meaning: Selected writings in semiotic theory*. (P. J. Perron & F. H. Collins, Trans., pp. vi–xxii). Minneapolis: University of Minnesota Press.

Jenness, A., & Rivers, A. (1989). *In two worlds: A Yup'ik Eskimo family*. Boston: Houghton Mifflin.

Johnson, S., & Recktenwald, W. (1991, October 31). When it comes to doughnuts, do cops ever miss a dunk? *The Chicago Tribune*, Section 1, pp. 1, 16.

Jones, M. O. (1975). *The hand made object and its maker*. Berkeley: The University of California Press.

Jones, M. O. (1989). *Craftsman of the Cumberlands: Tradition and creativity*. Lexington: University of Kentucky Press.

Jones, M. O., Giuliano, B., & Krell, R. (Eds.). (1981). Special issue: Foodways and eating habits: Directions for research. *Western Folklore, 40*, 1–137.

Jones, S. (1983). Art by fiat, and other dilemmas of cross-cultural collecting. In J. M. Vlach & S. Bronner (Eds.), *Folk art and art worlds* (pp. 243–266). Ann Arbor: UMI Research Press.

Jones, W. T. (1961). *The romantic syndrome: Toward a new method in cultural anthropology and history of ideas*. The Hague: Martiuns Nijhoff.

Joos, S. K. (1985). Economic, social, and cultural factors in the analysis of disease: Dietary change and diabetes mellitus among the Florida Seminole Indians. In L. K. Brown & K. Mussell (Eds.), *Ethnic and regional foodways in the United States: The performance of identity* (pp. 217–237). Knoxville: University of Tennessee Press.

Joselit, J. W. (1991). "A Set Table": Jewish domestic culture in the new world, 1880–1950. In S. L. Braunstein & J. W. Joselit (Eds.), *Getting comfortable in New York: The American Jewish home, 1880–1950* (pp. 21–73). Bloomington: Indiana University Press.

Joseph, N. (1986). *Uniforms and nonuniforms: Communication through clothing*. New York: Greenwood.

Joyce, R. O. (1983). "Fame don't make the sun any cooler": Folk artists and the marketplace. In J. M. Vlach & S. Bronner (Eds.), *Folk art and art worlds* (pp. 225–241). Ann Arbor: UMI Research Press.

*J. Peterman* (1991). Fall catalog: Owner's manual No. 12.

Kaiser, S. B. (1985). *The social psychology of clothing*. New York: MacMillan.

Kalčik, S. (1985). Ethnic foodways in America: Symbol and the performance of identity. In L. K. Brown & K. Mussell (Eds.), *Ethnic and regional foodways in the United States: The performance of identity* (pp. 37–65). Knoxville: University of Tennessee Press.

Katriel, T. (1986). *Talking straight: Dugri speech in Israeli Sabra culture*. Cambridge: Cambridge University Press.

Katriel, T. (1987). Rhetoric in flames: Fire inscriptions in Israeli youth movement ceremonials. *Quarterly Journal of Speech, 73*, 444–459.

Katriel, T. (1991). *Communal webs: Communication and culture in contemporary Israel*. Albany: State University of New York Press.

Katriel, T. (1992, May). *Re-making place: Cultural production in Israeli pioneer settlement museums*. Paper presented at the meeting of the International Communication Association, Miami.

Katriel, T., & Farrell, F. (1991). Scrapbooks as cultural texts: An American art of memory. *Text and Performance Quarterly, 11*, 1–17.

Katz, A. M., & Katz, V. T. (Eds.). (1983a). *Foundations of nonverbal communication: Readings, exercises, and commentary*. Carbondale: Southern Illinois University Press.

Katz, A. M., & Katz, V. T. (1983b). Putting it all together: Encoding and decoding message patterns. In A. M. Katz & V. T. Katz (Eds.), *Foundations of nonverbal communication: Readings, exercises, and commentary* (pp. 205–207). Carbondale: Southern Illinois University Press.

Kazanjian, D. (1991, August 25). The real thing. *The New York Times Magazine*, pp. 122–123.

Keali'inohomoku, J. W. (1979). You dance what you wear, and you wear your cultural values. In J. M. Cordwell & R. A. Schwarz (Eds.), *The fabrics of culture: The anthropology of clothing and adornment* (pp. 77–83). The Hague: Mouton.

Kendon, A. (1990). *Conducting interaction: Patterns of behavior in focused encounters*. Cambridge: Cambridge University Press.

Kernan, J. B. (1973). Her mother's daughter? The case of clothing and cosmetic fashions. *Adolescence, 8*, 343–350.

Kirshenblatt-Gimblett, B. (1986). Objects of memory: Material culture as life review. In E. Oring (Ed.), *Folk groups and folklore genres: A reader* (pp. 329–338). Logan: Utah State University Press.

Kirshenblatt-Gimblett, B. (1991). Kitchen Judaism. In S. L. Braunstein & J. W. Joselit (Eds.), *Getting comfortable in New York: The American Jewish home, 1880–1950* (pp. 75–105). Bloomington: Indiana University Press.

Kitahara-Frisch, J. (1980). Symbolizing technology as a key to human evolution. In M. L. Foster & S. H. Brandes (Eds.), *Symbol as sense: New approaches to the analysis of meaning* (pp. 211–223). New York: Academic.

Knapp, M. L., & Hall, J. A. (1992). *Nonverbal communication in human interaction*. Fort Worth: Holt, Rinehart & Winston.

Kopytoff, I. (1986). The cultural biography of things: Commoditization as process. In A. Appadurai (Ed.), *The social life of things: Commodities in cultural perspective* (pp. 64–91). Cambridge: Cambridge University Press.

Krampen, M. (1979a). *Meaning in the urban environment*. London: Pion.

Krampen, M. (1979b). Survey of current work on the semiology of objects. In S. Chatman, U. Eco, & J. Klinkenberg (Eds.), *A semiotic landscape* (pp. 158–168). The Hague: Mouton.

Krampen, M. (1986). Code. In T. Sebeok (Ed.), *Encyclopedic dictionary of semiotics* (Vol. 1, pp. 123–132). Berlin: Mouton de Gruyter.

Kress, G. (1988a). Communication and culture. In G. Kress (Ed.), *Communication and culture: An introduction* (pp. 1–19). Kensington: New South Wales University Press.

Kress, G. (Ed.). (1988b). *Communication and culture: An Introduction*. Kensington: New South Wales University Press.

Krippendorff, K. (1990, October). *Two paths alongside the meaning of things*. Paper presented at the meeting of the Sixth International Congress "Sign (Theory) in Practice," Passau, Germany.

Kristeva, J. (1969). Le mot, le dialogue et le roman [The word, dialogue, and the novel]. In J. Kristeva, *Sémeiotiké: Recherches pour une sémanalyse* (pp. 143–175). Paris: Éditions du Seuil.

Kristeva, J. (1989). *Language, the unknown: An initiation into linguistics*. (A. M. Menke, Trans.). New York: Columbia University Press.

Kuper, H. (1973). Costume and identity. *Comparative Studies in Society and History, 15*, 348–367.

Laderman, C. (1981). Symbolic and empirical reality: A new approach to the analysis of food avoidance. *American Ethnologist, 8*, 468–93.

Langer, L. (1959). *The importance of wearing clothes*. New York: Hastings House.

Langer, S. K. (1967). On a new definition of symbol. In F. W. Matson & A. Montague (Eds.), *The human dialogue* (pp. 548–554). New York: The Free Press.

Lanigan, R. L. (1972). *Speaking and semiology*. The Hague: Mouton.

Lanigan, R. L. (1979). A semiotic metatheory of human communication. *Semiotica, 27*, 293–305.

Lanigan, R. L. (1982). Semiotic phenomenology: A theory of human communication praxis. *Journal of Applied Communication Research, 10*, 62–73.

Lanigan, R. L. (1983). *Semiotic phenomenology of rhetoric*. Washington, DC: University Press of America.

Lanigan, R. L. (1986). Semiotics, communicology, and Plato's sophist. In J. Deely, B. Williams, & F. E. Kruse (Eds.), *Frontiers in semiotics* (pp. 199–216). Bloomington: Indiana University Press.

Lanigan, R. L. (1990). Le même et l'autre [The same and the other]: Michel Foucault's semiotic quadrilateral of the phenomenology of discourse. In J. Deely, K. Haworth & T. Prewitt (Eds.), *Semiotics 1989* (pp. 117–123). Lanham, MD: University Press of America.

Lannamann, J. W. (1992). Deconstructing the person and changing the subject of interpersonal studies. *Communication Theory, 2*, 139–148.

Lathrop, L. (1984). Outer image, inner things: A study of the relationship between social organization and artistic expression. *Anthropology and Humanism Quarterly, 9*, 2–7.

Laumann, E. O., & House, J. S. (1970). Living room styles and social attributes: The patterning of material artifacts in a modern urban community. In E. O. Laumann, P. M. Siegel, & R. W. Hodge (Eds.), *The logic of social hierarchies* (pp. 189–203). Chicago: Markham.

Lawless, E. J. (1989). Brothers and sisters: Pentecostals as a religious folk group. In E. Oring (Ed.), *Folk groups and folklore genres: A reader* (pp. 99–113). Logan: Utah State University Press.

Leach, E. (1976). *Culture and communication: The logic by which symbols are connected*. Cambridge: Cambridge University Press.

Lee, D. D. (1964). Symbolization and value. In L. Bryson, Finkelstein, L., MacIver, R. M., & McKeon, R. (Eds.), *Symbols and values: An initial study* (pp. 73–85). New York: Cooper Square.

Leeds-Hurwitz, W. (1987). The social history of the *Natural history of an interview*: A multidisciplinary investigation of social communication. *Research on Language and Social Interaction, 20*, 1–51.

Leeds-Hurwitz, W. (1989). *Communication in everyday life: A social interpretation*. Norwood, NJ: Ablex.

Leeds-Hurwitz, W. (1990a). Culture and communication: A review essay. *Quarterly Journal of Speech, 76*, 85–96.

Leeds-Hurwitz, W. (1990b). Notes in the history of intercultural communication: The Foreign Service Institute and the mandate for intercultural training. *Quarterly Journal of Speech, 76*, 262–281.

Leeds-Hurwitz, W. (1992a, August). *Connecting interpersonal to intercultural research by way of ethnography*. Paper presented at the Ways of Speaking, Ways of Knowing: Ethnography of Communication Conference, Portland, OR.

Leeds-Hurwitz, W. (1992b). Forum introduction: Social approaches to interpersonal communication. *Communication Theory, 2*, 131–139.

Leeds-Hurwitz, W., & Sigman, S. J., with Sullivan, S. J. (in press). Communication structures and performed invocations: A revision of Scheflen's notion of programs. In S. J. Sigman (Ed.), *The consequentiality of communication*. Hillsdale, NJ: Lawrence Erlbaum Associates.

Lennon, S. J. (1986). Additivity of clothing cues in first impressions. *Social Behavior and Personality, 14*, 15–21.

Lennon, S. J., & Davis, L. L. (1989). Clothing and human behavior from a social cognitive framework: Part I: Theoretical perspectives. *Clothing and Textiles Research Journal, 7*, 41–48.

Leone, M. P. (1977). The new Mormon temple in Washington, D.C. In L. Ferguson (Ed.), *Historical archaeology and the importance of material things* (pp. 43–61). New York: Society for Historical Archaeology.

Lerner, D. (Ed.). (1963). *Parts and wholes*. New York: Free Press of Glencoe.

Levenstein, H. A. (1988). *Revolution at the table: The transformation of the American diet*. New York: Oxford University Press.

Levi-Strauss, C. (1963). *Structural anthropology* (Vol. 1, C. Jacobson & B. G. Schoepf, Trans.). New York: Basic Books.

Levi-Strauss, C. (1966a). The culinary triangle. *Partisan Review, 33*, 586–595.

Levi-Strauss, C. (1966b). *The savage mind*. Chicago: University of Chicago Press.

Levi-Strauss, C. (1966c). The scope of anthropology. *Current Anthropology, 7*, 112–123.

Levi-Strauss, C. (1969). *The raw and the cooked*. (J. Weightman & D. Weightman, Trans.). New York: Harper & Row.

Levi-Strauss, C. (1973). *From Honey to Ashes*. (J. Weightman & D. Weightman, Trans.). New York: Harper & Row.

Levi-Strauss, C. (1976). *Structural anthropology* (Vol. 2). New York: Basic Books.

Levi-Strauss, C. (1978). *The origin of table manners*. (J. Weightman & D. Weightman, Trans.). New York: Harper & Row.

Levrant de Bretteville, S. (1979). The "parlorization" of our homes and ourselves. *Chrysalis: A Magazine of Women's Culture, 8*, 33–45.

Lewis, I. M. (Ed.). (1977). *Symbols and sentiments: Cross-cultural studies in symbolism*. London: Academic.

Lincourt, J. (1978). Communication as semiotic. *Communication, 3*, 3–20.

Lindsay-Hogg, M. (1991, March 17). Jeremy Iron's effortless style. *The New York Times Magazine*, Part 2, pp. 48–51, 72.

Littlejohn, S. W. (1977). Symbolic interactionism as an approach to the study of human communication. *Quarterly Journal of Speech, 63*, 84–91.

Littlejohn, S. W. (1978). Theories of signs: Verbal and nonverbal coding. In S. W. Littlejohn (Ed.), *Theories of human communication* (pp. 79–110). Columbus, OH: Charles E. Merrill.

Lockwood, Y. R., & Lockwood, W. G. (1991). Pasties in Michigan's Upper Peninsula: Foodways, interethnic relations, and regionalism. In S. Stern & J. A. Cicala (Eds.), *Creative ethnicity: Symbols and strategies of contemporary ethnic life* (pp. 3–20). Logan: Utah State University Press.

Lofland, L. H. (1988). Communication and construction: The built environment as message and medium. In D. R. Maines & C. J. Couch (Eds.), *Communication and social structure* (pp. 307–322). Springfield, IL: Charles C. Thomas.

Logue, C. M., & Patton, J. H. (1982). From ambiguity to dogma: The rhetorical symbols of Lyndon B. Johnson on Vietnam. *Southern Speech Communication Journal, 47*, 310–329.

Lönnqvist, B. (1979). Symbolic value in clothing. *Ethnologia Scandinavica, 9*, 92–105.

Lotman, Y. M. (1970). *The structure of the artistic text*. Ann Arbor: University of Michigan.

Lotman, Y. M. (1985). The poetics of everyday behavior in eighteenth-century Russian culture. In A. D. Nakhimovsky & A. S. Nakhimovsky (Eds.), *The semiotics of Russian cultural history* (pp. 67–94). Ithaca, NY: Cornell University Press.

Lotman, Y. M. (1990). *Universe of the mind: A semiotic theory of culture*. (A. Shukman, Trans.). London: I. B. Tauris.

Lotman, Y. M., & Uspensky, B. A. (1978). On the semiotic mechanism of culture. *New Literary History, 9*, 211–232.

Lucid, D. P. (Ed.). (1977). *Soviet semiotics*. Baltimore: Johns Hopkins University Press.

Lurie, A. (1981). *The language of clothes*. New York: Random House.

Lydon, M., with Woodruff, L., & Warren, S. (1989). In memoriam Roland Barthes. The contract: A stele for Roland Barthes. In S. Ungar & B. R. McGraw (Eds.), *Signs in culture: Roland Barthes today* (pp. 37–45). Iowa City: University of Iowa Press.

Lyne, J. R. (1980). Rhetoric and semiotic in C. S. Peirce. *Quarterly Journal of Speech, 66*, 155–168.

Lyne, J. R. (1981a). Arguing as "Speaking a language": Semiotic consistency. In G. Ziegulmuller & J. Rhodes (Eds.), *Dimensions of argument* (pp. 820–847). Annandale, VA: Speech Communication Association.

Lyne, J. R. (1981b). Speech acts in a semiotic frame. *Communication Quarterly, 29*, 202–208.

MacCannell, D. (1973). A note on hat tipping. *Semiotica, 7*, 300–312.

MacCannell, D., & MacCannell, J. F. (1982). *The time of the sign: A semiotic interpretation of modern culture*. Bloomington: Indiana University Press.

MacVean, M. (1990, December 19). It's a holiday food some love to hate. *The Milwaukee Journal*, p. D17.

Maines, D. R., & Couch, C. J. (Eds.). (1988). *Communication and social structure*. Springfield, IL: Charles C. Thomas.

Manning, P. K. (1991). Semiotic ethnographic research. *American Journal of Semiotics, 8*, 27–45.

Maquet, J. (1982). Introduction: The symbolic realm. In J. Maquet (Ed.), *On symbols in anthropology: Essays in honor of Harry Hoijer, 1980* (pp. 1–12). Malibu: Undena.

Marriott, M. (1990, December 9). In Arizona's King vote, debate on a school role. *The New York Times*, p. Y16.

Marshall, L. (1961). Sharing, talking and giving: Relief of social tensions among !Kung Bushmen. *Africa, 31*, 231–249.

Martindale, C. (1990). *The clockwork muse: The predictability of artistic change.* New York: Basic.

Marvin, C. (1988). *When old technologies were new.* New York: Oxford University Press.

Mascia-Lees, F. E., & Sharpe, P. (Eds.). (1992). *Tattoo, torture, mutilation, and adornment: The denaturalization of the body in culture and text.* Albany: State University of New York Press.

Masumoto, D. M. (1983). Brown rice *sushi. Western Folklore, 42*, 140–144.

Matejka, L., Shiskoff, S., Suino, M. E., & Titunik, I. R. (Eds.). (1977). *Readings in Soviet semiotics.* Ann Arbor: University of Michigan.

Matejka, L., & Pomorska, K. (Eds.). (1971). *Readings in Russian poetics: Formalist and structuralist views.* Cambridge, MA: MIT Press.

Matejka, L., & Titunik, I. R. (Eds.). (1976). *Semiotics of art: Prague School contributions.* Cambridge: MIT Press.

Mauss, M. (1990). *The gift.* London: Routledge. (Original work published 1954)

McCracken, G. (1988). *Culture and consumption: New approaches to the symbolic character of consumer goods and activities.* Bloomington: Indiana University Press.

McLaughlin, P. (1989, December 6). Training bras define a rite of passage. *The Milwaukee Journal,* p. C2.

Mead, G. H. (1922). A behavioristic account of the significant symbol. *The Journal of Philosophy, 19*, 157–163.

Mead, G. H. (1974). *Mind, self, and society.* (C. W. Morris, Ed.). Chicago: University of Chicago Press.

Mead, M. (1943). The problem of changing food habits. *National Research Council Committee on Food Habits, Bulletin 108* (pp. 20–31). Washington, DC: National Academy of Sciences.

Mechling, E. W., & Mechling, J. (1983). Sweet talk: The moral rhetoric against sugar. *Central States Speech Journal, 34*, 19–32.

Menkes, S. (1986, July 24). Romance, history and fun: A dress to match the bride. *The [London] Times,* p. 5.

Mennell, S. (1985). *All manners of food: Eating and taste in England and France from the Middle Ages to the present.* Oxford, England: Basil Blackwell.

Merriam, A. H. (1975). Symbolic action in India: Gandhi's nonverbal persuasion. *Quarterly Journal of Speech, 61*, 290–306.

Mertz, E., & Parmentier, R. J. (Eds.). (1985). *Semiotic mediation: Sociocultural and psychological perspectives.* New York: Academic.

Messer, E. (1984). Anthropological perspectives on diet. *Annual Reviews in Anthropology, 13*, 205–249.

Messing, S. D. (1960). The nonverbal language of the Ethiopian toga. *Anthropos, 55*, 558–561.

Metz, C. (1974). *Film language: A semiotics of the cinema.* New York: Oxford University Press.

Meyerowitz, J. (1979). Television and interpersonal behavior: Codes of perception and response. In G. Gumpert & R. Cathcart (Ed.), *Inter/media: Interpersonal communication in a media world* (pp. 56–76). New York: Oxford University Press.

Middendorf, J. (1990). Semiotics and naturalistic inquiry. In J. Deely, K. Haworth, & T. Prewitt (Eds.), *Semiotics 1989* (pp. 305–313). Lanham, MD: University Press of America.

Miles, E. M., & Leathers, D. G. (1984). The impact of aesthetic and professionally-related objects as credibility in the office setting. *Southern Speech Communication Journal, 49*, 361–379.

Millen, J. H. (1992, October). *Teaching communication students about social reality: A cross-cultural example.* Paper presented at the meeting of the Speech Communication Association, Chicago.

Mintz, S. W. (1985). *Sweetness and power: The place of sugar in modern history.* New York: Viking.

Mitchell, S. (1990, February 21). Boutique puts stars in your wardrobe. *The Milwaukee Journal,* pp. G1, G4.

Moore, B., Jr. (1984). *Privacy: Studies in social and cultural history.* Amonk, NY: M. E. Sharpe.

Moore, H. (1990). Paul Ricoeur: Action, meaning and text. In C. Tilley (Ed.), *Reading material culture: Structuralism, hermeneutics and post-structuralism* (pp. 85–120). Oxford, England: Basil Blackwell.

Moore, H. B. (1957). The meaning of food. *The American Journal of Clinical Nutrition, 5*, 77–82.

Moore, S. F. (1975). Epilogue. In S. F. Moore & B. Myerhoff (Eds.), *Symbol and politics in communal ideology* (pp. 210–238). Ithaca, NY: Cornell University Press.

Moore, S. F. (1978). *Law as process*. London: Routledge & Kegan Paul.

Moore, S. F., & Myerhoff, B. G. (Eds.). (1977). *Secular ritual*. Assen, The Netherlands: Van Gorcum.

Morawski, S. (1970). The basic functions of quotation. In A. J. Greimas, R. Jakobson, M. R. Mayenowa, S. K. Šaumjan, W. Steinitz, & S. Żółkiewski (Eds.), *Sign, language, culture* (pp. 690–705). The Hague: Mouton.

Morgan, G., Frost, P. J., & Pondy, L. R. (1983). Organizational symbolism. In L. R. Pondy, P. J. Frost, G. Morgan, & T. C. Dandridge (Eds.), *Organizational symbolism* (pp. 3–35). Greenwich: JAI Press.

Morgan, T. E. (1985). Is there an intertext in this text? Literary and interdisciplinary approaches to intertextuality. *American Journal of Semiotics, 3*, 1–40.

Morris, C. (1938). *Foundations of the theory of signs*. Chicago: University of Chicago Press.

Mukarovsky, J. (1977). *The word and verbal art*. (J. Burbank & P. Steiner, Ed. and Trans.). New Haven: Yale University Press.

Mukarovsky, J. (1978). *Structure, sign, and function*. (J. Burbank & P. Steiner, Ed. and Trans.). New Haven: Yale University Press.

Mullen, J. (1992, March 15). I sold clothes in the naked city. *The New York Times Magazine*, Part 2, p. 16.

Mumby, D. K. (1989). Ideology and the social construction of meaning: A communication perspective. *Communication Quarterly, 37*, 291–304.

Murcott, A. (Ed.). (1983). *The sociology of food and eating*. Hants, England: Gower.

Murphy, R. F. (1964). Social distance and the veil. *American Anthropologist, 66*, 1257–1274.

Musello, C. (1992). Objects in process: Material culture and communication. *Southern Folklore, 49*, 37–59.

Napier, A. D. (1986). *Masks, transformations, and paradox*. Berkeley: University of California Press.

Nemy, E. (1989, April 9). For generations, this special bassinet has been a good-luck charm. *The New York Times*, p. Y29.

Neusner, J. (1990). Intertextuality and the literature of Judaism. *American Journal of Semiotics, 7*, 153–182.

Nöth, W. (1990). *Handbook of semiotics*. Bloomington: Indiana University Press.

Noyes, D. (1989). *Uses of tradition: Arts of Italian Americans in Philadelphia*. Philadelphia: Philadelphia Folklore Project and Samuel S. Fleisher Art Memorial.

Nwankwo, R. L. (1973). Communication as symbolic interaction: A synthesis. *Journal of Communication, 23*, 195–215.

Ogibenin, B. L. (1975). Mask in the light of semiotics: A functional approach. *Semiotica, 13*, 1–9.

Olson, C. D. (1985). Materialism in the home: The impact of artifacts on dyadic communication. *Advances in Consumer Research, 12*, 388–393.

O'Neill, M. (1989, September 20). By any name: If you don't know the local food terms, you're marked as a foreigner. *The Milwaukee Journal*, p. 3E.

Ortner, S. B. (1973). On key symbols. *American Anthropologist, 75*, 1338–1346.

Ortner, S. B. (1975). Gods' bodies, Gods' food: A symbolic analysis of a Sherpa ritual. In R. Willis (Ed.), *The interpretation of symbolism* (pp. 133–169). London: Malaby.

Ortner, S. B. (1984). Theory in anthropology since the sixties. *Comparative Studies in Society and History, 26*, 126–165.

Osborn, M. (Ed.). (1983). A symposium: The power of the symbol. *Southern Speech Communication Journal, 48*, 211–268.

O'Sullivan, T., Hartley, J., Saunders, D., & Fiske, J. (Eds.). (1983). *Key concepts in communication*. London: Methuen.

Page, J. (1988). Do animals think? In W. Leeds-Hurwitz (Ed.), *Communication and the evolution of civilization: A book of readings* (pp. 43–45). Needham Heights, MA: Ginn.

Parents of Poplar Indian varsity players honor their sons. (1992, February 27). *Wotonia Wowapi, 23*(9), 9.

Parman, S. (1990). *Orduighean*: A dominant symbol in the Free Church of the Scottish Highlands. *American Anthropologist, 92*, 295–305.

Parmentier, R. J. (1985). Semiotic mediation: Ancestral genealogy and final interpretant. In E. Mertz & R. J. Parmentier (Eds.), *Semiotic mediation: Sociocultural and psychological perspectives* (pp. 359–385). New York: Academic.

Payne, R. (1969). *The life and death of Mahatma Gandhi.* New York: E. P. Dutton.

Pearce, W. B. (1989). *Communication and the human condition.* Carbondale: Southern Illinois University Press.

Pearce, W. B., & Cronen, V. E. (1980). *Communication, action, and meaning: The creation of social realities.* New York: Praeger.

Peirce, C. S. (1931–1958). *Collected papers.* (C. Hartshorne & P. Weiss, Eds. [Vols. 1–6] & A. W. Banks, Ed. [Vols. 7–8]). Cambridge, MA: Harvard University Press.

Peirce, C. S. (1985). Logic as semiotic: The theory of signs. In R. E. Innis (Ed.), *Semiotics: An introductory anthology* (pp. 4–27). Bloomington: Indiana University Press.

Pepin, J. (1990, December 2). All in a roe. *The New York Times Magazine,* pp. 111–112.

Peterson, S. (1988). "They know the rule for what will make it pretty": Hmong material traditions in translation. In S. D. Staub (Ed.), *Craft and community: Traditional arts in contemporary society* (pp. 107–118). Philadelphia: Balch Institute for Ethnic Studies and the Pennsylvania Heritage Affairs Commission.

Petitot-Concorda, J. (1985). *Morphogénèse du sens* [Morphogenesis of meaning]. Paris: Presses Universitaires de France.

Pilotta, J. J., Widman, T., & Jasko, S. A. (1988). Meaning and action in the organizational setting: An interpretive approach. *Communication Yearbook, 11,* 310–334.

Pines, M. (1982, September 28). What's the real message of "Casablanca"? Or of a rose? *The New York Times,* pp. C1, C6.

Pogrebin, L. C. (1992, November 29). To tell the truth. *The New York Times Magazine,* pp. 22, 24.

Polacco, P. (1988). *The keeping quilt.* New York: Simon & Schuster.

Polhemus, T., & Procter, L. (1978). *Fashion and anti-fashion: An anthropology of clothing and adornment.* London: Ames & Hudson.

Ponce, M. H. (1989). *The wedding.* Houston: Arte Publico.

Porter, M. J. (1983). Applying semiotics to the study of selected primetime television programs. *Journal of Broadcasting and Electronic Media, 27,* 69–75.

Powers, W. K., & Powers, M. M. N. (1984). Metaphysical aspects of an Oglala food system. In M. Douglas (Ed.), *Food in the social order: Studies of food and festivities in three American communities* (pp. 40–96). New York: Russell Sage Foundation.

Pratt, G. (1982). The house as an expression of social worlds. In J. S. Duncan (Ed.), *Housing and identity: Cross-cultural perspectives* (pp. 135–180). New York: Holmes & Meier.

Propp, V. J. (1968). *Morphology of the folktale.* Austin: University of Texas Press. (Original work published 1928)

Prosterman, L. (1985). Food and celebration: A kosher caterer as mediator of communal traditions. In L. K. Brown & K. Mussell (Eds.), *Ethnic and regional foodways in the United States: The performance of identity* (pp. 127–142). Knoxville: University of Tennessee Press.

Putnam, L. L., & Pacanowsky, M. E. (Eds.). (1983). *Communication and organizations: An interpretive approach.* Beverly Hills: Sage.

Rabinow, P., & Sullivan, W. M. (Eds.). (1979). *Interpretive social science: A reader.* Berkeley: University of California Press.

Rakow, L. (1992). *Gender on the line.* Carbondale: University of Illinois Press.

Ramsey, S. J. (1976). Prison codes. *Journal of Communication, 26,* 39–45.

Rapoport, A. (1982). Identity and environment: A cross-cultural perspective. In J. S. Duncan (Ed.), *Housing and identity: Cross-cultural perspectives* (pp. 6–35). New York: Holmes & Meier.

Raspa, R. (1985). Exotic foods among Italian-Americans in Mormon Utah: Food as nostalgic enactment of identity. In L. K. Brown & K. Mussell (Eds.), *Ethnic and regional foodways in the United States: The performance of identity* (pp. 185–194). Knoxville: University of Tennessee Press.

Rauch, I., & Carr, G. F. (Eds.). (1980). *The signifying animal: The grammar of language and experience*. Bloomington: Indiana University Press.

Rawlins, W. K. (1992). *Friendship matters: Communication, dialectics, and the life course*. New York: Aldine de Gruyter.

Regan, J. (1984). Metaphors of information. In R. P. Fawcett, M. A. K. Halliday, S. M. Lamb, & A. Makkai (Eds.), *The semiotics of culture and language. Vol. 1: Language as social semiotic* (pp. 37–47). London: Frances Pinter.

Rey, A. (1978). Communication vs. semiosis: Two conceptions of semiosis. In T. A. Sebeok (Ed.), *Sight, sound, and sense* (pp. 48–110). Bloomington: Indiana University Press.

Reynolds, B., & Stott, M. A. (Eds.). (1987). *Material anthropology: Contemporary approaches to material culture*. New York: University Press of America.

Richards, A. (1932). *Hunger and work in a savage tribe*. London: Routledge.

Richardson, J., & Kroeber, A. L. (1940). Three centuries of women's dress fashions: A quantitative analysis. *Anthropological Records, 5*, 1–153.

Richardson, M. (1974). Images, objects, and the human story. In M. Richardson (Ed.), *The human mirror: Material and spatial images of man* (pp. 3–14). Baton Rouge: Louisiana State University Press.

Richardson, M. (1987). A social (ideational-behavioral) interpretation of material culture and its application to archaeology. In D. W. Ingersoll, Jr., & G. Bronitsky (Eds.), *Mirror and metaphor: Material and social constructions of reality* (pp. 381–403). Lanham, MD: University Press of America.

Roach, M. E., & Eicher, J. B. (1979). The language of personal adornment. In J. M. Cordwell & R. A. Schwarz (Eds.), *The fabrics of culture: The anthropology of clothing and adornment* (pp. 7–21). The Hague: Mouton.

Roach, M. E., & Musa, K. E. (1983). Functions of dress. In A. M. Katz & V. T. Katz (Eds.), *Foundations of nonverbal communication: Readings, exercises, and commentary* (pp. 170–176). Carbondale: Southern Illinois University Press.

Roberts, H. E. (1977). The exquisite slave: The role of clothes in the making of the Victorian woman. *Signs, 2*, 554–569.

Roberts, W. E. (1988). *Viewpoints on folklife: Looking at the overlooked*. Ann Arbor: UMI Research Press.

Robinson, G., & Straw, W. O. (1984). Semiotics and communications study: Points of contact. *Progress in Communication Sciences, 4*, 91–114.

Rogov, D. (1991, February/March). The daily portion. *Israel Scene*, p. 18.

Rosaldo, M. Z., & Atkinson, J. M. (1975). Man the hunter and woman: Metaphors for the sexes in Ilongot magical spells. In R. Willis (Ed.), *The interpretation of symbolism* (pp. 43–75). London: Malaby.

Rosencranz, M. L. (1972). *Clothing concepts: A social-psychological approach*. New York: Macmillan.

Rosenfeld, L. B., & Plax, T. G. (1977). Clothing as communication. *Journal of Communication, 27*(2), 24–31.

Rothenbuhler, E. W. (1989). Values and symbols in orientations to the Olympics. *Critical Studies in Mass Communication, 6*, 138–157.

Rowen, J. (1992, May 31). A catch to quit on. *The Milwaukee Journal*, Wisconsin Magazine, pp. 24–25.

Royce, J. R. (Ed.). (1965). *Psychology and the symbol: An interdisciplinary symposium*. New York: Random House.

Rubinstein, D. H. (1987). The social fabric: Micronesian textile patterns as an embodiment of social order. In D. W. Ingersoll, Jr. & G. Bronitsky (Eds.), *Mirror and metaphor: Material and social constructions of reality* (pp. 63–82). Lanham, MD: University Press of America.

Rubinstein, R. P. (1985). Color, circumcision, tattoos, and scars. In M. R. Solomon (Ed.), *The psychology of fashion* (pp. 243–254). Lexington: Lexington Books.

Rudofsky, B. (1955). *Behind the picture window*. New York: Oxford University Press.

Ruesch, J., & Kees, W. (1956). *Nonverbal communication: Notes on the visual perception of human relations*. Berkeley: University of California Press.

Russell, J. (1991, May 10). Paul Mellon's life in art: Understated, oversubscribed. *The New York Times*, pp. H1, H37.

Rutz, H. J., & Orlove, B. S. (Eds.). (1989). *The social economy of consumption*. Lanham, MD: University Press of America.

Sacks, M. (1989). Computing community at Purim. *Journal of American Folklore, 102*, 275–291.

Sahlins, M. (1976a). Colors and cultures. *Semiotica, 16*, 1–22.

Sahlins, M. (1976b). Food preference and tabu in American domestic animals. In *Culture and practical reason* (pp. 169–176). Chicago: University of Chicago Press.

Sahlins, M. (1976c). Notes on the American clothing system. In *Culture and practical reason* (pp. 179–203). Chicago: University of Chicago Press.

Salmans, S. (1989, November 26). Collections: Favorites divide along gender lines. *The Milwaukee Journal*, p. 5F.

Salomon, G. (1979). *Interaction of media, cognition, and learning*. San Francisco: Jossey-Bass.

Saussure, F. de. (1969). *Course in general linguistics*. New York: McGraw-Hill. (Original work published 1916)

Schlereth, T. J. (1990). *Cultural history and material culture: Everyday life, landscapes, museums*. Ann Arbor: UMI Research Press.

Schneider, D. M. (1976). Notes toward a theory of culture. In K. H. Basso & H. A. Selby (Eds.), *Meaning in anthropology* (pp. 197–220). Albuquerque: University of New Mexico Press.

Schneider, J. (1987). Anthropology of cloth. *Annual Review of Anthropology, 16*, 409–448.

Schudson, M. (1989). How culture works: Perspectives from media studies on the efficacy of symbols. *Theory and Society, 18*, 153–180.

Schutz, A. (1967). *The phenomenology of the social world*. Evanston: Northwestern University Press.

Schwartz, G., & Merten, D. (1971). Participant observation and the discovery of meaning. *Philosophy of the Social Sciences, 1*, 279–298.

Schwarz, R. A. (1979). Uncovering the secret vice: Toward an anthropology of clothing. In J. M. Cordwell & R. A. Schwarz (Eds.), *The fabrics of culture: The anthropology of clothing and adornment* (pp. 23–45). The Hague: Mouton.

Schwichtenberg, C. (1989). The "Mother lode" of feminist research: Congruent paradigms in the analysis of beauty culture. In B. Dervin, L. Grossberg, B. J. O'Keefe, & E. Wartella (Eds.), *Rethinking communication. Vol. 2: Paradigm exemplars* (pp. 291–306). Newbury Park: Sage.

Schwimmer, E. (1977). Semiotics and culture. In T. A. Sebeok (Ed.), *A perfusion of signs* (pp. 153–179). Bloomington: Indiana University Press.

Sciolino, E. (1992, May 24). The will to adorn, the will of Allah. *The New York Times*, p. Y20.

Sebeok, T. A. (1976). The semiotic web: A chronicle of prejudices. In *Contributions to the doctrine of signs* (pp. 149–188). Bloomington: Indiana University Press.

Sebeok, T. A. (1986a). The doctrine of sign. In J. Deely, B. Williams, & F. E. Kruse (Eds.), *Frontiers in semiotics* (pp. 35–42). Bloomington: Indiana University Press.

Sebeok, T. A. (Ed.). (1986b). *Encylopedic dictionary of semiotics* (Vols. 1–3). Berlin: Mouton de Gruyter.

Sebeok, T. A., Hayes, A. S., & Bateson, M. C. (Eds.). (1964). *Approaches to semiotics*. The Hague: Mouton.

*Second Nature* (1992). Fall catalog, p. 32.

Seligman, K. L. (1974). Shakespeare's use of Elizabethan dress as a comedic device in *The Taming of the Shrew*: "Something mechanical encrusted on the living." *Quarterly Journal of Speech, 60*, 39–44.

Shannon, C. E., & Weaver, W. (1949). *The mathematical theory of communication*. Urbana: University of Illinois Press.

Shapiro, E. (1992, May 3). A dowdy soft drink in search of a new age remake. *The New York Times*, p. F10.

Sharman, A., Theophano, J., Curtis, K., & Messer, E. (1991). Introduction. In A. Sharman, J. Theophano, K. Curtis, & E. Messer (Eds.), *Diet and domestic life in society* (pp. 3–14). Philadelphia: Temple University Press.

Sherman, E., & Newman, E. S. (1977–1978). The meaning of cherished personal possessions for the elderly. *International Journal of Aging and Human Development, 8*, 181–92.

Sherzer, D., & Sherzer, J. (1979). Système de la mode en Darien: Towards a semiotic analysis of Cuna *molas*. In S. Chatman, U. Eco, & J. Klinkenberg (Eds.), *A semiotic landscape* (pp. 1073-1079). The Hague: Mouton.

Shirer, W. L. (1979). *Gandhi: A memoir*. New York: Simon & Schuster.

Shops quick to copy royal gown. (1986, July 25). *The [London] Times*, p. 16.

Shotwell, J. M., Wolf, D., & Gardner, H. (1980). Styles of achievement in early symbol use. In M. L. Foster & S. H. Brandes (Eds.), *Symbol as sense: New approaches to the analysis of meaning* (pp. 175-199). New York: Academic.

Shukman, A. (1978). Soviet semiotics and literary criticism. *New Literary History, 9*, 189-198.

Sigman, S. J. (1987). *A perspective on social communication*. Lexington: Lexington Books.

Sigman, S. J. (1990). Toward an integration of diverse communication contexts. *Communication Yearbook, 13*, 554-563.

Sigman, S. J. (1991). Handling the discontinuous aspects of continuous social relationships: Toward research on the persistence of social forms. *Communication Theory, 1*, 106-127.

Silverman, K. (1983). *The subject of semiotics*. New York: Oxford University Press.

Silverstein, M. (1976). Shifters, linguistic categories, and cultural description. In K. H. Basso & H. A. Selby (Eds.), *Meaning in anthropology* (pp. 11-55). Albuquerque: University of New Mexico Press.

Singer, E. A. (1985). Conversion through foodways enculturation: The meaning of eating in an American Hindu sect. In L. K. Brown & K. Mussell (Eds.), *Ethnic and regional foodways in the United States: The performance of identity* (pp. 195-214). Knoxville: University of Tennessee Press.

Singer, M. (1978). For a semiotic anthropology. In T. A. Sebeok (Ed.), *Sight, sound, and sense* (pp. 202-231). Bloomington: Indiana University Press.

Singer, M. (1982). Emblems of identity: A semiotic exploration. In J. Maquet (Ed.), *On symbols in anthropology: Essays in honor of Harry Hoijer, 1980* (pp. 73-133). Malibu: Undena.

Singer, M. (1984). *Man's glassy essence: Explorations in semiotic anthropology*. Bloomington: Indiana University Press.

Skillman, A. E. (1988). No smoke? No fire: Contemporary hamming the ol' fashioned way. In T. C. Humphrey & L. T. Humphrey (Eds.), *"We gather together": Food and festival in American life* (pp. 125-136). Ann Arbor: UMI Research Press.

Sless, D. (1986). *In search of semiotics*. London: Croom Helm.

Smith, A. G. (1966). Introduction: Communication and culture. In A. G. Smith (Ed.), *Communication and culture: Readings in the codes of human interaction* (pp. 1-10). New York: Holt, Rinehart & Winston.

Smith, R. E. F., & Christian, D. (1984). *Bread and salt: A social and economic history of food and drink in Russia*. Cambridge: Cambridge University Press.

Solomon, M. R. (Ed.). (1985). *The psychology of fashion*. Lexington: Lexington Books.

Sperber, D. (1974). *Rethinking symbolism*. (A. L. Morton, Trans.). Cambridge: Cambridge University Press.

Sperber, D. (1985). *On anthropological knowledge: Three essays*. Cambridge/Paris: Cambridge University Press/Éditions de la Maison des Sciences de l'Homme.

Spierenburg, P. (1991). *The broken spell: A cultural and anthropological history of pre-industrial Europe*. New Brunswick, NJ: Rutgers University Press.

Spivak, G. C. (1990). *The post-colonial critic: Interviews, strategies, dialogues*. (S. Harasym, Ed.). New York: Routledge.

Spooner, B. (1986). Weavers and dealers: The authenticity of an Oriental carpet. In A. Appadurai (Ed.), *The social life of things: Commodities in cultural perspective* (pp. 195-235). Cambridge: Cambridge University Press.

Spotswood, B. (1975). Toys: A portfolio of magic. In National Geographic Society, Special Publications Division (Ed.), *The craftsman in America* (pp. 150-163). Washington, DC: National Geographic Society.

Spradley, J. (1970). *You owe yourself a drunk: An ethnography of urban nomads*. New York: Little, Brown.

Stacy, S. (1988). Tartan. In J. Ash & L. Wright (Eds.), *Components of dress: Design, manufacturing and image-making in the fashion industry* (pp. 52–53). London: Routledge.

Staub, S. D. (1989). *Yeminis in New York City: The folklore of ethnicity*. Philadelphia: Balch Institute Press.

Steele, V. (1985). *Fashion and eroticism: Ideals of feminine beauty from the Victorian Era to the Jazz Age*. New York: Oxford University Press.

Steele, V. (1988). Le five o'clock tea. In *Paris fashion: A cultural history*. New York: Oxford University Press.

Steier, F. (Ed.). (1991). *Research and reflexivity*. London: Sage.

Steinberg, S. (1990, December 2). Traveler's mission: Search and acquire. *The New York Times*, Travel section, p. 37.

Steiner, W. (1978). Modern American semiotics (1930–1978). In R. W. Bailey, L. Matejka, & P. Steiner (Eds.), *The sign: Semiotics around the world* (pp. 99–118). Ann Arbor: Michigan Slavic Publications.

Sterba, J. P. (1987, March 26). Cut from CEO cloth. *The Wall Street Journal*, pp. 7D, 8D.

Stewart, J. (1972). Concepts of language and meaning: A comparative study. *Quarterly Journal of Speech, 58*, 123–133.

Stewart, J. (1986). Speech and human being: A complement to semiotics. *Quarterly Journal of Speech, 72*, 55–73.

Stewart, J. (1991). A postmodern look at traditional communication postulates. *Western Journal of Speech Communication, 55*, 354–379.

Stewart, J. (in press). Structural implications of the symbol model for communication theory. In R. Conville (Ed.), *Structure and communication*. New York: Praeger.

Stewart, S. (1991). *Crimes of writing: Problems in the containment of representation*. New York: Oxford University Press.

Stinchecum, A. M. (1990, August 26). Cool eating during Kyoto's dog days. *The New York Times*, Travel section, pp. 19, 32.

Stone, G. P. (1962). Appearance and the self. In A. M. Rose (Ed.), *Human behavior and social processes: An interactionist approach* (pp. 86–118). New York: Houghton Mifflin.

Stott, M. A. (1987). Object, context and process: Approaches to teaching about material culture. In B. Reynolds & M. A. Stott (Eds.), *Material anthropology: Contemporary approaches to material culture* (pp. 13–30). New York: University Press of America.

Striedter, J. (1989). *Literary structure, evolution, and value: Russian formalism and Czech structuralism reconsidered*. Cambridge, MA: Harvard University Press.

Stromberg, P. G. (1990). Ideological language in the transformation of identity. *American Anthropologist, 92*, 42–56.

Super, J. C. (1988). *Food, conquest, and colonization in sixteenth-century Spanish America*. Albuquerque: University of New Mexico Press.

Switzer, J. Y., Fry, V. H., & Miller, L. D. (1990). Semiotic and communication: A dialogue with Thomas A. Sebeok. *Southern Communication Journal, 55*, 388–401.

Tannahill, R. (1989) *Food in history*. New York: Crown.

Tax, S. (1979). Preface. In J. M. Cordwell & R. A. Schwarz (Eds.), *The fabrics of culture: The anthropology of clothing and adornment* (pp. v–vii). The Hague: Mouton.

Taylor, A. (1991). *Quench the lamp*. New York: St. Martin's.

Teske, R. T. (1979). Living room furnishings, ethnic identity, and acculturation among Greek Philadelphians. *New York Folklore, 5*, 21–32.

Theophano, J. S. (1978). Feast, fast and time. *Pennsylvania Folklife, 27*, 25–32.

Theophano, J. S. (1982). "It's really tomato sauce, but we call it gravy." Unpublished doctoral dissertation, University of Pennsylvania, Department of Folklore and Folklife.

Theophano, J. S. (1991). "I gave him a cake": An interpretation of two Italian-American weddings. In S. Stern & J. A. Cicala (Eds.), *Creative ethnicity: Symbols and strategies of contemporary ethnic life* (pp. 44–54). Logan: Utah State University Press.

Thibault, P. J. (1991). *Social semiotics as praxis: Text, social meaning making, and Nabokov's Ada.* Minneapolis: University of Minnesota Press.

Thomas, J. (1989). System vs. code: A semiologist's etymology. In S. Ungar & B. R. McGraw (Eds.), *Signs in culture: Roland Barthes today* (pp. 49–62). Iowa City: University of Iowa Press.

Thomas, N. (1991). *Entangled objects: Exchange, material culture and colonialism in the Pacific.* Cambridge, MA: Harvard University Press.

Thompson, L. (1969). *The secret of culture.* New York: Random House.

Thompson, R. F., & Cornet, J. (1987). Bottomless vessels: Sounding the sea of Kalunga. In D. W. Ingersoll, Jr. & G. Bronitsky (Eds.), *Mirror and metaphor: Material and social constructions of reality* (pp. 83–111). Lanham, MD: University Press of America.

Thorpe, W. H. (1988). The comparison of vocal communication in animals and man. In W. Leeds-Hurwitz (Ed.), *Communication and the evolution of civilization: A book of readings* (pp. 23–27). Needham Heights, MA: Ginn. (Original work published 1972)

Threadgold, T. (1986). The semiotics of Vološinov, Halliday, and Eco. *American Journal of Semiotics, 4,* 107–142.

Tilley, C. (1990a). Preface. In C. Tilley (Ed.), *Reading material culture: Structuralism, hermeneutics and post-structuralism* (pp. vii–x). Oxford, England: Basil Blackwell.

Tilley, C. (Ed.). (1990b). *Reading material culture: Structuralism, hermeneutics and post-structuralism.* Oxford, England: Basil Blackwell.

Tobin, Y. (1990). *Semiotics and linguistics.* London: Longman.

Todorov, T. (1982). *Symbolism and interpretation.* (C. Porter, Trans.). Ithaca, NY: Cornell University Press.

Todorov, T. (1984). *Mikhail Bakhtin: The dialogical principle.* (W. Godzich, Trans.). Minneapolis: University of Minnesota Press.

Tokarev, S. A. (1985). Toward a methodology for the ethnographic study of material culture. (P. Voorheis, Trans.). In S. J. Bronner (Ed.), *American material culture and folklife: A prologue and dialogue* (pp. 77–96). Ann Arbor: UMI Research Press. (Original work published 1970)

Tuerina, E. S., & Edmund, M. (1992, November 25). Teen wearing Raiders jacket chased, killed. *The Milwaukee Journal,* pp. B1, B5.

Turner, V. (1967). *Forest of symbols.* Ithaca, NY: Cornell University Press.

Turner, V. (1969). Forms of symbolic action: Introduction. In R. F. Spencer (Ed.), *Forms of symbolic action: Proceedings of the 1969 annual spring meeting of the American Ethnological Society* (pp. 3–25). Seattle: American Ethnological Society, distributed by the University of Washington Press.

Turner, V. (1974). *Dramas, fields, and metaphors: Symbolic action in human society.* Ithaca, NY: Cornell University Press.

Turner, V. (1975). Symbolic studies. *Annual Review of Anthropology, 4,* 145–161.

Turner, V. (1977). Symbols in African ritual. In J. L. Dolgin, D. S. Kemnitzer, & D. M. Schneider (Eds.), *Symbolic anthropology: A reader in the study of symbols and meanings* (pp. 183–194). New York: Columbia University Press.

Turner, V. (1985). *On the edge of the bush: Anthropology as experience.* Tucson: University of Arizona Press.

Tylor, E. B. (1958). *Primitive culture.* New York: Harper & Row. (Original work published 1871)

Tynjanov, J., & Jakobson, R. (1971). Problems in the study of literature and language. In L. Matejka & K. Pomorska (Eds.), *Readings in Russian poetics: Formalist and structuralist views* (pp. 79–81). Cambridge, MA: MIT Press. (Original work published 1928)

Ulrich, G. (1989). Masks. *Lore, 39,* 2–9.

Umiker-Sebeok, D. J. (1977). Semiotics of culture: Great Britain and North America. *Annual Review of Anthropology, 6,* 121–135.

Umiker-Sebeok, J. (Ed.). (1987). *Marketing and semiotics: New directions in the study of signs for sale.* Berlin: Mouton de Gruyter.

Ungar, S., & McGraw, B. R. (1989). Introduction. In S. Ungar & B. R. McGraw (Eds.), *Signs in culture: Roland Barthes today* (pp. xi–xxv). Iowa City: University of Iowa Press.

Unruh, D. (1983). Death and personal history: Strategies of identity preservation. *Social Problems, 30,* 340-351.

Upton, D. (1985). [Comments in] Material culture studies: A symposium. *Material Culture, 17,* 85-88.

Upton, D. (1991). Form and user: Style, mode, fashion, and the artifact. In G. L. Pocius (Ed.), *Living in a material world: Canadian and American approaches to material culture* (pp. 156-169). St. John's, Newfoundland, Canada: Institute of Social and Economic Research.

Urban, G. (1981). The semiotics of tabooed food: The Shokleng case. *Social Science Information, 20,* 475-507.

Uspensky, B. A. (1973). *A poetics of composition: The structure of the artistic text and typology of a compositional form.* (V. Zavarin & S. Wittig, Trans.). Berkeley: University of California Press.

Uspensky, B. A., Ivanov, V. V., Toporov, V. N., Piatigorskij, A. M., & Lotman, Y. M. (1973). Theses on the semiotic study of cultures (As applied to Slavic texts). In J. van der Eng & M. Grygar (Eds.), *Structure of texts and semiotics of culture* (pp. 1-28). The Hague: Mouton.

Valverde, M. (1989). The love of finery: Fashion and the fallen woman in nineteenth-century social discourse. *Victorian Studies: A Journal of the Humanities, Arts and Sciences, 32,* 169-188.

Van den Berghe, P. L. (1984). Ethnic cuisine: Culture in nature. *Ethnic and Racial Studies, 7,* 387-397.

Van der Veer Hamilton, V. (1991, March 10). As old as you drive. *The New York Times Magazine,* pp. 22-23.

Van Matre, L. (1992, March 12). Creating a social fabric. *The Chicago Tribune,* Section 5, pp. 1-2.

Vanden Brook, T. (1993, May 2). Remember when Donna Shalala was UW President? *The Milwaukee Journal,* Wisconsin Magazine, pp. 5-8, 10-13.

Varenne, H. (1973). American culture and the school: A case study. In C. J. Calhoun & F. A. J. Ianni (Eds.), *The anthropological study of education* (pp. 227-237). The Hague: Mouton.

Voloshinov, V. N. (1971). Reported speech. In L. Matejka & K. Pomorska (Eds.), *Readings in Russian poetics: Formalist and structuralist views* (pp. 149-175). Cambridge, MA: MIT Press. (Original work published 1930)

Voloshinov, V. N. (1973). *Marxism and the philosophy of language.* (L. Matejka & I. R. Titunik, Trans.). New York: Seminar Press. (Original work published 1929)

Von Bertalanffy, L. (1965). On the definition of the symbol. In J. R. Royce (Ed.), *Psychology and the symbol: An interdisciplinary symposium* (pp. 26-72). New York: Random House.

Wagner, R. (1986). *Symbols that stand for themselves.* Chicago: University of Chicago Press.

Warner, D. (1978). Fashion, emancipation, reform and the rational undergarment. *Dress: Journal of the American Costume Society, 14,* 24-29.

Warnick, B. (1979). Structuralism vs. phenomenology: Implications for rhetorical criticism. *Quarterly Journal of Speech, 65,* 250-261.

Watrous, P. (1992, April 26). Tiny voices, funny clothes. *The New York Times,* p. H31.

Weaver, W. W. (1983). White gravies in American popular diet. In A. Fenton & E. Kisban (Eds.), *Food in change: Eating habits from the Middle Ages to the present day* (pp. 41-54). Glasgow, Scotland: John Donald Publishers in association with the National Museums of Scotland.

Webb, D. (1990, August 29). TV: Does it sway eating habits? *The Milwaukee Journal,* p. D17.

Weiner, A. B., & Schneider, J. (Eds.). (1989). *Cloth and human experience.* Washington, DC: Smithsonian Institution Press.

Weitman, S. R. (1973). National flags: A sociological overview. *Semiotica, 8,* 328-367.

Welsch, R. L. (1981). An interdependence of foodways and architecture: A foodways context on the American plains. In A. Fenton & T. M. Owen (Eds.), *Food in perspective.* Edinburgh, Scotland: John Donald.

Werbner, R. P. (1989). *Ritual passage, sacred journey: The process and organization of religious movement.* Washington, DC: Smithsonian Institution Press.

Wertsch, J. W. (1985). The semiotic mediation of mental life: L. S. Vygotsky and M. M. Bakhtin. In E. Mertz & R. J. Parmentier (Eds.), *Semiotic mediation: Sociocultural and psychological perspectives* (pp. 49-71). New York: Academic.

White, L. A. (1962). Symboling: A kind of behavior. *Journal of Psychology, 53*, 311–317.

Whitehead, A. N. (1959). *Symbolism: Its meaning and effect.* New York: G. B. Putnam's Sons. (Original work published 1927)

Whorf, B. L. (1956). *Language, thought and reality.* Cambridge, MA: Technologist Press.

Wieder, D. L. (1988). *Language and social reality: The case of telling the convict code.* Washington, DC: Center for Advanced Research in Phenomenology and University Press of America. (Original work published 1974)

Wieder, D. L., & Pratt, S. (1990). On being a recognizable Indian among Indians. In D. Carbaugh (Ed.), *Cultural communication and intercultural contact* (pp. 45–64). Hillsdale, NJ: Lawrence Erlbaum Associates.

Williams, B. (1985). Why migrant women feed their husbands tamales: Foodways as a basis for a revisionist view of Tejano family life. In L. K. Brown & K. Mussell (Eds.), *Ethnic and regional foodways in the United States: The performance of identity* (pp. 113–126). Knoxville: University of Tennessee Press.

Williams, M. A. (1991). *Homeplace: The social use and meaning of the folk dwelling in southwestern North Carolina.* Athens: University of Georgia Press.

Williams, R. (1980a). Advertising: The magic system. In R. Williams, *Problems in materialism and culture* (pp. 170–195). London: Verso.

Williams, R. (1980b). *Problems in materialism and culture.* London: Verso.

Wills, G., & Midgley, D. (Eds.). (1973). *Fashion marketing: An anthology of viewpoints and perspectives.* London: Allen & Unwin.

Wilson, C. S. (1973). Food habits: A selected annotated bibliography. *Journal of Nutrition Education, 5*(1, Suppl. 1), 40–72.

Wilson, E. (1985). *Adorned in dreams: Fashion and modernity.* London: Virago.

Winkin, Y. (1983). Eating topics and talking food. *Le Langage et l'Homme, 51*, 17–23.

Winner, I. P. (1986). Semiotics of culture. In J. Deely, B. Williams, & F. E. Kruse (Eds.), *Frontiers in semiotics* (pp. 181–184). Bloomington: Indiana University Press.

Winner, I. P., & Umiker-Sebeok, J. (Eds.). (1979). *Semiotics of culture.* The Hague: Mouton.

Winner, I. P., & Winner, T. G. (1976). The semiotics of cultural texts. *Semiotica, 18*, 101–156.

Wolf, E. (1972). The Virgin of Guadalupe: A Mexican national symbol. In W. A. Lessa & E. Z. Vogt (Eds.), *Reader in comparative religion: An anthropological approach* (3rd ed., pp. 149–153). New York: Harper & Row.

Wollen, P. (1987). Fashion/Orientalism/the body. *New Formations, 1*, 5–33.

Worth, S., & Gross, L. (1974). Symbolic strategies. *Journal of Communication, 24*, 27–39.

Wray, H. (1981). Semiotics: Fad or revolution? The study of signs is attracting students and controversy. *Humanities Report, 3*, 4–9.

Wright, G. (1980). *Moralism and the model home: Domestic architecture and cultural conflict in Chicago, 1873–1913.* Chicago: University of Chicago Press.

Yoder, D. (1972). Folk cookery. In R. Dorson (Ed.), *Folklore and folklife: An introduction* (pp. 325–350). Chicago: University of Chicago Press.

Yoder, D. (1989). *Discovering American folklife: Studies in ethnic, religious, and regional culture.* Ann Arbor: UMI Research Press.

Young, M. J. (1991). Permeable boundaries: Ambiguity and metaphor in Zuni ceremonialism and daily life. *Southern Folklore, 48*, 159–189.

Zito, G. V. (1984). *Systems of discourse: Structures and semiotics in the social sciences.* London: Greenwood.

# Author Index

# Subject Index

## A

Aberrant coding, 108
Acculturation, 148, 150
Acquisition, *see* Gifting, Theft, Trade
Adidas, 141
Adornment, 123–124
Adventurous consumerism, 142
Advertisement(s), xxv, 132, 163
Advertising, 123, 132, 135, 149
Afghanistan, 142
African Americans, 103, 115
Age
   and clothes, 116–117
   and food, 91
   and objects, 127, 129, 131, 134–135, 140
Alaska, 55, 165
Alcohol, 90, 94, 103
Alphabet, 52
Amber, 148
Ambiguity, 72, 174
Ambivalence, 81
America, *see* USA
American civilization studies, 128, 148
Amish, 64, 142
Analogic, *see* Codes
*Angarkha*, 120
Animal communication, 19, 29
*Animal symbolicum*, 13
Animals, drawings of, 145

Anthropology, xxiv, xxix, 18, 21, 24, 44, 47,
   69, 72, 77, 80, 87, 102, 128, 130,
   148–150, 175
Anthroposemiosis, 20
Anti-culture, 72
Anti-language, 72
Antiques, 168
Apples, 47
Appropriation, 159, 168–169
Apron, 112
Arab, 108
Archaeologists, 128, 132, 148–149
Architects, 128
Architecture, 149
Art, 77, 80, 145, 150, 164, 169, 176
Art historians, 132
Art history, 131
Artefacts, 128
Artifacts, 33, 48, 81, 128
Assimilation, 159, 168
Assumptions, xx, xxviii
Audience, 60
Authenticity, 142
Automobiles, *see* Cars
Awards, 147
Axes of bias, xxix

## B

Babies, 115–116, 129
Backpack, 159, 161, 163